Welsh*lives*

Gone but not forgotten

Welsh*lives*
Gone but not forgotten

M e i c   S t e p h e n s

First impression: 2012

© Copyright Meic Stephens and Y Lolfa Cyf., 2012

The contents of this book are subject to copyright, and may
not be reproduced by any means, mechanical or electronic,
without the prior, written consent of the publishers.

The publishers wish to acknowledge the support of
Welsh Books Council

Cover design: Y Lolfa
Thanks to Emyr Young for the Ray Gravell photograph

ISBN: 978 1847714879

FSC

Published and printed in Wales
on paper from well maintained forests by
Y Lolfa Cyf., Talybont, Ceredigion SY24 5HE
website www.ylolfa.com
e-mail ylolfa@ylolfa.com
tel 01970 832 304
fax 832 782

CONTENTS

NOTE

THIS BOOK BRINGS together 75 obituaries that first appeared, for the most part, in the pages of *The Independent* between January 1999 and August 2012; five were published in *The Guardian* and one in *The Times*. I am grateful for permission to reprint them here, particularly to Chris Maume, Obituaries Editor at *The Independent*.

Whereas an earlier selection, published as *Necrologies* by Seren in 2008, included 72 obituaries of writers, painters, musicians, film-makers, historians, graphic designers, actors, editors, scholars, librarians, cultural mandarins and publishers, the present volume is even more capacious and various in that it mixes creative people with politicians, sportsmen, civil servants, film critics, broadcasters, arts administrators, doctors and judges, all of whom may be deemed to have made a contribution to 'this world of Wales'. Five Bretons and seven English people closely associated with our country have been added to their number.

The obituaries are arranged this time in alphabetical, rather than chronological order, although as a matter of record the date of publication is given at the foot of each one. As before, no attempt has been made to bring them up to date: they appear here just as they did in the newspapers that first published them, albeit with a few minor blemishes silently removed.

Readers who are familiar with things Welsh are asked once again to bear in mind that these tributes were written for a worldwide audience, so that a certain amount of explanation, translation and repetition was required that some may find unnecessary, though I hope not too tedious. I regret that a number of eminent Welsh people who have died in recent years do not appear here, the only reason being that I was not acquainted with them and therefore felt unable to write their obituaries.

The publisher and I thought long and hard about a suitable title for this book. We think *Welsh Lives: Gone but not Forgotten*, despite its provenance on Victorian monumental masonry, sums up what we want to convey: that the people gathered here are remembered for their life's work and that, in this special sense, they live on in the Wales and world they helped to shape.

Meic Stephens
Whitchurch, Cardiff
September 2012

A.M. ALLCHIN

Theologian who fostered unity
between Christianity's major strands

THE ANGLICAN THEOLOGIAN A.M. Allchin wrote prolifically
on Christian spirituality and, in particular, the relationship
between Eastern Orthodoxy and the Christianity of the
West. During a distinguished life as priest and academic,
he strove to foster an awareness of the underlying unity
between the major strands of Christianity, throwing new
light on our understanding of diverse traditions and belief
systems.

He travelled widely, making available what he had
experienced in places like Mount Athos and Romania in
lectures, conferences, pamphlets and a score of books that
are among the most readable, and stimulating, studies in
their fields. He was for many years the editor of *Sobornost*,
the journal of the Fellowship of St Alban and St Sergius
which is devoted to the life and thought of the Eastern
Churches and their relationship with Western Christendom.
He was also involved in dialogue with representatives of
the Lutheran tradition.

Arthur Macdonald Allchin, known as Donald, was
born in London in 1930. During the Second World War
Westminster School was evacuated to Malvern where he
sang choral works in Worcester cathedral. From there he
went up to Christ Church, Oxford, before studying for the
priesthood at Cuddesdon College. The subject of his MA
thesis was the origin of the Anglican Religious Communities
and his belief that they played a vital role in the Church was
one of his lifelong passions; this conviction was set forth
with characteristic vigour in his book *The Silent Rebellion*

(1958), which became the definitive account of the 19th-century revival of the religious life in the Anglican church.

From 1956 to 1960 he was curate of St Mary Abbots in Kensington and librarian at Pusey House in Oxford from 1960 to 1969. His time at Canterbury, from 1973 to 1987, was particularly fruitful in the contacts he made with Roman Catholic communities in Europe. During these years monks and nuns from Bec, Mont de Cats, and Chevetogne frequently came to stay and share the life of the cathedral. From 1987 to 1996 he was Programme Director at the St Theosevia Centre for Christian Spirituality in Oxford. As a freelance theologian with private means but no ambition, he was free to lecture and teach at many institutions in America and France.

His most important books include *The Spirit and the Word* (1963), *The World is a Wedding* (1978), *The Kingdom of Love and Knowledge* (1979), *The Dynamic of Tradition* (1981), *A Taste of Liberty* (1982), *The Joy of all Creation* (1984), *Threshold of Light* (1986), *Participation in God* (1988), *The Heart of Compassion* (1989), and *God's Presence Makes the World* (1997). All are written with an attractive lucidity and effortless charm. His magisterial study of the Danish patriot and hymn-writer N.F.S. Grundtvig (1997) is much admired.

A walking holiday in Wales led to a major influence on Donald's thinking and writing. In the work of poets such as Dafydd ap Gwilym, Thomas Traherne, Williams Pantycelyn, Ann Griffiths and D. Gwenallt Jones he found the well-springs of Christian belief and 'a deep, hidden joy' which he had long sought.

Having learnt to read Welsh, he wrote a percipient study of Ann Griffiths, the great 18th-century hymn-writer, for the *Writers of Wales* series (1976), returning to her work in *The Furnace and the Fountain* (1987); he also edited, with E. Wyn James, a volume of her hymns and letters.

In his book *Sensuous Glory* (2000, co-written with

D. Densil Morgan) he went into detail about how he had come to appreciate the language, literature and culture of Wales: 'Like most English people I grew up in almost total ignorance of the existence of Wales. Only in my thirties did I begin to discover that there was another people in the south of Britain with a language and a history of their own. While they were much less numerous than the English they certainly had inhabited this island which is both theirs and ours, considerably longer than we had.'

The book is still the best introduction in English to the poetry of D. Gwenallt Jones, whose spiritual odyssey from industrial south Wales to incarceration in Dartmoor as a conscientious objector, and then to a lectureship at Aberystwyth, from chapel to atheism and then from church to chapel again, he found fascinating.

A more wide-ranging view is to be found in *Praise Above All* (1991), in which he explored praise in the Welsh poetic tradition from the 9th century to the present. His purview extended to include such major names from the canon of modern Welsh literature as Bobi Jones, R.S. Thomas and Waldo Williams, who are shown as inheritors of a tradition that is coloured by the Bible and by prayer and worship. Among contemporary poets in whom he had an interest are Ruth Bidgood and Gwyneth Lewis.

Donald Allchin, a genial and gracious man, was particularly fond of Ynys Enlli, the island known in English as Bardsey, and Pennant Melangell, the church in Montgomeryshire associated with the princess Monacella, who became the patron saint of all small creatures; he wrote guides to both places. The last 16 years of his life were spent contentedly in Bangor, close to the hill country which he so greatly enjoyed and where he held an honorary professorship at the University. In 2006 he was awarded a Lambeth doctorate in divinity but in 2009, and in failing health, he left for Oxford, where he was to die.

Arthur Macdonald Allchin, priest and theologian: born London 20 April 1930; librarian, Pusey House (1960–69); residentiary canon, Canterbury (1973–87); programme director, St Theosevia Centre for Christian Spirituality (1987–96); died Oxford 23 December 2010.

The Independent (29 March 2011)

P.C. BARTRUM

Scholar of Welsh genealogy

ALTHOUGH HE HAD no family connection with Wales, and was in some respects the quintessential Englishman, P.C. Bartrum devoted his immense scholarly skills to the study of Welsh genealogy, in which he was the foremost expert.

Peter Clement Bartrum was born in Hampstead, London, in 1907 and educated at Clifton College and the Queen's College, Oxford. Most of his career was spent as a meteorologist in the Colonial Service in Bermuda and West Africa, but during his spare time he learned to read Welsh, the better to understand medieval manuscripts in which the descent of prominent families is set out. The authors of most of these important works were heraldic bards who were employed by noble families to research their histories. One such was Gutun Owain, who in 1491 traced the ancestry of Owain Tudur of Penmynydd in Anglesey, the grandfather of Henry VIII.

Bartrum was especially interested in the legends associated with Arthur – not the later fanciful accretions dreamt up by writers such as Malory and Tennyson but the much earlier *Annales Cambriae* and *Historia Brittonum* dating from around the 9th and 10th centuries, in which Arthur appears as a *dux bellorum* (tribal military head) who leads the native Britons against the invading Saxons. His interest also took in the tale of Culhwch and Olwen, found in the *Mabinogion*, which dates from around 1100 and is thus the earliest composition on an Arthurian theme in any language.

But his *magnum opus* was the 26-volume *Welsh Genealogies AD 300–1400* and *Welsh Genealogies AD 1400–1500*, published by the University of Wales Press and the National Library of Wales in 1974 and 1983 respectively. It is these two works, together with *Early Welsh Genealogical Tracts* (1966), which form the basis of the archive that Bartrum presented to the Welsh Department at the University of Wales, Aberystwyth, in 2006. The work, which is now being put into an electronic database with the help of a grant from the Arts and Humanities Research Council, will be, when completed in 2009, an important source for academic researchers, historians and literary historians engaged in the study of medieval society.

The archive, consisting of thousands of names, will make it possible to trace the lineage of eminent people, their period and region – which would have otherwise taken months of research – with minimal effort. Members of the public who can already trace their families to the 16th century will also be able to go much further back.

Bartrum, who was awarded an Honorary DLitt by the University of Wales in 1988, also compiled *A Welsh Classical Dictionary: people in history and legend up to about AD 1000*, which the National Library of Wales published in 1993. His passion was madrigal music – he sang in several groups – and his other interests included the theory of relativity, on which he delivered a paper to the Royal Society in 1965.

When asked to say why he was prepared to spend so many years in the meticulous labour of collecting and deciphering medieval manuscripts, Bartrum modestly explained that he 'liked to put things in order'. The triumph of his scholarship will soon be plain to see by a wider public, thanks to technology which did not exist for most of his long life.

Peter Clement Bartrum, meteorologist and genealogist: born London 4 December 1907; meteorologist in Colonial Service 1932–55; married Barbara Spurling (died 2003; one son); died Hemel Hempstead, Hertfordshire 14 August 2008.

The Independent (20 September 2008)

DOUGLAS BASSETT

Geologist who became an inspirational
Director of the National Museum of Wales

ONE OF THE most distinguished Directors of the National
Museum of Wales in recent years, Douglas Bassett was by
training a geologist and an authority on such matters as the
use and conservation of water resources. Among the public
bodies which benefited from his expertise were the Welsh
Office, the Ordnance Survey and the Nature Conservancy
Council, forerunner of the Countryside Council for Wales,
which he chaired. He was also a founder member of the
National Welsh-American Foundation and its Vice-President
between 1996 and 1998.

During the 1960s he was the sole Welsh representative on
the Department of the Environment's Water Resources Board
at a time when the highly charged question of whether Welsh
valleys should be flooded to make reservoirs for English cities
added to the complexity of political discourse in Wales. The
Board advised the Government on future supplies of water
for industrial and domestic purposes, laying down guidelines
which are still largely in place.

Born the son of a miner in Llwynhendy, near Llanelli,
in industrial Carmarthenshire, where he grew up Welsh-
speaking, Doug Bassett was educated at the University
College of Wales, Aberystwyth, taking his first degree in
Geology in 1952 and then his doctorate in the same discipline.
From 1952 to 1959 he taught in the Geology Department at
Glasgow University while at the same time making geological
forays into north and mid-Wales, especially in the Bala
district in collaboration with Professors Alwyn Williams
and Harry Whittington, and his pioneering surveys came

to be considered models of their kind. Having joined the National Museum of Wales as Keeper of Geology in 1959, he was appointed to the post of Director in 1977 and remained in it until ill health forced him to retire in 1985.

His years in Cathays Park, Cardiff, saw a rapid development of the Museum's Geology Department. He encouraged colleagues and students working in Wales to donate their specimen collections and appointed additional staff to develop the Museum as a centre for research, especially in the Natural Sciences. The institution was promoted as an educational establishment of the first rank through his strong support of what was then the Museum Schools Service, and by the mounting of didactic exhibitions. Some of the galleries dating from before the war were replaced by better designed display areas. In 1960 he co-founded the South Wales Group of the Geologists' Association which flourishes to this day. His working-class origins, which he gladly acknowledged, proved a breath of fresh air in the rather stuffy milieu of the establishmentarian institution and he is remembered there with real affection. He was the first Welsh-speaking Director the Museum had had since receiving its charter in 1907.

Meticulous in his methods, he demonstrated particular skills as a bibliographer and historian of science. In 1961 he published his magisterial study, *Bibliography and Index of Geology and Allied Sciences for Wales and the Welsh Borders 1897–1958*, which made his name as a geologist. It was followed six years later by *A Source-book of Geological, Geomorphological and Soil Maps for Wales and the Welsh Borders 1800–1966*, which proved invaluable for town and country planners. Generous in sharing his specialist knowledge with lay people, he made substantial contributions to the Welsh Academy's *Encyclopaedia of Wales* which was published by the University of Wales Press in 2008.

A friend of Iorwerth C. Peate, former Curator of the Welsh Folk Museum, he made it his business to carry out enquiries into that irascible man's personal background, eliciting facts which had eluded his official biographers. For American visitors he produced a series of pamphlets explaining the significance of various places in Wales which had historical associations. This aspect of his interest in the heritage of Wales and its links with the United States was recognized by the Ivorite Award in 2008. He also edited the magazine *Nature in Wales* (1982–97) and, for the Museums Association, *A Manual of Curatorship*.

Among the honours to come his way were the Aberconway Medal from the Institute of Geologists and the Silver Medal of the Czechoslovak Society for International Relations, both awarded in 1985. He was made *Officier de l'Ordre des Arts et des Lettres* by the Ministry of Culture in Paris in recognition of the National Museum's loan of its important collection of Impressionist paintings, including several Renoirs, for exhibition at various venues in France. He was also an honorary professorial fellow at the University of Wales College of Cardiff (1977–97), a member of the White Robe Order of the Gorsedd of Bards, said to be for the patriotic Welshman the equivalent of the CBE, and honorary resident fellow at the National Museum (from 1986).

His committee skills were exceptionally well honed and he seemed to revel in the work of the myriad committees of which he was an active member. At the same time he retained an impish sense of humour and enjoyed anecdotes about the great and the good with whom he often rubbed shoulders. Nor was he averse to recounting episodes from his own career, beginning in Glasgow where, he said, his landlady was so negligent she would line a drawer with greaseproof paper and fill it with enough porridge to feed him and his housemates for a whole term. He never figured out why the food didn't go off and always found it delicious.

Although divorced from his wife Menna, whom he had married in 1955, they remained on friendly terms for the rest of his life.

Douglas Anthony Bassett, geologist and Director, National Museum of Wales (1977–86): born Llwynhendy, Carmarthenshire 11 August 1927; married 1955 Menna Roberts (three daughters, marriage dissolved); died Cardiff 8 November 2009.

The Independent (3 December 2009)

EILEEN BEASLEY

Welsh language campaigner of remarkable resilience

THE ROSA PARKS of the language movement in Wales was a polite but steel-willed housewife who, with her husband, refused to pay rates on their house in Llangennech, Carmarthenshire, while Llanelli Rural District Council issued demands in English only.

In this Eileen and Trefor Beasley had, at first, the support of nobody but themselves. They reasoned that as they lived their lives through the Welsh language, and their village was Welsh-speaking, as were the majority of Council members, it was reasonable that they should be able to use the language in their dealings with officialdom.

But the Council, like most others in Wales in the 1950s, had never thought of providing services in Welsh. They flatly refused to comply with the Beasleys' request, continuing to communicate with them in English only. In this they greatly underestimated the couple's strong wills.

Bailiffs began calling at their home and removing household goods such as chairs and tables, and then the family's piano, the carpets, the bookcases and even food from the larder, distraining goods to the value of the rates that remained unpaid.

Having bailiffs in the house was, for the law-abiding Beasleys, a distressing experience, especially as they would arrive without warning and, without consultation, take items of furniture that had been wedding presents.

Legal proceedings for the non-payment of rates were taken against the Beasleys on twelve occasions but still they would not accept demands in English. They could hardly afford to pay the fines, especially as they lived on a coal-miner's wage and had two small children, and they stoutly refused to do so as a matter of principle.

The campaign that had begun in 1952 came to an end in 1960 when the Council grudgingly issued a Welsh form and the Beasleys promptly paid their rates. In 1958 Eileen was elected as a Plaid Cymru member of the same District Council, where she continued to press for a degree of official status for the language.

In 1962 their determination proved a stimulus to the activities of *Cymdeithas yr Iaith Gymraeg* (the Welsh Language Society), especially as Saunders Lewis, in his famous radio broadcast of that year, *Tynged yr Iaith* (The Fate of the Language), singled out the Beasleys for praise and urged supporters to emulate their civil disobedience.

His aim was to persuade Plaid Cymru to adopt 'direct action' techniques which would win for Welsh the legal status it had enjoyed before the loss of political independence, a condition he considered essential if the language was to be saved from extinction. But Plaid Cymru felt unable to contemplate unconstitutional methods, preferring to use electoral methods only. Lewis's other aim was to make the governance of Wales impossible while the authorities, both local and central, refused to employ Welsh for public purposes.

The challenge was taken up instead by the *Cymdeithas* which, over the last half-century, has played a leading role in the achievement of many important goals in such areas as broadcasting, education, the law, and local government, while Plaid Cymru has been left free to concentrate on its political agenda. Today the language is much more visible and used in an ever-increasing variety of contexts.

The Beasleys' stand inspired a generation of young Welsh Nationalists to challenge the law, for which many were fined and some imprisoned, and they remained heroes of the movement ever after. Trefor spent a week in prison for refusing to acknowledge an English-only fine for the non-payment of road-tax.

Like her husband, who was the very type of a cultured miner, widely read, politically aware and radically inclined, Eileen was highly literate; she published a selection of her short stories as *Yr Eithin Pigog* ('The prickly gorse') in 1997.

At the 2012 National Eisteddfod held near Cowbridge in the Vale of Glamorgan there was an empty stall, representing the Beasleys' living-room stripped of its furniture, which was meant to be a tribute to the courage and dignity of a couple who were well-liked and generally admired. It was a poignant reminder of what sometimes has to be done to persuade officialdom on a point of principle whenever it is a question of the public use of the Welsh language.

Catherine Eileen James, teacher and Welsh language campaigner, born Henllan Amgoed, Carmarthenshire, 4 April 1921; married Trefor Beasley (died 1994; one son, one daughter); died Henllan Amgoed, Carmarthenshire, 12 August 2012.

DAVE BERRY

Historian and critic of film and television in Wales

'FILM WAS NEVER made to feel very welcome in Wales. As a two or three year old infant, stinking slightly of gin and the sweat of the fairground, it ran slap up against Evan Roberts and the religious revival of 1904, and was severely mauled. It survives, but remains retarded to this day,' wrote the distinguished film-maker Wil Aaron in *The Arts in Wales 1950–1975*, a symposium I edited for the Arts Council in 1979.

David Berry set out to test the veracity of this provocative statement by researching the origins of cinema in Wales and showing, the fire-and-brimstone evangelist notwithstanding, that there had indeed been a thriving industry in places like Cardiff, Swansea and the old coal and iron towns of upland Glamorgan from about 1894, when entertainments such as Edison's Peepshows had been very popular. Two years later Birt Acres's Kineopticon had put on a display of early movies at the Fine Art and Industrial Exhibition held in Cardiff at which a film of the visit by Edward VII had been screened.

In his *magnum opus*, *Wales and Cinema: the First Hundred Years*, published by the University of Wales Press in association with the Wales Film Council and the British Film Institute in 1994, Berry charted the rise of travelling picture showmen, mountebanks and pioneers who operated at fairgrounds and music-halls in Edwardian Wales, which was always his favourite era because it was the moment when moving films emerged from still photography.

Foremost among them was William Haggar, maker of thirty-four films which were distributed by Gaumont; the most controversial was *The Life of Charles Peace* (1905), which appealed to audiences in south Wales weaned on penny dreadfuls but shocked many progressively-minded people with its brutal hanging scene. In north Wales Haggar's counterpart was Arthur Cheetham; Berry's research into the work of both men brought him great acclaim as a historian of early film in Britain.

The book's first section focussed on the silent melodramas made when Wales was 'discovered' by Hollywood and on the career and influence of Ivor Novello, who starred in D.W. Griffith's film *The White Rose* (1923), Cutts's *The Rat* (1925) and Hitchcock's *The Lodger* (1926). Berry was the first to bring a critical mind to these films and put them in the context of their time. Suddenly, it seemed, Wales had a tradition of film-making that was far from being retarded, and had produced actors and film-makers who could be compared with the most famous stars and technicians of their day.

With the coming of sound and the boom of the inter-war years, Wales became the setting for films portraying working-class communities, often with quasi-propagandist messages. Berry wrote a detailed analysis of such films as *The Citadel* (1938), based on a novel by A.J. Cronin, *Proud Valley* (1940), starring Paul Robeson, and John Ford's *How Green Was My Valley* (1941).

He was particularly informative in his account of how Ford, who was of Irish descent, shot his version of Richard Llewellyn's famous novel in the back lot of 20th Century-Fox's studios and on its ranch near Malibu, employing with just one exception a cast of American-Irish actors (including Maureeen O'Hara, Roddy McDowall and Walter Pidgeon) whose accents were, at best, only approximately Welsh. The film presented a heavily romanticised vision of industrial south Wales which went round the world and was to retain its mythic quality even for the Welsh themselves until critics like Berry began to deconstruct it.

He also delved into the film careers of some of the best-known screen actors produced in Wales, including Emlyn Williams, Stanley Baker, Richard Burton and Anthony Hopkins, showing how their talents had been nurtured in their home country before they won fame in the wider world.

A final section discussed television and film-making since the Second World War and up to the creation in 1982 of S4C, the fourth channel in Wales, casting a cold eye over reputations which had hitherto not had much critical attention paid them. The directors John Grierson, John Ormond, Karl Francis, Endaf Emlyn, Chris Monger, Colin Thomas, Joanna Quinn and Stephen Weeks featured prominently at this point in Berry's narrative. The book had a useful filmography of actors and directors and some fascinating photographs unearthed during his research and a comprehensive appendix listing about 400 films of specifically Welsh interest.

Dave Berry first came to Wales in 1974 and was by trade a print journalist. Born in Farnworth, Lancashire, in 1943, he had worked on the *Lancashire Evening Post* in Preston, *The Journal* in Newcastle, the *Birmingham Post*, the *Bristol Evening News* and for Northcliffe Newspapers in London, where he had honed his skills as a sports correspondent. A proud Lancastrian, he was a lifelong supporter of Bolton Wanderers, Rugby League, Speedway and the game of cricket. From 1974 to 1989 he worked in Cardiff for the *South Wales Echo* as education correspondent and until 1994 as film critic.

He was research officer with the Wales Film Council and from 1997 to 2004 with the National Screen and Sound Archive of Wales. In 1986 he wrote and directed a four-part series for HTV about the film industry, *The Dream that Kicks* – the title is taken from a poem by Dylan Thomas – which was also shown on Channel Four and S4C.

Among the mysteries which exercised him was why a silent film depicting David Lloyd George had been 'lost' shortly after it was made in 1918: he concluded that it had almost certainly been banned by the Government for not showing the statesman in a wholly favourable light. Berry discovered the spools in 1994 and made the film available again for general release; Norman Page played the part of Lloyd George and Alma Reville, who became Alfred Hitchcock's wife in 1926, played his daughter Megan. With Simon Horrocks, Berry wrote *David Lloyd George: the Movie Mystery* (1998).

A kindly and modest man, with an encyclopaedic knowledge of film and television, Dave Berry was always ready to share it, his infectious enthusiasm inspiring others, especially young film-makers and animators, and this role gave him oracular status. In 2002, for his services to the industry, he received the Anthony Hopkins Award and at the Cyfrwng Conference held at the University of Glamorgan in 2005, where Kenneth Griffith was among those who paid him tribute, he was given the equally prestigious Siân Phillips Prize.

David John Berry, journalist and film historian: born Farnworth, Lancashire 29 December 1943; features writer with the South Wales Echo *(1974–94), Research Officer, Wales Film Council (1989–97) and the National Screen and Sound Archive of Wales (1997–2004); died Cardiff 22 January 2010.*

The Independent (15 March 2010)

GERAINT BOWEN

Archdruid of Wales who campaigned against
nuclear dumping and championed Welsh-language television

As ARCHDRUID OF Wales from 1979 to 1981, Geraint Bowen was renowned for his hard-hitting speeches from the Logan Stone in the ceremonies of the Assembly of Bards of the Isle of Britain (the Gorsedd). Not only did he speak out against the Anglicization of Wales and in defence of the Welsh language, as Archdruids are expected to do, but also lent his authority to the campaign for a fourth television channel broadcasting in Welsh and against the burying of nuclear waste. In this he ran the risk of upsetting some of the more pusillanimous officers of the National Eisteddfod, to which the Gorsedd is closely affiliated.

He also called for unity among Celtic peoples and denounced the French government's intransigence towards the Breton language and the movement calling for a wider measure of Breton autonomy. His pan-Celtic sentiments were reported in the Parisian press and made him something of a hero among militant Bretons.

In 1977 he became editor of the Welsh-language weekly *Y Faner*, though he did not last long in that capacity. Understaffed, underfunded and housed in Dickensian offices at Bala in Merioneth, the paper was fast losing readers and Bowen's rather gruff editorials put many off. When the Arts Council insisted that the paper should make an effort to win new readers by carrying more popular copy, or lose its subsidy, the editor resigned. 'I was not asked to edit a paper of that sort,' he wrote contemptuously in his autobiography, *O Groth y Ddaear* ('From the womb of the earth', 1993), 'and so I resigned after six months.'

Some thought Bowen's outspokenness may have been a reaction against the restrictions of having been employed between 1961 and 1975 as a member of Her Majesty's Inspectorate of Schools. But that was to misunderstand the nature of the man and the forces that went to his making. Geraint Bowen was born in Llanelli, the former steel and tinplate town in Carmarthenshire, in 1915, and brought up in a strictly religious home at New Quay in Cardiganshire. His father, an ex-collier, was a minister with the Independents, or Congregationalists, always the most radical of the Welsh denominations, and one of his brothers was the poet Euros Bowen.

After attending the grammar school in Aberaeron, Bowen entered University College, Cardiff, graduating in economics and politics in 1938, and went on to Liverpool University, where he took an MA in Celtic. His doctoral thesis was on the literature of Recusancy, the Catholic response to the Protestant Reformation in south-east and north-east Wales, and on which he was to write extensively.

Bowen was a member of Plaid Cymru, and its candidate in the safe Labour seat of Wrexham at the 1950 general election. During the war he registered as a conscientious objector on Welsh Nationalist grounds and was ordered to work on the land. The poem with which he won the Chair at the National Eisteddfod in 1946, '*Yr Amaethwr*' ('The farmer'), drew from Thomas Parry, the foremost literary critic of the day, the comment that it was the most technically accomplished poem of the half-century.

It was based on one of the farmers who employed him, John Jones, a monolingual countryman of Blaen-cwm, Cwm Cynllwyd, in the Berwyn hills. The poet wrote of him: '*Caled oedd fel clwydi og / A mwyn fel gofer mawnog.*' ('He was hard as a harrow's spikes and soft as newly cut peat.') The lines were written about my wife's grandfather but, for all his seriousness, fierce countenance, brusque manner and ultra-nationalist opinions, they might have applied to Bowen.

29

He published one slim volume of his own verse, *Cerddi* ('Poems', 1984), which received an Arts Council prize. He was a master of *cynghanedd*, the prosody in which much Welsh verse is written, particularly of the *englyn*, the four-line verse composed according to rules of devilish complexity.

Much of his life was given to scholarship. First he edited *Gwasanaeth y Gŵyr Newydd* by the Recusant Robert Gwyn, the most prolific Welsh writer of the Elizabethan age, who also wrote *Y Drych Cristianogawl* ('The Christian mirror', 1586), the first book to be printed in Wales, which appeared in 1970. His last book was *Ar Drywydd y Mormoniaid* ('In search of the Mormons', 1999).

Despite his academic absorption in Welsh Catholic literature, Bowen was a forthright atheist. Some thought an over-pious upbringing had caused him to turn against religion, but it is more likely that his Yorkshire-born, Welsh-speaking wife, Zonia, militantly atheist, was a crucial influence. The appointment of an Archdruid who openly admitted he had no God caused consternation in neo-druidic circles and several members resigned in protest.

As an editor he was industrious and meticulous. He compiled three volumes on the Welsh prose tradition, as well as a collection of essays on Celtic civilisation. But his main achievement was a history of the Gorsedd of Bards, that bastion of the nation's literary and linguistic heritage founded by the brilliant forger Iolo Morganwg, which he wrote with his wife and published in time for its second centenary in 1992.

Geraint took his role as Archdruid seriously. In 1980 he led a deputation to Hallein, near Salzburg in Austria, one of the cradles of Celtic civilisation, for the opening of an exhibition entitled *Die Kelten in Mitteleuropa*. He cut an imposing figure in his neo-druidic robes and was much feted as a living presence from 'the enchanted woods of Celtic antiquity'.

In 1980, when he was living near Tal-y-llyn in Merioneth, he became part of the campaign to prevent the burial of nuclear waste at various sites in southern Gwynedd and northern Powys. He served as chairman of Madryn, a movement with branches throughout the area, and presided over a policy of non-violent action against such bodies as the Forestry Commission and the Institute of Geological Sciences, which were searching for suitable sites.

Eventually successful, the campaign led to a famous declaration that Wales was 'a non-nuclear country'. It had the support of Dafydd Wigley, Neil Kinnock, A.J.P. Taylor and Joan Ruddock, but it was Bowen's denunciation of Nirex, the Nuclear Waste Inspectorate, during the Eisteddfod of that year, which received most publicity. Few Archdruids can claim to have stopped Leviathan dead in its tracks.

Geraint Bowen, poet: born Llanelli, Carmarthenshire 10 September 1915; Archdruid of Wales 1979–81; married 1947 Zonia North (two sons, two daughters); died Bangor, Gwynedd 16 July 2011.

The Independent (5 August 2011)

RACHEL BROMWICH

Celtic scholar celebrated for
her masterly dictionary of Welsh legend

RACHEL BROMWICH WAS a distinguished Celtic scholar whose *magnum opus* was *Trioedd Ynys Prydein: the Welsh Triads*, an index of legendary characters, arranged in groups of three, a characteristic feature of the traditional lore of Britain and Ireland since earliest times. In medieval Wales, a society in which oral instruction was the chief means of conserving and transmitting bardic culture, the cryptic triad served as a mnemonic device for cataloguing facts and ideas. Bromwich's book, first published in 1961 but reissued several times since then, is an invaluable dictionary of Welsh and British legend.

Working from a collation of manuscripts of the 13th and 14th centuries, she provided a translation of the texts, together with a commentary, thus throwing a great deal of light on allusions to heroes, places and events from the distant British past. In so doing she elucidated many of the more problematic references in early Welsh poetry, particularly that written in 'the Old North' – what are now parts of southern Scotland and northern England.

The erudition and meticulous scholarship displayed in her edition of the Triads was typical of all her work. She brought to it a formidable intellect and wide reading in the literatures and cultures of the Celtic countries which had begun long before she had personal contact with any of them.

She was born Rachel Amos in Hove, Sussex, in 1915, but spent her early childhood in Egypt, where her father was a barrister and Professor of Law. On his retirement in 1925 the family returned to England, settling in Cumberland, a county with old British associations which she was later to study as belonging to the traditions of 'the Old North'.

At Newnham College, Cambridge, she took the first part of the English Tripos in 1936 and the second part, consisting of Anglo-Saxon, Norse and Celtic, two years later, graduating with a First in both. The principal influence on English studies in Cambridge at the time was H.M. Chadwick, the foremost authority on the archaeology and languages of early Britain. It was his pupil, Kenneth H. Jackson, who persuaded Rachel Amos to go on to the University College of North Wales, Bangor, to study Welsh under Sir Ifor Williams.

The Second World War interrupted her studies at Bangor. Her husband, John Bromwich, a lecturer in Anglo-Saxon at St John's College, Cambridge, was posted to Northern Ireland, and she joined him there in 1940. For a while she was able to attend the Old Irish classes of Professor Michael O'Brien at Queen's University, Belfast, but when Bromwich was sent overseas his wife returned to Cumbria with their child.

In 1945 she was invited to teach Old Welsh and Old Irish as part of the English Tripos at Cambridge, and there she was to remain for the rest of her academic career. Among her first publications were studies of Gaelic tradition in 18th-century Ireland, including an essay on the 'Lament for Art O'Leary', and of the Arthurian tradition in Scotland and the Breton Lays. Her chapter on the drowned kingdoms of Cantre'r Gwaelod and Ker Ys in *The Early Cultures of North-West Europe* (the H.M. Chadwick memorial volume, 1950) is a model of lucidity and comparative scholarship. She was made University Reader in Celtic Languages and Literatures in 1973 and, in the year following, held the Sir John Rhys Fellowship at Oxford, where she was one of the first women to be elected Fellow of Jesus College.

Her work on Dafydd ap Gwilym, generally considered to be the outstanding Welsh poet of the medieval period, is much admired. In *Tradition and Innovation in the Poetry of Dafydd ap Gwilym* (1964) she demonstrated the French influences on his work, a theme she continued to explore in numerous essays which were collected under the title *Aspects of the Poetry of Dafydd ap Gwilym* in 1986. For readers with no Welsh she translated a generous selection of Dafydd's poems which appeared as a Penguin paperback in 1985. She was among those who in 1984 unveiled a memorial stone to Dafydd ap Gwilym in the churchyard at Talley in the belief that the poet was buried there and not, as is traditionally believed, at Strata Florida.

As a tribute to her old teachers, Sir Ifor Williams at Bangor and Sir Idris Foster at Oxford, she edited *The Beginnings of Welsh Poetry* (1972) for one and (with R. Brinley Jones) *Astudiaethau ar yr Hengerdd* (1978) for the other. The second of these consisted of essays written by members of the group devoted to the study of the earliest Welsh poetry in Oxford.

On her retirement in 1976 Rachel Bromwich went to live in Bethesda, the former slate-quarrying village in Gwynedd, where she renewed her contact with the University College of North Wales at Bangor by accepting an Honorary Professorial Fellowship in the Department of Welsh. The University of Wales awarded her the honorary degree of DLitt in 1985 and in the same year, the thirteenth volume in the prestigious series *Ysgrifau Beirniadol*, including a full bibliography of her writings, was presented to her. Her last years were spent in Aberystwyth, where she worked indefatigably at the National Library of Wales and the University of Wales Centre for Advanced Welsh and Celtic Studies.

Rachel Bromwich, Celtic scholar: born Hove, Sussex 30 July 1915; Lecturer and Reader in Celtic Languages and Literatures, University of Cambridge 1945–76 and Emeritus; married 1940 John Bromwich (deceased, one son); died Aberystwyth, Ceredigion 15 December 2010.

The Independent (14 January 2011)

MICHAEL BURN

Journalist, soldier and writer
who took part in the Commando raid on St Nazaire

MICHAEL BURN HAD a long life strewn with risks, setbacks, disenchantments and deceptions, and illumined by love affairs, literary acclaim and marvellous friendships. Man about town, journalist, soldier, poet, novelist and playwright, and latterly a breeder of mussels on the Dwyryd and Glaslyn estuaries of north-west Wales, he lived his life with panache and a debonair grin for whatever befell him, be it incarceration in Colditz during the Second World War or the gloomy spectacle of the Communist show-trials of central Europe which he covered for *The Times*.

There were contradictions in his character, flaws and conflicts even, which he wrote about with self-knowledge and a gentlemanly regard for others that won him the affection of many friends. Born into a well-to-do home in Mayfair in 1912, he observed unemployment and the most appalling poverty while living with a Yorkshire miner's family in the early 1930s and the experience left an indelible mark on him. By instinct republican, he was sent to cover the royal visit to Canada and the United States in 1939 and reported it rapturously.

For a while he was duped by the Nazis but became a Marxist while a prisoner of war after taking part in a commando raid against the German fortified harbour of St Nazaire in 1942. A convert to Roman Catholicism, he left the Church as a consequence of its teachings on homosexuality which he had practised intermittently since his schooldays. Unhappy with his sexuality, he gave up homosexual relations soon after meeting Mary Booker, and they lived happily as man and wife from their marriage in 1947 until her death in 1974.

Michael Burn's father, Sir Clive Burn, was a solicitor employed as Secretary to the Duchy of Cornwall, a royal fief with huge estates in the West Country and on the South Bank of the Thames. The boy was sent to Winchester and spent his holidays with grandparents in a villa near Le Touquet on the Normandy coast.

He soon rebelled against the class into which he had been born: the Wykehamist became an agnostic and only the study of History held any appeal for him. At New College, Oxford, he did no work whatsoever, left after his first year and, intent on joining the Fourth Estate, and in 1933, drawn by his love of Wagner, took flight for Germany, where he moved from Schloss to Schloss as the guest of aristocrats deeply implicated in the rise of National Socialism. He was briefly taken in by the Nazis, mainly because of what they seemed to be doing about reviving the German economy and abolishing the class system which he saw as a cancer eating at the heart of British society.

Back in London by 1934, Burn found a reporter's job with *The Gloucester Citizen*, which belonged to Lord Rothermere, the pro-Nazi owner of *The Daily Mail*. Still preoccupied with the scourge of mass unemployment, he took up the cause of Forest of Dean miners while, at the same time, enjoying the hospitality of the Earl of Berkeley. On holiday in Germany in 1935 he attended a Nazi rally at Nuremburg, met Hitler who signed a copy of *Mein Kampf* for him, and visited the Dachau concentration camp in the company of Unity Mitford and her sister Diana Guinness, soon to be married to Oswald Mosley.

The scales dropped from his eyes on his return to London. What changed his mind about Hitler was a week spent as a paying guest in the home of a Barnsley miner, where he saw the effects of economic depression and social deprivation at their most baneful; he remained in contact with the family for the rest of his life.

Soon afterwards, in 1937, he 'was received into *The Times*', whose policy of appeasement had held sway throughout the 1930s. Micky Burn was given the job of covering the abdication crisis, following the paper's line that the king should not enter into a morganatic marriage with Mrs Simpson. It was at this time he met and went to bed with the promiscuous Guy Burgess.

At the outbreak of war Burn joined the Territorials and, after the most basic training, saw guerrilla action around Mosjoen in German-occupied Norway which ended in disarray for the British troops. The audacious Commando raid of 1942 on the German-held port of St Nazaire, in which Burn took part, was more successful in that it denied sanctuary to the *Tirpitz*, the largest of all the German battleships. The Commandos rammed *HMS Campbeltown*, packed with explosives, into the harbour defences and then fought their way ashore. Though typically modest about his role in blowing up installations, Burn was awarded the Military Cross for his part in the assault. He was captured twice in twenty-four hours, the first time talking his way out of a tight corner in fluent German.

As he was led away by his captors, Burn put up his hands with fingers in a V for Victory sign, in defiance of Nazi cameras recording the surrender for Goebbels. The incident was seen in a cinema newsreel by a woman named Ella van Heemstra living in the occupied Netherlands whom Burn had befriended just before the war and whose daughter later became the filmstar Audrey Hepburn. The shot appeared in his autobiography, *Turned towards the Sun*, which appeared in 2003.

Burn spent the rest of the war in POW camps, including Spangenburg and Rothenburg, ending it at Colditz, where he specialised in making short-hand transcripts of the BBC news from a clandestine wireless set. By now 'slightly to the

Left of Major Atlee', he became a Marxist under the tutelage of a brother officer, gave talks on politics and economics to 'a captive audience', and wrote the drafts of two books. For years thereafter his parents corresponded with the families of those who had lost their lives on the St Nazaire raid and Burn served as President of the Society that was formed to keep survivors in touch with one another.

After the war, by which time he had fallen in love with Mary Booker, he was sent by *The Times* to Vienna and then to Central Europe with special responsibility for the Balkans, where he made friends with the hitherto unapproachable Soviet press corps. Among the events he covered were the rigged trial of Cardinal Mindszenty, the Roman Catholic primate of Hungary who was imprisoned by the Communist government in 1949, and for whom Burn, now a practising Catholic, had great sympathy.

His conversion to Catholicism, his wife's religion, lasted from about 1940 to 1994, when he felt obliged to leave the Church of Rome on account of its teachings on homosexuality. His sexual proclivities caused him great anguish but he was able to write about them with a light touch. Mary knew of his homosexuality, considering it 'a part of a general male retardation', but their marriage turned out to be extremely happy.

The house known as Beudy Gwyn, with its stunning views across the Dwyryd estuary near Minffordd in what is now Gwynedd, was renovated by the Burns in 1951. There he resumed his writing career. He had begun as a playwright with *The Modern Everyman* (1947) and now had some critical success as the author of *The Night of the Ball* (1956). His first novel, *Yes, Farewell* (1946), was followed by *Childhood at Oriol* (1951), *The Midnight Diary* (1952) and *The Trouble with Jake* (1967). He published five collections of poetry, including *The Flying Castle*, a fantasy demonstrating his mastery of rhyming quatrains, and was awarded the Keats Poetry Prize in 1973. He also wrote on political and sociological subjects in such books as *The Labyrinth of Europe*, *Mr Lyward's Answer* and *The Debatable Land*.

Micky Burn's autobiography deals with important events and famous people, but at its heart, as with all good examples of the genre, it is the author's own personality – intelligent, modest, painfully honest, drily witty, courageous, highly principled and unfailingly urbane – that shines through. The same qualities are to be seen in his book *Poems as Accompaniment to a Life* which was published in 2006.

Michael Clive Burn, journalist, soldier and author: born London 11 December 1912; MC 1942; Times reporter 1936–9 and Central Europe Correspondent 1946–9; married 1947 Mary Booker née Walter (died 1974); died Minffordd, Gwynedd 3 September 2010.

The Independent (24 September 2010)

STUART CABLE

Drummer with the Stereophonics and broadcaster

STUART CABLE WAS, by general assent, the most technically proficient drummer in the world. This unabashed extrovert put so much passion and physical effort into his drumming it had a charm of its own and seemed an extension of the man. With his abundant curls, broad grin, gravelly voice, raucous laugh and boisterous personality, he was a huge presence on the rock scene, and for a few years enjoyed fame as the drummer who played with the Stereophonics, one of the most successful British bands of recent times. Five out of their nine albums topped the UK charts and they were asked to perform at all the major venues. But Cable's career was marked by acrimony and alcohol and drugs took their toll.

As his rock'n'roll lifestyle began to have adverse effects, and to everyone's surprise, he made a new career as a broadcaster with BBC Wales: in 2002 he was given his own television chat show, *Cable TV*, which was followed by *Cable Connects* and then his own radio show, *Cable Rock*. Ever the joker in the pack, he also appeared as a guest on umpteen shows in Wales, enjoying a reputation as a larger-than-life character who could make audiences laugh.

It was his burgeoning career as a broadcaster that was to cause the bitter split with the Stereophonics in September 2003 when they sacked the percussionist on the grounds that he often missed rehearsals because he had commitments elsewhere. Full details of his fraught relationship with his erstwhile band-mates are given in his autobiography (written with the help of Anthony Bunko), *Demons & Cocktails: My Life with Stereophonics* (2009), an updated paperback version of which appeared in the same week as his death. Even so, his differences with Kelly Jones, with whom he had fallen out so spectacularly, were eventually patched up, for Cable had a sunny personality that didn't bear grudges for long.

Born in the former mining village of Cwmaman in the Cynon Valley in 1970, Stuart Cable grew up there and retained a strong commitment to his community. Even after fame and fortune came his way, he steadfastly resisted the temptation to move to more fashionable places so that he could be near his family and the friends with whom he had grown up, and for this he was admired as one of Wales's favourite sons. He learned a little Welsh as part of BBC Wales's *Big Welsh Challenge* and this seemed to connect him with his roots, in which he took great pride and from which he drew strength. On the day of his death the affection in which he was held by local people was attested by the flowers left at the gates of his house in Llwydcoed, near Aberdare, which he called Castle Cable, and heaped on his car parked outside the Welsh Harp pub in nearby Trecynon. Among the many tributes that came up on the internet from all over the world was one referring to him as 'a diamond geezer, a top dude'.

Determined to be a rock-star from an early age, having been given a drum kit by his widowed mother Mabel, he practised drumming with two friends, namely Richard Jones on bass guitar, and Kelly Jones, the singer-songwriter and guitarist who lived in the same street. In 1992 they began performing in workmen's clubs in south Wales under the name Tragic Love Company but changed to Stereophonics after Cable spotted the word on an old record-player belonging to his father. At first he was also playing drums with such combos as Nail Bombs and Ritch Bitch, the gigs supplementing his wages as a double glazing salesman. The only setback to the lads' early success was when their instruments were stolen but this was soon put right with financial help from the Prince's Trust.

It was not long before they were encouraged by their agent John Brand to set their sights on higher things, especially after he had made sure they became the first group to sign up with the newly-formed record label V2, created by Richard Branson, in a deal worth £265,000. Their first recording, *Word Gets Around*, sold 800,000 copies in 1996. They also recorded the EP *Raw Sex for Breakfast* at Sound Space's studios in Cardiff on which Cable sang the vocals. Among the group's many hits were 'Traffic', 'Have a Nice Day', 'Local Boy in the Photograph', 'Just Looking' and 'The Bartender and the Thief', all of which were performed before an audience of 30,000 at the Cardiff City Stadium the weekend of his death.

The band won more than its share of awards. They were voted Best New British Band by *Kerrang!* in 1998 and in the same year they won the Brit Award for Best Newcomer and were named Best Live Act of the Year by *Q* magazine. They were twice voted Number 2 in the Top Ten 'Sexiest Lads' by readers of *Melody Maker* and in May 2000 Kelly Jones was voted Number 6 in *Company* magazine's Top One Hundred Men. In 2000 the Stereophonics were named Band of the Year by *Loaded*. They revelled in such accolades as 'the bastard sons of rock 'n'roll, possessed with the demon swagger of Dylan, Hendrix and Angus Young'. In the late 1990s, together with Super Furry Animals, Manic Street Preachers and Catatonia, they were riding high as part of the scene known as 'Cool Cymru'.

So began the rollercoaster years in which Stuart Cable experienced all the highs and lows of a rock-star's career. The 'Phonics played with some of the most famous bands in the world, including the Rolling Stones, U2 and Oasis, and were household names for more than a decade. Their second album, *Performances and Cocktails*, reached the top of the UK charts, selling 600,000 copies, and world tours followed. After the split with his old butties, followed by 'dark and difficult' days for Cable, he formed a new band, Killing for Company, which was due to play at the Download Festival, heavy rock's annual shindig in Donnington Park, Leicestershire, a few days after his death. He had said he never expected to live beyond the age of forty and now his demons began to close in.

Confessing in his autobiography to being a hard drinker and drug user, especially of cocaine, he described himself at the height of the Stereophonics' fame as 'a coke-taking zombie'. He had moved back to his home area, he said, 'because if I hadn't I'd have probably ended up dead or round the bend – or both.' Although he had recently settled to a calmer way of life and was a devoted father, the percipience of this remark was borne out when his body was found at his home in the early hours of 7 June after what was said to have been a heavy drinking session.

He had nevertheless managed to keep up his broadcasting, interviewing such stars as Cerys Mathews and Tom Jones with his usual cheery manner and winning a BAFTA award for his voice part in the BBC animation series *Colin and Cumberland*. In 2002 he also lent his active support to a BBC Wales campaign to encourage men to look out for warning signs of testicular cancer. Three years later he hosted the *Kerrang!* awards and in November 2007 joined XFM South Wales, hosting a weekend show until the station was sold a year later. He then returned to BBC Radio Wales as presenter of *Saturday Night Cable*, playing old and new rock music which he introduced with infectious enthusiasm. He used his star status in the interests of child safety, notably in 'Stuart's Campaign', after the death of a schoolboy, Stuart Cunningham-Jones, who had died aboard a bus.

Stuart Cable, drummer and broadcaster: born Cwmaman, near Aberdare, Glamorgan 19 May 1970; married 1999 Nicola Damon (marriage dissolved; one son); died Llwydcoed, near Aberdare, Rhondda Cynon Taf 7 June 2010.

The Independent (9 June 2010)

HUW CEREDIG

Actor who was a mainstay of the
Welsh soap opera *Pobol y Cwm* for 29 years

HUW CEREDIG'S BEST-KNOWN role was as Reg Harries in the long-running nightly soap-opera *Pobol y Cwm* ('People of the valley'), the most popular programme in the history of television in Wales, which has been broadcast by BBC Cymru and S4C since 1974 and is now a cornerstone of the service.

From the first episode he had a huge screen presence that never faltered – he was a large man with a gravelly, instantly recognisable voice and a bushy beard – and the part established him as one of the most talented and well-liked television actors of his generation.

The story is set in Cwmderi, a fictitious village which, if it were on the map, would be located somewhere to the west of Llanelli. Conveniently for the plot, it has both a rural and industrial character, and is not far from Llanarthur, a thinly disguised Carmarthen town. It is predominantly Welsh-speaking and, as society in Wales has changed over the years so has life in the village, which now has its share of unemployment, crime, divorce, domestic violence and the problems associated with drug addiction. A deliberate attempt was made from the start to appeal to the whole of Wales by featuring characters, accents and idioms from all parts of the country.

The series has provided many actors, directors and scriptwriters with a living, not least Huw Ceredig, who acted in it for 29 years and thus became a household name. At the outset, when the series went out weekly, Reg Harries was a union official and local councillor striving to keep his pit open. But like many talented working-class men in south

Wales he goes up to Ruskin College to get an education. After the miners' strike of 1984–85 and the closure of so many pits by the Thatcher government, the village's social life declines and Reg marries Megan James (played by Lisabeth Miles), the licensee of the Deri Arms, and it is as the pub's landlord that many viewers will remember him. Warm-hearted Reg listens to everyone's problems and tries to solve them, with tact and a twinkle in his eye.

When his own marital difficulties come to a head Reg separates from his wife and marries again. Eventually, after many twists and turns that are the stuff of soap operas, he sees his old mine acquired by his arch-rival Ieuan Griffiths, one of the villains of the series whom everyone loves to boo and hiss. Reg's son, Gareth Wyn, was played by a young Ioan Gruffudd, who has joined many of his fellow-actors in paying tribute to Huw Ceredig's generosity and patience in taking novices under his wing and putting them at their ease in front of the camera. Ceredig's part was eventually written out of the series against the actor's wishes.

Born in 1942 in Brynaman in the industrial part of Carmarthenshire, a village not unlike Cwmderi, Huw Ceredig Jones spent part of his youth in Llanuwchllyn, near Bala, in Merioneth. Educated at Llandovery and Trinity College, Carmarthen, he taught at the village school in Laleston, near Bridgend, until he became a full-time actor. He was one of the four sons of Fred Jones, a minister who was among the early members of Plaid Cymru.

Although he dropped the surname Jones for professional purposes he was always proud to be known as his father's son. One of his brothers, Dafydd Iwan, is a professional folk-singer and leading member of Plaid Cymru; another, Alun Ffred Jones, is a prominent Plaid member of the National Assembly and has held ministerial posts in Cardiff Bay; and another, Arthur Morus, owns a woollen mill in Drefach Felindre.

Besides his Welsh television work, including voice-overs

for the *Super Ted* series, Ceredig had smaller parts in London soaps such as *Z Cars*, *Ennal's Point*, *District Nurse*, *Emmerdale*, *Heartbeat* and *Doctors*, and in the BBC Wales series *The Life and Times of David Lloyd George*. The last of these was made in 2005, after which he had to retire from television owing to ill-health. But he was seen in the visually stunning, though factually risible Dylan Thomas biopic *The Edge of Love* in 2008, which starred Keira Knightley, Sienna Miller, Mathew Rhys and Simon Armstrong. His most memorable screen appearance was in *Twin Town* (1997), the anarchic revenge comedy set in the 'ugly lovely town' of Swansea, in which the careers of Rhys Ifans (Spikey in *Notting Hill*) and his brother Llŷr were launched. He was also a memorable First Voice in Dylan Thomas's *Under Milk Wood*, played the Judge in Ibsen's *Hedda Gabler* and was seen in *Y Llosgwr*, about the Chartist and pioneer of cremation, Dr William Price.

In 2006 he published his autobiography (co-written with Aled Islwyn), *Cofio Pwy Ydw I* ('Remembering who I am'), where something of his larger-than-life personality shines through. He revelled in good company, particularly late at night, and was among those who founded Clwb Ifor Bach, a club for Welsh-speakers in Cardiff. He gave substantial sums to Welsh causes like the Welsh Language Society and Plaid Cymru, usually without fuss and anyone knowing. For a while he was chairman of Bridgend Rugby Club. A lifelong fan of Manchester United, he never missed a game and, in 1999, flew to Barcelona to see his team play, returning the same day in order not to miss rehearsals for *Pobol y Cwm*.

Huw Ceredig Jones (Huw Ceredig), actor: born Brynaman, Carmarthenshire 22 June 1942; married 1965 Margaret Grey (two daughters); died Morriston, Swansea 16 August 2011.

The Independent (22 August 2011)

JOHN CLEMENT

Canny civil servant who played
a key role in the growth of the Welsh Office

JOHN CLEMENT'S MOTIVATION as a senior civil servant in the Welsh Office was shaped by two experiences: growing up in south Wales as one of a collier's five children during the grim Depression of the 1930s; and his service with the RAF during the Second World War.

He volunteered in 1940, at the age of 20, from a junior job as a clerical officer in the Welsh Board of Health in Cathays Park, Cardiff and was immediately sent for training as a navigator in Pensacola, Florida, where he passed at the very top of his intake. On his return to Britain he was commissioned and posted to 44 (Rhodesia) Squadron based at Waddington in Lincolnshire, the first in the air force to be equipped with Lancaster bombers.

Chosen by Sqn Ldr John Nettleton VC to be his navigator, Clement soon won his confidence. On his test flight, over parts of north Wales in thick cloud, Nettleton wanted to drop below cloud level in order to verify the instrument-based position which Clement had just given him. But Clement, who had been plotting their course every six minutes by reference to speed, wind and compass bearings, advised against it because such a descent would mean flying into the side of Snowdon. Nettleton was adamant until, just then, the clouds parted to reveal the mountain's summit directly below them; he never doubted his navigator's judgement again.

Clement went on 30 bombing missions over Germany. He was so adept that he was lined up as one of the reserves for the famous Dam Busters' raid of 16 May 1943. When, in later life, he was hauled before the formidable Dame Evelyn

Sharp, Permanent Secretary at the Ministry of Housing in Whitehall, and told that perhaps he had been under a good deal of pressure at the Welsh Office, he replied that it wasn't the case: 'Flying over the Ruhr at 20,000 feet with anti-aircraft shells bursting all around you and the night fighters strafing you – now that was pressure!'

Clement was determined for the rest of his life to use the good fortune of his survival to address the other passion which motivated him, namely the need to create economic conditions in Wales which would go some way to alleviating the social problems which had blighted his own boyhood in Felindre, a coalmining village near Swansea.

Returning to the Civil Service after the war, and with no formal academic qualifications, he made steady progress up the career ladder. Appointed Principal in the Welsh office of the Ministry of Housing and Local Government in 1960 and Assistant Secretary in the new Welsh Office in 1966, he served as Private Secretary to Cledwyn Hughes, the second Secretary of State for Wales, and then from 1971 to 1981 as Under-Secretary for Economic Planning and Director of Industry. From 1955 to 1959 he was Secretary of the Council for Wales and Monmouthshire and Chairman of the Welsh Planning Board from 1971 to 1976.

With a reputation for competence and a dogged determination 'to get things done', Clement worked with some of the leading figures in the postwar revival of the Welsh economy, particularly the trade-union leader Huw T. Edwards, Chairman of the Council for Wales. It was Clement who wrote the council's famous third memorandum which recommended the setting up of a Welsh Office under its own Secretary of State, a policy adopted by the Labour Party in its manifesto of 1964.

As a civil servant, Clement's forte was writing policy reports whose main thrust was to indentify Wales as a political entity. In these years he had to tread a very tortuous line between the advocacy of policies he believed to be right for Wales and his departmental brief, which was often much less adventurous. The Welsh Office, established in 1964, had not got off to the most auspicious of starts and took until 1969 to produce its first economic development strategy, *Wales: the way ahead*. It was no accident that Clement was chosen to lead its implementation.

His work in the Economic Planning Division and subsequently as Under-Secretary in charge of the Industry Division at the Welsh Office during the 1970s was an important part of the long process of devolution which has continued to our own day. His special tactic was always to provide ministers, whether Labour or Conservative, with arguments for timing the closure of coal mines and steelworks to coincide with the growth of new industries. He had seen enough of unemployment in his youth and did not wish to see its baneful effects repeated.

At the time the Government was relocating parts of the Civil Service out of London and Clement worked tirelessly to ensure that Wales had its share of jobs. The Development Board for Rural Wales and the Welsh Development Agency were set up on his watch, as well as the Royal Mint at Llantrisant, the DVLC in Morriston and the Inland Revenue in Llanishen, Cardiff. His expertise was grudgingly recognised by Whitehall mandarins: he was a first-class 'operator' and his canniness made for confidence that the Welsh Office was clearly capable of developing its own policies and becoming an effective and credible Department of State.

But Clement paid a price for this success: he was refused promotion at least once on the grounds that he was too 'nationalist' and emotional in his approach, though he had never sought preferment in London. In a newspaper interview published in 1999, Rhodri Morgan – now First Minister at the third National Assembly – referred to Clement as one of 'the select crew' who were prepared to stand up to the power of Whitehall on behalf of Welsh interests.

Every Secretary of State for Wales under whom he served

paid public tribute to Clement. On one occasion he went to meet James Callaghan, the Prime Minister, on the platform of Cardiff station to accompany him to a meeting in the city. Clement was offered a lift in the PM's car but politely declined because he wanted to stretch his legs. Callaghan, anxious for a conversation with someone whose opinion he respected, said he would walk with him and the two proceeded up St Mary's Street followed slowly by an entourage of flabbergasted minders in their chauffeur-driven cars; no one, in their experience, had ever turned down a lift with the PM. For his services to the governance of Wales, Clement was appointed CB in 1980 and was awarded an honorary MA by the University of Wales in 1982.

His means of relaxation were following the fortunes of the Cardiff XV and the Glamorgan XI, reading poetry and trout-fishing – though he never once thought to buy a licence. In retirement he served as a member of the Wales Tourist Board from 1982 to 1988 and of the Midland Bank's Advisory Council in Wales from 1985 to 1994.

A fluent Welsh-speaker, for more than 50 years he was regular in his attendance at the Welsh Congregationalist chapel in Minny Street, Cardiff.

John Handel Clement, civil servant: born Felindre, Glamorgan 24 November 1920; Principal, Welsh office, Ministry of Housing and Local Government 1960–66; Assistant Secretary, Welsh Office 1966–71, Under-Secretary 1971–81, Director of Industry Department 1976–81; Private Secretary to the Secretary of State for Wales 1966; Chairman, Welsh Planning Board 1971–76; CB 1980; married 1946 Anita Jones (one daughter, and one daughter deceased); died Cardiff 24 May 2007.

The Independent (7 June 2007)

HAFINA CLWYD

Feisty journalist, diarist and essayist

ONE OF THE liveliest women journalists ever produced in Wales, Hafina Clwyd wrote perceptively and sometimes provocatively in both Welsh and English, often focussing on personalities making the news but sometimes on topics nearer her heart such as broadcasting, the press and cultural matters. Her weekly column in *The Western Mail*, the 'national newspaper of Wales', was always worth reading, as was her radio and television column in *Y Cymro*, the weekly Welsh-language newspaper. Some of her most entertaining pieces, deliciously waspish, caused sparks to fly in the best tradition of engaged, not to say opinionated journalism, but the reader was always left with the impression that she meant precisely what she said and was prepared to stand by it. This taste for controversy and a willingness to raise the hackles of the pompous and complacent went hand-in-hand with a more academic trait in her personality which found expression in her keen interest in local history and genealogy.

She was born a farmer's daughter at Gwyddelwern, near Corwen in Merioneth, in 1936, and brought up at Llanychan in the Vale of Clwyd. Educated at the Girls' Grammar School in Bala, she went on to the Normal College in Bangor to train, despite her atheism, as a teacher of Religious Education. There she threw herself into student life with a gusto that left most of her contemporaries breathless.

The same conviviality and vivacity were displayed in the dizzy social whirl of the London Welsh Association, of which she became a leading light soon after arriving in the city in 1957 as a schoolteacher; she ended her career as a head of department at a comprehensive in Islington. She often drew on her years in London, where she lived until 1979, in her essays and newspaper columns.

The early 1960s were a golden age in the life of the London Welsh. The young, especially those from rural, Welsh-speaking areas, had a freedom largely denied them at home by the last vestiges of a chapel culture and they grasped their opportunities in the metropolis with both hands. Those who attended the evening service in Charing Cross would often repair to a pub or to private parties, and Hafina Clwyd – she soon dropped the surname Jones – was usually to be seen where the fun was most rumbustious.

That is not to say she did not have a more serious side. She helped form *Clwb Llyfrau Cymraeg*, the Welsh Books Club which was a forerunner of the Welsh Books Council, and was a keen member of the Honourable Society of Cymmrodorion, the ancient and most pinstripe of all the Welsh expatriate societies in London, of which she served as a Vice-President.

This interest in books and antiquities she brought back to Wales in 1979, when she returned with her husband, teacher and compatriot Cliff Coppack, to live in Ruthin. From 1981 to 1989 she edited *Y Bedol* ('The horseshoe'), the local community newspaper, and became a stalwart of the town's History Group and the Clwyd Family History Society, which she later chaired. She also served as a member and, in her turn, mayor of Ruthin Town Council. Many of her articles, meticulously researched, appeared in the *Transactions of the Denbighshire Historical Society*. Her special interest was in family history, on which she was ever-ready to dilate in the manner often observed in those who know a person's history *i'r nawfed ach* – 'to the ninth generation'. Between 1986 and 1992 she also edited *Y Faner* ('The flag'), the venerable weekly newspaper whose radical traditions she tried valiantly to maintain in the face of a dwindling readership, but it folded soon afterwards.

A prolific author, she published eleven books, mostly collections of essays in which her feisty but engaging personality was given free rein. In *Clychau yn y Glaw* ('Bells in the rain', 1973) she described an idyllic childhood on the family farm; one of her anecdotes is about her small brother, a monoglot Welsh-speaker, pointing up at the sun and saying '*Haul!*' to a German prisoner-of-war who thought he was being offensive until it was explained to him that '*haul*' is the Welsh word for 'sun'. In *Defaid yn Chwerthin* ('Sheep laughing', 1980) she looked back at her college days with impish humour and disarming candour.

An inveterate diarist from the age of seven, she published a racy selection of her London diaries in *Buwch ar y Lein* ('A cow on the line', 1987); the cover has a photograph of her in the role of Polly Garter in a production of *Under Milk Wood*. With the autobiographical *Merch Morfydd* ('Morfydd's daughter', 1987) she came second in the Prose Medal competition at the National Eisteddfod. She co-edited *Welsh Family History: a Guide to Research* (1993). A selection of her articles first published in *The Western Mail* is to be found in *Clust y Wenci* ('The weasel's ear', 1997). In *Pobol sy'n Cyfri* ('It's people who count', 2001) she delved into the 1891 Census of Denbighshire, unearthing in a house-by-house analysis of the returns a wealth of detail about a rural community on the cusp of change. Her last collection of essays, published in 2009, was *Prynu Lein Dillad* ('Buying a clothes line') but yet another appeared in time for the National Eisteddfod in August 2011.

Among the honours that came her way was the White Robe Order of the Gorsedd of Bards in 1992 for her services to journalism in Wales and an Honorary Fellowship from the University of Bangor in 2005.

Mair Hafina Clwyd Jones (Hafina Clwyd), journalist and essayist: born Gwyddelwern, Merioneth 1 July 1936; editor of Y Faner *(1986–92); first marriage dissolved; married 1971 Clifford Coppack (deceased, one step-daughter); died Ruthin 14 March 2011.*

The Independent (22 March 2011)

DENNIS COSLETT

Dashing Commandant of the Free Wales Army

THE FREE WALES Army enjoyed a brief notoriety between 1963, when it began to attract attention with its marches and press releases, and 1969, when some of its members were sentenced at the end of a 53-day trial which culminated (too neatly to be a coincidence, some observers thought) on the very day of the investiture of the Prince of Wales at Caernarfon. Dennis Coslett was among the nine men charged under the Public Order Act with a variety of offences that included membership of a paramilitary organization and the handling of firearms and explosives.

The FWA's declared aim was to do for Wales what the IRA had done for Ireland: to initiate a revolution that would lead to independence. The group, including Coslett, carried the Red Dragon flag through the streets of Dublin in 1966 in the ceremonies marking the 50th anniversary of the Easter Rising.

Its leader was a charismatic young man named Julian Cayo Evans, a breeder of Palomino horses and an accomplished accordionist, who had a flair for publicity and, in particular, for hoodwinking the more gullible among the reporters who flocked to west Wales to cover a story about 'insurrection in the hills'.

He and Coslett came to wider notice when they were interviewed by a facetious David Frost on a late-night television programme in 1967. It was this thirst for publicity that was to prove fatal for the FWA: the case against them rested largely on the evidence provided by journalists who had witnessed their drills and rifle practice, though all agreed that, in fact, these idealistic young men were, if a little naive, quite harmless.

Dennis Coslett, a dashing figure who, like Moshe Dayan, the Israeli general, sometimes wore a black patch over his glass eye, was often to be seen at the head of the marches staged by the FWA. He was usually accompanied by his beloved dog Gelert, an impeccably well-behaved Alsatian, and dressed in the homemade uniform, complete with bandolier, pistol and insignia fashioned from the White Eagle of Snowdonia, in which the rebels liked to parade.

On one occasion, for the benefit of a reporter, he fitted a harness to Gelert's back which he said would take sticks of gelignite, thus making the animal a lethal missile. He had, he said, dozens more dogs hidden in the Black Mountains of Carmarthenshire, all trained to carry magnetic devices under the vehicles of the British army which would be sent to put down the Welsh rising. The story about these 'kamikaze dogs' duly appeared in *The Herald of Wales* and was then taken up by the colour supplement of *The Daily Telegraph*, after which Coslett received hundreds of angry letters from dog-lovers.

The FWA, never more than 20 in number (to say nothing of the dogs), made extravagant claims about their strength and firepower, and put on manoeuvres in which explosives and small arms were used. They were wont to claim responsibility whenever there was an attack on a reservoir or public building in Wales, though it subsequently transpired that these acts of arson, which caused a good deal of damage, were the work of a much more shadowy group calling itself *Mudiad Amddiffyn Cymru* ('Movement for the defence of Wales'), known as MAC.

For all the FWA's shenanigans, there was a more serious side to their activities in the fraught atmosphere of the 1960s when *Cymdeithas yr Iaith Gymraeg* (the Welsh language society) and other militant groups on the fringes of the nationalist movement were taking direct action against symbols of the British state. They no doubt drew attention to some genuine grievances but they also divided nationalist opinion and had an adverse effect on the electoral fortunes of Plaid Cymru, whose President Gwynfor Evans won the Carmarthen by-election of July 1966, only to lose it four years later.

The party was inevitably tarred by its opponents, cynically enough, with the same brush as the one used against the FWA, and Evans believed it was largely responsible for slowing up Plaid's advance in parliamentary terms. The veteran nationalist Saunders Lewis, on the other hand, who had served in the First World War and was no pacifist, regarded the FWA as soldiers fighting for Wales and made a point of attending their trial, while many others showed sympathy for the accused men.

Dennis Coslett was born in Carmarthen in 1939. Short, dark-haired, lean and hard-bodied, he seemed the archetypal Welshman, or at least the physical type that passes as such in the world's view. He had considerable reserves of nervous energy and his speech, in both Welsh and English, was fluent and excitable.

He always maintained that he was anti-English only in so far as England ruled Wales, and wanted total separation for his country, a republic no less. Having been conscripted at the age of 18, he did his military service as an infantryman with the Royal Welch Fusiliers and later sailed the world as a merchant seaman. Returning to Wales, he worked as a shot-firer in the small private mines that proliferated in the anthracite coalfield of west Wales after nationalization of the industry in 1947. It was an accident underground that had cost him the sight in his left eye.

The path that led him to the dock in Swansea in 1969 had begun in the late 1950s when it became clear that, despite united opposition in Wales to the flooding of the Tryweryn Valley in Merioneth, Liverpool Corporation was nevertheless able to turn it into a reservoir, with the loss of a Welsh-speaking community. The sense of injustice which thousands felt at this brazen trampling on the sensibilities of the Welsh people was exacerbated, in Coslett's view, by the ceremony at Caernarfon Castle in which the young

Englishman whom he called Charles Windsor was invested as Prince of Wales.

Coslett and Cayo Evans also offered their services to the stricken villagers of Aberfan near Merthyr Tydfil where, in October 1966, a coaltip slid into the valley, killing 116 schoolchildren; it is not clear what they did, but Coslett considered the gold watch with which he was presented as his most treasured possession.

Exasperated by Plaid Cymru's steadfast refusal to take a tougher line on such issues as Tryweryn, the investiture and Aberfan, he sought other means of promoting the nationalist cause. He had formed a cell of five friends who styled themselves the Welsh Republican Army which, after drilling by their commandant, soon merged with Cayo Evans's FWA.

Coslett believed an independent Wales would never be won by constitutional means alone because the only language understood by the British state was one backed up by violence. 'Force is to diplomacy what bullion is to banknotes,' he said, quoting John Jenkins, a sergeant in the British army who was subsequently sentenced to 10 years' imprisonment for his part in carrying out explosions in the name of MAC.

Having set his face against the non-violent methods of Plaid Cymru, Coslett was to remain outside mainstream politics for the rest of his days. His last years were spent in practising the martial arts at which he was adept and writing *Rebel Heart* (2000) and *Patriots and Scoundrels* (2004), in which he collected his poems and speeches and gave his own defiant account of the turbulent events in which he had played a part. His books are full of the high rhetoric, heavily influenced by Patrick Pearse and Michael Collins, which he habitually employed to express his views.

Of the nine members of the FWA who were arrested in dawn raids, roughly handled by the police and brought to trial at Swansea on 1 July 1969, one was dismissed, two were found not guilty and six sentenced to terms of imprisonment, with three sentences suspended. Cayo Evans and Coslett, rightly deemed to be the ringleaders, were each given 15 months.

In the latter's speech from the dock, which he delivered in Welsh before sentence was passed, he reminded the judge, Mr Justice Thompson, that he had learned violence in the British army, ending with a typical flourish: 'I sought to serve Wales and now I am prepared to suffer for Wales. I am ready for your sentence. Free Wales!'

Dennis Coslett, political activist: born Carmarthen 12 September 1939; married Averil Webb (one daughter, and two sons deceased); died Llanelli, Carmarthenshire 20 May 2004.

The Independent (21 May 2004)

GORONWY DANIEL

Civil servant and university administrator

GORONWY DANIEL'S CAREER as a public servant spanned 45 years, during which he won a reputation not only as a safe pair of hands, always an essential prerequisite for appointments in Wales, but as a committee man who could get the best out of his colleagues and officers without too much cajoling or having to use his somewhat gruff manner in anything but the most courteous way.

He was already well versed in the mandarin culture of Whitehall when he took up his appointment as Permanent Under-Secretary of State at the Welsh Office in 1964. Having lectured in Economics at Bristol University for just a year, he had been appointed temporary clerk attached to the Select Committee on National Expenditure in the House of Commons in 1941 and in the Ministry of Town and Country Planning two years later. From 1947 to 1955 he had worked as Chief Statistician at the Ministry of Fuel and Power and as Under-Secretary in the Coal Division from 1955 to 1964.

He was to spend only five years at the Welsh Office, from 1964 to 1969, under the first Secretary of State for Wales, James Griffiths, thereafter under Cledwyn Hughes and, briefly, under the prickly George Thomas, all of whom were Labour MPs for Welsh constituencies. Those were tempestuous times, with the Young Turks of the Welsh Language Society campaigning hard for official status for the language and Plaid Cymru beginning to make electoral headway after Gwynfor Evans won a by-election at Carmarthen in July 1966. Other events in the same year were the Aberfan disaster and the opening of the Severn Bridge and, three years later, the Investiture of the Prince of Wales.

Goronwy Daniel, a Welsh-speaker and patriot, was true to Whitehall tradition in never wearing his political colours on his sleeve and always maintaining his aplomb. The main challenge of the Permanent Secretary's job was to establish the credibility of the fledgling Welsh Office which, at the outset, was little more than a regional arm of the Ministry of Housing and Local Government with a staff of only 250, and he did that with great success.

Soon, under his leadership, it acquired additional responsibilities for health and agriculture, thus setting in train the process of devolution of which he was in favour. He was also an effective voice for Wales in lobbying Whitehall and Westminster on such major economic issues as pit closures. Unfailingly courteous and famously able to remember his colleagues by name, he won the lasting affection of all who worked with and under him, including Rhodri Morgan, now First Minister at the Welsh Assembly.

Born the son of a colliery manager in the industrial village of Ystradgynlais, Breconshire, in 1914, Goronwy Daniel was educated at Pontardawe Grammar School, the Amman Valley County School and the University College of Wales, Aberystwyth, where he took first class Honours in Geology in 1937; he then went on to Jesus College, Oxford, where he took a DPhil in Economic Statistics. In 1940 he married Lady Valerie, daughter of the second Earl Lloyd George and a granddaughter of the statesman. At the time of their marriage Valerie Lloyd George was Statistical Assistant to Sir William Beveridge, the Minister of Labour whose reports on insurance and employment became a blueprint for legislation ushering in the Welfare State during the years after the Second World War.

It was with a keen sense of loyalty to his old college that Daniel accepted the post of Principal at Aberystwyth in 1969. From among 22 names considered, his was unanimously and enthusiastically recommended by the selection committee. His 10 years at the 'College by the Sea' were happy and fruitful. The college had weathered the turbulence of the Investiture of July 1969 – for his own part in which the future Principal received a knighthood (Prince Charles had controversially spent the summer term at Aberystwyth as an undergraduate) – and now began a period of fresh growth on all fronts.

Daniel was particularly supportive of various initiatives in teaching through the medium of Welsh. One of his favourite schemes was the inauguration of a bilingual Drama Department in 1973 which he saw as providing theatre and broadcasting in Wales with fully trained actors and dramatists. In 1988–89 he chaired the Powers and Functions Working Party set up to consider the future of the University of Wales, whose 'Daniel Report' came out clearly in favour of the institution's federal structure.

He was physically very fit and apparently impervious to cold. Tales are still told of the consternation among coastguards on Cardigan Bay whenever Sir Goronwy took his small boat out in inclement weather, often sailing alone as far as Ireland. When the College Registrar once asked for permission to turn up the heating system at the approach of winter, the Principal advised him to instruct his staff to don extra pullovers and gloves.

A vital part of Goronwy Daniel's character was his egalitarian spirit: he treated everyone with the same warm geniality, however exalted or lowly their place in the scheme of things. Even so, it must be said that for those who did not know him well his rather forthright way of speaking could be disconcerting. I remember taking the French dramatist Eugene Ionesco to lunch at Plas Penglais, the Principal's official residence, during a tour of the University Colleges of Wales in 1972. Ionesco had no English and so there were some awkward silences during the pre-lunch drinks, relieved only when Lady Valerie addressed him in her fluent and elegant French. Sir Goronwy, a hospitable man, was not to be outdone in taking his responsibilities as host seriously, but unfortunately his French was not quite up to it.

At one point, in an effort to entertain his guest, he began prancing around the room, tapping on the valuable pieces of Welsh oak furniture and asking, *'Combien coute ça?'* When Ionesco, with that clown-like mask of his, ventured to guess the value of the antiques (in millions of francs), the Principal would exclaim, *'Non, non, non! Beaucoup plus, beaucoup plus!'* For much of the rest of the visit I had my work cut out having to explain to a perplexed master of the absurd how distinguished a man Daniel really was.

After leaving Aberystwyth in 1979, the Daniels retired to their farm at Treletert in Pembrokeshire, where they enjoyed country pursuits. For some time interested in the provision of a television service for Wales, Goronwy Daniel now became involved in the campaign for a fourth channel broadcasting mainly in Welsh. Under his chairmanship, the university published an influential feasibility study in which many of the old chestnuts used by opponents of the idea – Wales did not have sufficient talent to maintain such a service, and so on – were finally shown to have no substance.

He also played a vital role behind the scenes. When, in 1980, William Whitelaw reneged on the Conservative government's promise to create a Welsh-language Fourth Channel, and Gwynfor Evans was threatening to fast unto death unless it kept its word, Daniel was one of 'the three wise men' – with the Archbishop of Wales and Cledwyn Hughes – who went to see the Home Secretary in London. About a week later, the Secretary of State for Wales, Nicholas Edwards, announced that the Government would set up a Welsh-language channel after all.

A Bill received the royal assent on 13 November 1980, the new service came on air in 1982 and Daniel was appointed its first Chairman. S4C, as the Fourth Channel is known in Wales, is now an integral part of the Government's provision for television broadcasting. It may be properly considered as a monument not only to the readiness of Gwynfor Evans to sacrifice himself for the sake of a principle but also to the practical skills of Sir Goronwy Daniel, who guided the frail bark through what were then uncharted and choppy waters.

It was Daniel, together with Professor Alwyn Roberts, a leading member of S4C's board, who drew up contracts, made the first appointments and laid the financial foundations for the channel. Elan Closs Stephens, whom Daniel appointed as Professor of Drama at Aberystwyth in 1975 and who is now Chair of S4C, recalls how Daniel took a hands-on approach and was in his element whenever he had audience statistics to analyse.

Among his many honours, he received in 1980 the honorary degree of LLD from the University of Wales in recognition of his outstanding service to the life of the Welsh nation.

Goronwy Hopkin Daniel, civil servant and university administrator: born Ystradgynlais, Breconshire 21 March 1914; CB 1962; Permanent Under-Secretary of State, Welsh Office 1964–9; KCVO 1969; Principal, University College of Wales, Aberystwyth 1969–79; Vice-Chancellor, University of Wales 1977–9; Lord-Lieutenant for Dyfed 1978–89; Chairman, Welsh Fourth Channel Authority (S4C) 1981–6; married 1940 Lady Valerie Lloyd George (died 2000; one son, two daughters); died St Fagans, Cardiff 16 January 2003.

The Independent (20 January 2003)

GARETH ALBAN DAVIES

Poet who combined Welsh and Hispanic interests in his work

GARETH ALBAN DAVIES, the former Professor of Spanish at Leeds University, was also a Welsh poet who brought a genuinely European perspective to his writing, especially a scholarly knowledge of Lorca, the poet murdered during the civil war in Spain, and of Fernando Arrabál, the Spaniard who writes in French.

He translated a good deal of Spanish poetry into Welsh and, for the Welsh Academy, edited an anthology, *Y Ffynnon sy'n Ffrydio* ('The bubbling well', 1990), in which the eponymous fountain refers to the well-spring of poetic inspiration in Spain in the first three decades of the 20th century – until Franco's dictatorship poisoned it.

Gareth combined his Welsh and Hispanic interests in research on the writer David Rowland, whose translation of *La vida de Lazarillo de Tormes* (1554) was published as *The Pleasant History of Lazarillo de Tormes* in 1586. This anonymous work, the prototype of all picaresque literature and a scurrilous satire on the Catholic Church, was edited by Gareth for the prestigious Gregynog Press, which brought out a particularly fine edition with wood engravings by Frank Martin in 1991. His interest in the picaresque genre took in *La Celestina*, the short name for the famous dialogue novel by Fernando de Rochas, first published in 1499, on which he was an authority.

Gareth was also among a small but gallant band of Welsh writers whose knowledge of other European languages has been put to the service of Welsh literature. With Gareth Jones, sometime Professor of Russian at Bangor, he edited a symposium on 20th-century literature under the title *Y Llenor yn Ewrop* (1976), contributing chapters on Lorca and André Gide. With his wife Caryl, a distinguished scholar in her own right, he translated Gide's masterpiece, *La Symphonie Pastorale*, as *Y Deillion* (1965), in which the Protestant ethos and the pastor's love for the blind girl Gertrude are movingly rendered in Welsh.

Gareth was born at Tonpentre in the Rhondda Fawr during 'the angry summer' of 1926, when the miners were locked out for seven months by intransigent coal-owners after the General Strike of the previous May. His father, the Reverend T. Alban Davies, was a former miner, a pillar of the community and an early member of Plaid Cymru who instilled in his son a social conscience and the egalitarian and patriotic principles which remained with him for the rest of his life. He was the minister of Bethesda, a bastion of Congregationalism, whose lamp-lit piety his son was to recall with affection. Both father and son had broad shoulders, deep voices and a handshake that could crush the knuckles of lesser men.

The mass unemployment and economic deprivation of the Rhondda in the inter-war years do not figure much in Gareth's writing, but in an essay which I translated into English as 'The Fur Coat' he recalled the subtle class distinctions of the Valley – from the extravagant Siberian fox and Persian lamb worn in chapel by the managers' wives to the sealskin for which colliers' wives had to scrimp and save. He was particularly percipient about the superior social status of women teachers, the proud daughters of colliers set apart by their salaried profession in a sub-class of their own.

As a schoolboy, Gareth was introduced to *Cylch Cadwgan*, a coterie of Welsh writers who used to meet at the home of J. Gwyn Griffiths at Pentre in the Rhondda, and he later contributed poems to a group anthology. In such congenial company he was able to hone his skills as a poet and discuss the Spanish and French literature he was studying at Porth Grammar School. Thanks to his teacher, the Swiss expatriate

Georges Rochat, the school had a high reputation for the teaching of Romance languages, and by the time he left Gareth was a fluent Spanish-speaker.

In this he was helped by the existence in London of the bookseller Joan Gilli, who satisfied his voracious reading by supplying him, at generous discounts, with books in Catalan and Castilian. Gareth was able to repay his debt in 1988 by writing a glowing article in the magazine *Planet* about Martin Gilli, the bookseller's son, who carried on the business from a warehouse near Llangrannog in Ceredigion.

At the age of 18 Gareth became a Bevin Boy. For those readers too young to remember the 1940s, Bevin Boys were men conscripted to work in local mines in lieu of military service, under a scheme introduced by the Minister for Labour, Ernest Bevin. Gareth, who had inherited his father's sturdy build, spent three years working underground and, despite the physical hardship, enjoyed the experience because it brought him into closer contact with Rhondda men with whose lives he was already familiar. Even so, the son of the manse was regarded as very odd by his work-mates because he didn't smoke, didn't drink, didn't swear and didn't chase women.

In 1948, free at last to pursue an academic career, he went up to The Queen's College, Oxford, where he took a degree in Romance Languages, after which he was appointed to a lectureship in Spanish and Portuguese at Leeds University. He was given the chair of Spanish at Leeds in 1975. His doctoral thesis was on Antonio Urtado de Mendoza, poet and dramatist at the court of Philip IV in the 17th century, the entry for whom in *The Oxford Companion to Spanish Literature* names Gareth as the best critic of his work.

Although Gareth and Caryl spent some thirty years in Yorkshire, mainly near Otley, they kept in close touch with Welsh cultural life and managed to bring up their children as Welsh-speakers. After Gareth's retirement in 1986, they moved back to Wales, making their home in Llangwyryfon.

Gareth Alban, as he was generally known in Wales, was an accomplished poet who was not averse to letting his knowledge of the Romance languages show in his writing. His three collections, *Baled Lewsyn a'r Mor* (1964), *Trigain* (1986) and *Galar y Culfor* (1992), include poems addressed to the Spanish writer Unamuno and the Portuguese José Maria de Eça de Quéroz, while others are set in Galicia, Asturias, Valladolid, Barcelona, Estremadura, the Balearics and El Escoriál. Saunders Lewis thought Gareth's verse was more influenced by what he called Eluard's 'crystalline simplicity' than by any Spanish poet, but that is to ignore the echoes of Lorca, Quasimodo and Neruda to be heard in it. His poems have a voice of their own, especially when probing the faith he had inherited from his father and the more cerebral complexities learned from his extensive reading.

Gareth Alban was 'a Welshman with an international accent'. Though he was steeped in the Welsh literary tradition, his horizons were wide and his sympathy with other peoples deep and lasting. Much travelled, he wrote two journals, one dealing with a sabbatical year spent teaching at Dartmouth College in New Hampshire and the other with a visit to Australia. In both books he suppressed personal anecdote in favour of social observation.

In *Tan Tro Nesaf* ('Until next time', 1976), he gave an account of several months spent in Patagonia, the southernmost province of Argentina, during which he met descendants of the Welsh people who in 1865 had settled in the Chubut valley and the foothills of the Andes. Because many are bilingual in Spanish and Welsh, he was the ideal visitor and his book a valuable account of that distant place and its dual culture.

Gareth had a keen interest in the visual arts. His book *Y Llaw Broffwydol*, sumptuously produced by Y Lolfa in 2004, is a magisterial study of the life and work of Owen Jones, the son of Owain Myfyr, author of *The Grammar of*

Ornament and architect of many of the crystal palaces which proliferated in the London of his day.

Largely on account of his European interests and the universal themes of his verse, Gareth Alban stood slightly apart from many of his contemporaries in Wales and, in a culture that prefers the performer to the philosopher, his work has received comparatively little critical attention. The 'Collected Poems' I suggested to him several times did not materialize, though I hope that will soon be put right. For here was a Welsh writer fully equipped to deal with the modern world in all its complexity. Gareth was a scholar to his fingertips, a true poet, a staunch patriot and a man for whom the things of the mind always took precedence.

Gareth Alban Davies, writer and Hispanist: born Tonpentre, Rhondda Fawr, Glamorgan 30 July 1926; married 1953 Caryl Jones (one son, three daughters); Professor of Spanish, University of Leeds, 1975–86; died Aberystwyth, Ceredigion 9 February 2009.

The Independent (12 March 2009)

J.A. DAVIES

Airman betrayed to the Gestapo

J.A. Davies spent the latter part of the Second World War in hiding and as a POW, after baling out of his Lancaster over the Netherlands in February 1944. Having taken off with 101 Squadron from Ludford Magna in Leicestershire, the plane had been hit by German flak as it approached Leipzig on what was only the young Special Duty Operator's second sortie. The aircraft was in flames and, the last of the crew to jump, Jim Davies pulled the rip-cord on his parachute with the Welsh words *'Ein Tad, dyma dy gyfle di'* ('Our Father, this is your chance!') as he plunged into the darkness.

He landed near Groningen in the north of occupied Holland, sustaining only a sprained ankle on a night when the RAF lost 79 bombers and 553 aircrew. Two days later, his parents were informed by the Casualty Branch of the Air Ministry that his plane had been shot down over enemy territory and that he might be dead, and his personal effects were forwarded from Ludford Magna. It was not until the following August, when he was captured by the Germans, that they heard from the same source that he was alive and well. After a few weeks of being moved from house to house under the supervision of the Dutch Resistance, Davies had been taken into rural Friesland, where he was given sanctuary by a farmer on the outskirts of Oosterwolde. When that became too dangerous, he was moved to Garijp, about 10km from the provincial capital Leeuwarden, where the family of Pieter Dijkstra hid him in the secret compartment of a cellar.

It was not long before the Welshman had learned enough Dutch to be able to read the Bible, one of the few books in the Dijkstra household, and to walk the fields at night without arousing suspicion. He fitted well into the frugal life of the devoutly Protestant Dijkstras, though he was increasingly impatient to be repatriated. One of the small gestures of defiance he witnessed involved a comedian who came on to the stage of a village concert with his right hand raised in what appeared to be a Nazi salute. German soldiers in the audience sprang to attention shouting, 'Sieg Heil!' – only to hear the comedian go on, 'The snow was this high in Friesland in 1928.'

Eventually, after about six months, Davies was taken 'down the line' by the clandestine Witte Brigade and by August 1944 he was in Antwerp, where he was betrayed and handed over to the Gestapo by his guide, a woman he knew as 'Anna'. After the war he was one of many who testified against 'Anna', whom he had taken to be a member of the Resistance but who turned out to be a double agent, and she was given a long prison sentence.

Davies spent the rest of the war in the notorious St Giles Prison in Brussels, where he was in constant fear of execution because he had been captured in civilian clothes, and latterly in Stalag Luft 7 at Bankau, near Kreuzburg in Upper Silesia. During his incarceration he organized a choir and Welsh class for some 40 of his compatriots, among whose covert activities was an unsuccessful attempt to dig a tunnel out of the camp.

As the Allies advanced into Europe during the harsh winter of 1945, 1,500 prisoners were taken on a forced 300-mile march in sub-zero temperatures, many dying of exposure, malnutrition and dysentery. They were eventually liberated by the Soviet army from a camp near Luckenwalde, southwest of Berlin, Davies having survived by eating potato peelings which he had scrounged from the cooks.

Six weeks later, he was repatriated by American troops via Belgium. White bread, soap and hot water, he once told me, had never lost their fascination for him since. Severely malnourished and weighing under six stone, he returned to Blaen-ffos in Pembrokeshire where he had been brought up and, in the Baptist chapel of his childhood, received an emotional welcome which culminated in the singing of Pantycelyn's great hymn 'Cwm Rhondda', at which, for the first time since he had enlisted, he broke down and could not be comforted. He was now 22.

From Blaen-ffos he had gone, one of only two boys whose parents could afford it, to the grammar school at Cardigan and thence to Trinity College, Carmarthen, where he had joined the RAF Cadet Squadron and the Volunteer Reserve. After enlistment in the RAF in 1943, he had learned German so well that he was chosen to broadcast false codes in the language, the exact words of which he was to remember for the rest of his life.

In 1946, after a period of convalescence at Sunningdale Park in Berkshire, Davies went to study under Harold Laski at the London School of Economics, where he took his first degree and then his doctorate. The fruits of his research were later published as *Education in a Welsh Rural County, 1870–1973* (1973). The direction of his career was now set.

He taught for four years at schools in London and was then appointed to a post in Further Education in his home county of Pembrokeshire, with special responsibility for providing services for young people. A series of jobs followed including those of lecturer at Trinity College, Carmarthen, Deputy Director of Education for Pembrokeshire and Director of Education for Montgomeryshire. 'Dr Jim' was appointed Principal of the Normal College of Higher Education, Bangor, in 1969. The college, founded in 1858 as the first in Wales to admit the sons of Nonconformist parents, existed for the training of primary school teachers and had at the time about 700 students. Situated on the banks of the Menai Straits overlooking Anglesey, it had an enviable academic record.

It was, too, a bilingual institution in that most subjects were taught through the medium of Welsh and English, and the majority of its staff were Welsh-speakers. The Principal was staunch in his support for the college's language policy and proud that it turned out so many teachers capable of teaching in the Welsh-speaking parts of Wales and later in the officially designated bilingual schools in the English-speaking areas.

Jim Davies retired as Principal in 1985. Seven years later the Normal was integrated with the University College of North Wales, Bangor – a merger which Davies and his colleagues had stoutly resisted, fearing its implications for the bilingual policies they held so dear.

In retirement Davies kept in touch with his former comrades and his many friends in Friesland, visiting the districts where he had been hidden during the war. Some of his hosts, and their children, came to stay with the Davieses at their home on the Menai Straits. He described his wartime adventures in a book, *A Leap in the Dark* (1994).

Davies served as Chairman of the Welsh Film Board and on the executive committee of Cwmni Theatr Cymru, the Welsh-language theatre company. He was also prominent in the affairs of the University of Wales, the National Eisteddfod, the National Museum, the BBC and the Honourable Society of Cymmrodorion. In recognition of his services to Welsh culture he was made a member of the White Robe of the Gorsedd of Bards – the highest honour in Welsh-speaking Wales.

James Arthur Davies, educationist: born Boncath, Pembrokeshire 12 January 1923; Principal, Normal College, Bangor 1969–85; OBE 1989; married 1959 Nesta Williams (two daughters); died Bangor, Gwynedd 17 February 2007.

The Independent (27 February 2007)

LEWIS DAVIES

Philanthropist and librarian
whose generosity will benefit many Welsh writers

LEWIS DAVIES WAS the younger brother of the writer Rhys Davies (1901–78). Like him, he was born at Blaenclydach, a mining village near Tonypandy in the Rhondda Fawr. Their parents kept a small grocer's shop, known rather grandly as Royal Stores, and their mother was an uncertificated schoolteacher. Lewis, born in 1913, was the youngest of their six children.

The Davieses were set apart from a community wholly dependent on the coal industry by their status as shopkeepers. The father voted Liberal, played golf and had social aspirations which were linked with the Anglican Church, rather than the chapel which commanded the allegiance of the majority. Confirmed by the Bishop of Llandaf at the age of 17, Lewis was an acolyte for the Anglican priesthood but changed his mind on realising he was homosexual. The mother, rather like D.H. Lawrence's, was intent on securing for her children an education that would be the surest way of avoiding the pits. Two of her daughters became schoolteachers and one a nurse.

Lewis Davies could remember little of his more famous brother as a child. Rhys Davies, appalled by the endemic grime of industrial Rhondda and the narrowness of its social life, but also aware that his homosexuality had no place in the Valley's macho culture, left home at the age of 17 for a job in a Cardiff warehouse and, determined to become a writer, went to London shortly afterwards. By the time Lewis was a teenager Rhys, the author of several novels and collections of short stories, had a literary reputation comparable with that of H.E. Bates and A.E. Coppard.

It was not until the late 1930s, when they both lived in London, that the two brothers saw more of each other. Lewis was not admitted to the homosexual circles of Fitzrovia in which his brother moved, for Davies was notoriously secretive in all his liaisons and social contacts. The surviving correspondence between the brothers is confined, in the main, to advice from the older man on mundane matters such as finding a flat, confounding the demands of the income tax authorities and avoiding homosexuals whom he considered untrustworthy. The autobiographical novel, *Tomorrow to Fresh Woods* (1940), in which the principal characters are based on the Davieses, has no place for the Benjamin of the family.

Given this distance between them, it was all the more remarkable that, in 1990, Lewis set up a trust fund, with an initial endowment of £100,000, to keep his brother's name before the literary-minded public. When I first met him, he told me immediately that one of the reasons why he wished to offer me this sum was that, with intimations of mortality, he detested the idea of any part of his assets being taken, after his death, by 'that awful woman in Downing Street'. He spoke with great animus as if Margaret Thatcher were personally involved in meddling in his affairs.

He also explained that the money, which had come down to him after his brother's death, derived partly from the estate of the writer Anna Kavan, with whom Davies had had a strictly asexual relationship, and partly from that of Louise Taylor, an American who had been a close associate of Alice B. Toklas, the companion of Gertrude Stein. Davies, the most parsimonious of men, had come into this money towards the end of his life when he no longer had any use for it. Would I accept it as a first instalment of a much larger sum that would become available in due course?

I set up the Rhys Davies Trust, a registered charity

devoted to the promotion of Welsh writing in English, and have served as its Secretary ever since. Among the projects we have funded are the publication of three volumes of Rhys Davies's *Collected Stories*, a symposium of critical essays, an annual lecture delivered in his name at the University of Glamorgan and a short story competition organised by the Welsh Academy, the national association of writers in Wales. We have also put up plaques in memory of Welsh writers, beginning with one on the house that was once Royal Stores, and given prizes for creative writing at the comprehensive school in Tonypandy.

Lewis Davies was quietly pleased by what the Trust did with his money and, a cheerful, dapper man until well into his eighties, would turn up at events it sponsored, although he never interfered in its work except to express the hope that its awards would often go to young Welsh writers. He was aware that his brother, on first going to London as an impecunious writer, could have done with the financial support that the Trust was now able to provide, and he took great satisfaction from it.

He bore a physical resemblance to his brother, though was always quick to point out that he had not really known him. There is no mention of Lewis in Davies's autobiography, *Print of a Hare's Foot*; that book is, however, so unreliable an account that Lewis would only smile wryly whenever it came up in conversation.

He had no literary pretensions. After reading History at the University College of Wales, Aberystwyth, he trained as a librarian and, in 1937, found his first job, as an assistant librarian with *The Daily Mirror*. At the outbreak of war, he tried to register as a conscientious objector but his statement was refused by the tribunal; it was only with the help of a Dr Otto May, recommended by his brother for his sympathy for homosexuals, that he avoided conscription: he was rejected on medical grounds.

In 1947 he left his job at the *Mirror* because night shifts meant he had to miss many of the concerts and talks broadcast by the Third Programme, to which he was an avid listener. He joined Odham's Press, where in 1952 he was appointed Chief Librarian, remaining with the company after it became IPC and up to his retirement in 1978.

His last years were beset with physical infirmity and he was confined to a care home. He sold what remained of the writer's archive to the National Library of Wales and bequeathed his own estate to the Rhys Davies Trust, which will now benefit substantially. For such extraordinary generosity and for his genial personality, the last living link we had with his distinguished brother, Lewis Davies will long be remembered.

Arthur Lewis Davies, librarian and philanthropist: born Blaenclydach, Glamorgan 26 January 1913; assistant librarian, The Daily Mirror 1937–47; Chief Librarian, Odham's Press 1947–68, IPC 1968–78; died Lewes, East Sussex 9 December 2011.

The Independent (27 December 2011)

PER DENEZ

Writer and scholar who sought
recognition for the Breton language and culture

WHEN THE BRETON writer and scholar Per Denez was awarded
an honorary doctorate by the University of Wales in 1985,
he was astonished to hear its chancellor, Prince Charles, say
how sorry he was not to be able to address him in his own
language. He had never received such courtesy in France
and was more used to the insults which the French state
habitually flings at those who work on behalf of the Breton
language and its culture. The remark remained with him
as a sign of the comparatively kinder treatment received by
the Welsh, especially from their national university, where
the language and literature of Wales have been taught for a
hundred years or more.

Denez had long experience of fighting for the Breton
language and, during the post-war years when the Breton
movement was slowly recovering from the charge of
collaboration with the German invaders, was in the vanguard
of all attempts to restore the Breton language in schools and
the life of the people. At first he put his energies into the
publication of several small magazines which argued for a
measure of recognition for Breton by the French state and
the departmental authorities. In this he was associated with
Ronan Huon, who since 1948 had published an excellent
literary review entitled *Al Liamm* ('The link'). But in 1958
he started his own magazine, *Ar Vro* ('The country'), which
carried, besides articles about Breton culture, news from
the other Celtic countries, whose example was not lost on
those who were working for all things Breton. Another of
his magazines, *Hor Yezh* ('Our language'), still exists and

is the name of one of the leading publishing imprints in Breton.

But his most important contribution to Breton life was as a teacher. He had read English at the University of Rennes and stayed on to do a postgraduate diploma in Celtic Studies. A year in Aberdeen as a French-language assistant confirmed his interest in the Celtic lands and shortly afterwards he learnt Irish and Welsh, speaking them with great fluency and a charming accent, as well as Esperanto.

His first teaching post was at Quimper in Finistère but his proselytising on behalf of Breton soon came to the attention of the authorities and he was moved to Périgueux, where he promptly learned Catalan. After two years he was allowed to return to Brittany, taking a post as English teacher at Douarnenez in Finistère, where he lived for many years. Soon he was organising Breton classes for pupils and townspeople who wished to regain a grasp of their language.

Per Denez, or Pierre Denis as he was known to the French civil state, had a particular insight into the mindset of those who were anxious to learn Breton, the language of which they had been deprived by a centralist government virulently intolerant of 'regional dialects'. He had been born in Rennes, where no provision was made for Breton in the schools, and into a home which, although his mother was a Bretonne, was francophone. His interest in Brittany was awakened by a chance remark by one of his schoolmates at the Lycée St Martin that he was proud to be Breton. At the age of 13, he enrolled in Skol Ober, a correspondence course run for many years by the indefatigable Marc'harid Gourlaouen, and was soon at home in the language.

In 1969 he was appointed to the chair of Celtic at the University of Upper Brittany in Rennes, and was to remain there for 21 years, teaching the grammar and literature of Breton and specialising in research into the dialectology of

Douarnenez. Among his most startling achievements was to persuade Presidents Giscard d'Estaing and Mitterand of the case for introducing the licence, maîtrise, CAPES and DEUG through the medium of Breton. His department was responsible for turning out thousands of graduates who became the Young Turks of the revived Breton movement. Some, including one of his sons, Gwendal, who succeeded him to the chair at Rennes, have made major contributions to Breton scholarship and literature. Many became teachers in the Diwann primary-schools movement which, after 30 years of struggle, won a modicum of recognition from the French state in 2001.

Per Denez eschewed all party affiliations and was respected by most politicos in Brittany for his independent views. He served on myriad committees, including the Conseil Culturel de Bretagne and the Institut Culturel de Bretagne – though he was never tempted to stand for the regional council, which represents the furthest point to which the French government is prepared to take the process of administrative devolution. He also served as president of the Celtic Congress and the Kuzul ar Brezhoneg (Federation of Breton cultural organisations) and as a member of the Maison de la Culture at Rennes and the European Council of the Regions.

He saw this committee work as necessary if the cultural life of Brittany was to thrive, but preferred to apply his enormous energies to encouraging study of the language at the highest academic level, in particular the publication of texts and grammars, and in the training of teachers. For him, Breton was a living language which had to take its place in all sectors of public life.

His own list of books was held in great esteem. They include *Brezhoneg Buan hag Haes* ('Breton the quick and easy way', 1972), a textbook which went into Welsh, Irish, English, German and Catalan editions. He also wrote verse and prose in Breton, regularly contributing to a plethora of magazines and newspapers. Among his collections of stories are *Diougan Gwenc'hlan* ('The prophecy of Gwenc'hlan', 1979), *Glas evel daoulagad c'hlas* ('Blue like blue eyes', 1979) and *Evit an eil gwec'h* ('For the second time', 1982).

Many honours came his way: he was awarded Doctor in Litteris honoris causa by both the University of Wales and the National University of Ireland, and in 1990 he received the Ramon Llull prize from the Institute of Catalan Studies, the first time it had ever gone to a scholar the bulk of whose work had not been done in Catalan. In 1993 he received the Cross of Saint-Jordi, followed by the Prix Imram for Poetry and the Prix des Ecrivains Bretons. A Festschrift was published on the occasion of his retirement under the title *Breizh ha Pobloù Europa / Brittany and the Peoples of Europe*, to which 54 writers from a dozen countries, including Japan, Poland, Germany and Corsica, contributed articles.

The last time I saw Per Denez was during the Interceltic Festival at Lorient in 2000. He was not much interested in the folkloric aspect of things and we talked in Welsh mainly about the gains made by the Breton movement and, the subject always nearest his heart, the fortunes of the language. I had known him for 40 years and he seemed to be in his prime, buoyant with hope for Breton, cautious about the political situation in his country and anxious to learn about the latest developments in Wales. He was a gentle, modest, kind-hearted man, with an iron will and a beatific smile which faded only when he mentioned his wife, then suffering the last stages of Alzheimer's disease, whom he visited every day. Among the other topics we touched upon during that long sunny afternoon was what to do with his vast and valuable collection of papers and books. He had no confidence that they would be properly conserved in Brittany and liked the suggestion that he should give them to the National Library of Wales, where he knew they would be safe and available to researchers.

Per Denez (Pierre Denis), Breton writer and scholar: born Rennes, Brittany 3 February 1921; Professor of Celtic, Université de Haute-Bretagne, Rennes 1969–90; married 1949 Morwena Steven (died 2001; two sons, one daughter), 2003 Monique Macé (one son); died Romillé, Ille-et-Vilaine, Brittany 30 July 2011.

The Independent (2 September 2011)

HYWEL TEIFI EDWARDS

Historian of Victorian Wales and the National Eisteddfod

HYWEL TEIFI EDWARDS was Professor of Welsh at the University College of Swansea from 1989 until his retirement in 1995. He had spent some thirty years at Swansea prior to his appointment to a chair, during which he won a reputation as the pre-eminent authority on the literature of Wales in the 19th century, especially that produced under the aegis of the National Eisteddfod which was revived and put on a more secure footing in the 1860s. His knowledge of the colourful personalities and often bitter controversies animating the festival's affairs was encyclopaedic and his enthusiasm for its role in fostering the indigenous language and culture of Wales knew no bounds.

The fruits of his research first appeared in two substantial volumes, namely *Yr Eisteddfod 1176–1976* (1976) in which he traced the origins of the institution from the gathering of poets and musicians held at Cardigan under the patronage of the Lord Rhys in 1176, and *Gŵyl Gwalia* ('Festival of Gwalia', 1980), a magisterial study of the Eisteddfod between 1858 and 1868, when it was established as the paramount forum for the national culture of Wales.

Hywel Teifi, as he was known in Wales, was a great admirer of the Eisteddfod as a truly popular institution which did much to save the Welsh language from the oblivion into which Victorian values threatened to consign it, but he was no blinkered zealot and could be acerbically critical of its foibles and shortcomings, among which were nepotism and a false antiquarianism that undermined its legitimacy in some quarters.

He was particularly scathing about Hugh Owen (1804–81),

the influential civil servant who worked long and hard
to draw Wales more firmly into the orbit of the British
State, especially as far as its language was concerned: like
many members of the anglicized middle classes in his day,
Owen kept Welsh low on his list of priorities and urged his
countrymen, the majority of whom were Welsh monoglots,
to adopt English as the sole language of Progress, Empire
and Commerce.

Under the influence of Owen and his acolytes, the
Eisteddfod persuaded poets to yield their traditional pride of
place to musicians and singers, notably those who performed
for the Queen and won for Wales a reputation as 'the Land
of Song'. It also attracted the English-speaking gentry and
a small entrepreneurial class who insisted on introducing a
'Social Science Section' which offered prizes for essays on
social, commercial, industrial and scientific subjects, an
innovation soon abandoned, however, for lack of interest on
the part of a people hungry for poetry and music.

Hywel Teifi explored the psychology of this woeful
interlude in the history of Welsh culture in a memorable
lecture entitled *Baich y Bardd* ('The poet's burden') at the
National Eisteddfod held in Cardiff in 1978, an occasion
on which his laconic wit and trenchant views were warmly
appreciated by an audience of a thousand and more. There
was something attractively iconoclastic in his approach and
people enjoyed the demotic language he habitually used to
deflate the pompous and topple sacred cows from the Welsh
mantelpiece. A more sober account of the contribution made
by the Eisteddfod is to be found in his monograph in the
Writers of Wales series (1990), one of his rare publications in
English.

The attraction of music in Victorian Wales was particularly
potent. During the last decades of the 19th century the harpist
and the male voice choir came into their own, huge crowds
listening to the recitals in rapt awe and quasi-religious zeal
comparable to the fervour later seen at international rugby

matches. The choirs gave Wales a cultural identity when it most needed one: the 456-strong strong South Wales Choral Union, for example, conducted by the blacksmith-cum-hotelier Griffith Rhys Jones (known by his bardic name, Caradog), sang to tremendous acclaim at the Crystal Palace in 1872, after which the Welsh became renowned for this mode of singing.

Hywel Teifi made a special study of this phenomenon, which was social as much as it was musical, and in his short book *Eisteddfod Ffair y Byd* (1990) he wrote graphically about the impression made by Welsh choirs at the Chicago World Fair of 1893. He returned to this subject in *Jiwbilî y Fam Wen Fawr* ('Jubilee of the great white mother'), about how the Welsh celebrated Victoria's Jubilee in 1887, which was the subject of his lecture delivered at the National Eisteddfod in 2002.

On a wider canvas, Hywel Teifi traced the social fabric of Victorian and Edwardian Wales in his book *Codi'r Hen Wlad yn ei Hôl* (1989), the title of which –'To raise the old country to its feet'– was the motto of the great patriot Owen M. Edwards in his Herculean efforts to improve the teaching of Welsh in the schools of Wales and provide reading material for the common people. It focuses on the failure of the Welsh intelligentsia, after the infamous Blue Book reports of 1847 which had impugned the morality of the Welsh people, to mount an effective resistance to the imperial mindset which had confined Welsh to the home and chapel and refused it a place in law, education and public life.

The book also examines how a handful of writers, among them the polemicist Emrys ap Iwan and the novelist Daniel Owen, challenged the prevailing mood which revered all things English, and how Welsh literature, desperate to demonstrate the purity of the Welsh character to 'onlooking nationalities', reached a nadir from which it took a long time to recover. The most spirited chapters are those describing the raising of funds for the erection of a memorial to Llywelyn, the Last Prince of independent Wales, at Cilmeri near Builth where he was killed by Anglo-Norman forces in 1282, and a hilarious account of the National Pageant staged by members of the romantically-inclined gentry and industrialists of Cardiff in 1909.

The same regard for culture as the product of political and social attitudes informs *Arwr Glew Erwau'r Glo* ('Brave hero of the coal acres', 1994), a study of the miner in Welsh literature between 1850 and 1950. Although born in the village of Llanddewi Aber-arth in rural Cardiganshire (from which county, Sir Aberteifi, he was given his middle name), Hywel Teifi had his family roots in the coal valleys of Glamorgan. He now set about demolishing the image of the Welsh collier as, at best, a virtuous but pathetic victim and, at worst, a dangerous revolutionary. At the heart of the book is a discussion of the outrage caused by Kitchener Davies's play *Cwm Glo* ('Coal valley', 1935), which depicts the baneful effects of unemployment on the morals of a mining family during the Depression, the most shocking of which has the daughter walking the streets of Cardiff as a prostitute.

Hywel Teifi's keen interest in the theatre, especially amateur drama, is to be seen in *Codi'r Llen* ('Raising the curtain', 1998), an illustrated account of the myriad drama companies that flourished in all parts of Wales in the inter-war years.

It should come as no surprise that Hywel Teifi Edwards was not content to be confined to the groves of Academe. He was an active member of Plaid Cymru from his undergraduate days at the University College of Wales, Aberystwyth, and stood twice as the party's candidate. At the General Election of 1983 he contested Llanelli and, four years later, Carmarthen, where he made a large dent in the Labour vote. A left-winger, he had nothing but contempt for the Labour Party in Wales which survived the creation of the National Assembly in 1999.

An able public speaker, he often put me in mind of Aneurin Bevan in his mastery of the pregnant pause, the dramatic gesture and the swift delivery of the *coup de grace* that could be as devastating as it was wittily phrased, while his ebullient, not to say bullish manner, was always impressive. The same qualities brought him many invitations to take part in radio and television programmes, and he did so with a gusto, eloquence and erudition that were his trademarks. His stentorian voice and mischievous manner enlivened many a committee, public meeting and television programme.

He leaves a wife and two children, one of whom is the well-known broadcaster and BBC newsreader Huw Edwards. It gave him intense satisfaction to see his son, a Welsh-speaker, presenting a BBC Wales television series, *The Story of Welsh*, in the spring of 2003. A Festschrift in which some of his many admirers paid tribute to his scholarship and jovial personality was published as *Cawr i'w Genedl* ('A Giant for his Nation') in 2008.

Hywel Teifi Edwards, Welsh literary historian: born Llanddewi Aber-arth, Cardiganshire 15 October 1934; Professor of Welsh, University College, Swansea, 1989–1995 (and Emeritus); married Aerona (one son and one daughter); died Llanelli, Carmarthenshire 4 January 2010.

The Independent (7 January 2010)

OWEN EDWARDS

Pioneering television executive and architect of S4C

SOCIAL CLASS IN Wales is subtly different from that in England, but even by English standards Owen Edwards, broadcaster and first Chief Executive of S4C (Sianel 4 Cymru), the fourth television channel in Wales, was born with a silver spoon in his mouth.

His father, Sir Ifan ab Owen Edwards, was the founder in 1922 of Urdd Gobaith Cymru (Welsh League of Youth), which still flourishes in many parts of Wales. His grandfather, Sir Owen M. Edwards, was Chief Inspector of Schools with the Welsh Board of Education and, as writer, editor and publisher, made a major contribution to the Welsh national revival of the late 19th century.

Some of their forebears had been leaders of early Welsh Methodism and belonged to an intellectual elite which owed its status not to money but to their standing as pillars of a chapel society that amounted, in some parts of Victorian Wales, to a theocrcacy. The family's roots were in the monoglot, radical, Nonconformist peasantry of upland Merioneth, but over three generations they became the nearest Wales has had in recent times to a patrician line devoted to patriotic endeavour and public service.

Owen Edwards was born in Aberystwyth in 1933 and was among the first seven pupils to attend a pioneering Welsh-medium primary school which was opened by a group of prominent townspeople led by his father and under the aegis of the Urdd. Welsh was his first language and, although he acquired a pukka English accent at Leighton Park, a minor public school near Reading, it remained the language of his home and professional career for the rest of his life. Like his father and grandfather, he chose to serve the language and nation which had first claim on his allegiance, though like them he never revealed his political opinions and eschewed all affiliations which might have compromised him.

As an undergraduate reading Law at Lincoln College, Oxford, where his grandfather had been Fellow and Tutor in History before joining the Inspectorate, he showed little interest in party politics and confined his social activities to the convivial gatherings of the Dafydd ap Gwilym Society, where he came into contact with several compatriots who, like him, were later to take up influential posts in Wales.

His first job was in his home town: he became a cataloguer at the National Library of Wales, but remained in it for barely two years. It was only after he went to work in television, initially with Granada and, from 1961, with the BBC in Cardiff, that he came into his own. He had an authoritative voice, fluent Welsh, dark good looks, and an affable interviewing manner – all the very stuff of television – and it soon became clear that here was a man cut out for the new medium.

For the next six years he fronted the nightly current affairs programme *Heddiw* ('Today'), winning his spurs as an accomplished broadcaster who became in many ways the Welsh counterpart of Cliff Michelmore. It was not long before *Radio Times* would describe him as 'a friendly personality whose name has been made as widely known by the television camera as those of his father and grandfather who, in their turn, gave immeasureable service to Wales'.

The programme was the first of its kind in the Welsh language and proved to be a training-ground for a generation of broadcasters, many of whom went on to make their reputations as directors and administrators not only within the BBC but in commercial television and with independent production companies.

Edwards' promotion was swift and well-deserved. In 1967

he was appointed Programme Organizer with BBC Wales, Head of Programmes in 1970 and Controller in 1974. His seven years at the helm coincided with rapid development of the BBC's output in Wales, in both Welsh and English, so that by the mid-1970s it was producing some 1,500 hours of radio a year and 650 hours of television, in both languages.

But these were also some of the most turbulent years in the history of Welsh broadcasting. There was keen public debate about the structure of the BBC and vigorous, sometimes law-breaking campaigns were mounted by *Cymdeithas yr Iaith Gymraeg* ('Welsh Language Society') which was calling for greater provision and, in due course, for a single Welsh-language channel. There were attacks on the BBC's studios in Cardiff, Bangor, Manchester, Bristol, Newcastle and Plymouth, as well as a sit-in at Bush House and a demonstration in the House of Commons, followed by arrests, fines and prison sentences for hundreds of militants, young and old.

In the heated clashes between broadcasting executives and language activists over how many hours a week should be broadcast in Welsh, Edwards maintained a lofty insouciance towards the abuse that was often hurled at him, as the BBC's representative in Wales, but was always ready to talk to those who bothered to ascertain the facts before joining in the fray. Nevertheless, thousands refused to pay their television licence fee for as long as the broadcasting authorities remained intransigent.

It was, *inter alia*, Edwards' sympathy for the principle of a Welsh Channel – whatever the technical difficulties and political implications may have been – that encouraged the BBC's critics to go on pressing for it. 'The effectiveness with which nation can adequately speak unto nation,' he conceded in his coded manner during a lunch-time lecture in 1976, 'depends upon the extent to which a nation can adequately discharge its prime function and privilege of properly speaking to itself.' As a BBC man, he was not, however, in favour of an independent Welsh Broadcasting Authority and managed to stifle all talk of it.

When in 1974 the Crawford Committee was preparing its report on broadcasting in Wales, with particular regard to how a Welsh-language fourth channel might be funded and operated, Edwards made important contributions to its deliberations and brought his professional expertise to bear on some of the practical problems.

The cause of the channel suffered a setback in 1979, however, when William Whitelaw, the Home Secretary, announced that the Conservative government had changed its mind and would not, after all, set up a Welsh-language channel. It was only after the veteran leader of Plaid Cymru, Gwynfor Evans, threatened to fast to the death that Margaret Thatcher, making her first U-turn, announced that the government would keep its promise to set up the channel. Edwards, with others, worked hard behind the scenes in the fraught atmosphere of the time, using his diplomatic skills to excellent effect.

It seemed almost a foregone conclusion that when S4C was created in 1981, and began broadcasting on All Saints' Day in the year following, Edwards should be its Chief Executive. Gwynfor Evans referred to him in his memoirs, *For the Sake of Wales*, as 'the right man in the right job', and that was the general view of his appointment. Not least among his qualifications was that he was wholly conversant with the ways of the BBC and commanded a wide measure of respect in all camps – among independent programme makers, HTV and the BBC itself, in both Cardiff and London, all participants in the new enterprise.

Under his directorship the channel, even if the English-speaking Welsh viewed it with some envy, soon won its place in the affections of Welsh-speakers to an extent that it is now difficult to imagine a Wales without S4C. Owen Edwards was its architect and if he had not been obliged by Parkinson's disease to take early retirement in 1989, he would doubtless have continued to add cubits to his stature as the most outstanding broadcasting executive of his generation.

Even so, he maintained an interest in broadcasting as Chairman of the Association for Film and Television in the Celtic Countries, often speaking at its conferences and publishing papers in which he was always prepared to examine new concepts and structures. He served several of the organizations whose work was closest to his heart: as President of the Welsh Nursery Schools Movement, as Council member of Urdd Gobaith Cymru, and as Vice-Chairman of the National Eisteddfod. Among the awards he received in recognition of his contribution to the television industry were an honorary LLD from the University of Wales, the Gold Medal of the Royal Television Society and a special prize from BAFTA for a lifetime's achievement.

A genial man with a laconic sense of humour, fond of late-night company but allowing only a few of his closest colleagues a glimpse of the more relaxed side of his personality, he had one eccentricity which he made no attempt to hide. Railway timetables were for him a source of endless fascination: he knew the times of trains running on all the tracks in the United Kingdom and often tested his knowledge, and their reliability, by travelling its length and breadth by his favourite mode of transport. It was his way of relaxing from the arduous duties which he carried out with such exemplary diligence and courage.

In all that Owen Edwards did he proved worthy of his illustrious forebears and, like them, served the Welsh people to the utmost of his abilities. His grandfather's motto had been 'I godi'r hen wlad yn ei hôl' (To raise the old country to its feet) and to that ideal he devoted his life's work.

Owen Edwards, broadcaster and first Chief Executive of S4C (1981–9); born Aberystwyth, Cardiganshire 26 December 1933; Head of Programmes, BBC Wales (1970–4) and Controller (1974–81); married 1958, Shân Emlyn (two daughters, marriage dissolved, deceased); 1994, Rosemary Allen; died 30 August 2010.

The Independent (7 September 2010)

TOM ELLIS

Labour MP whose disillusion led
him into the ranks of the Liberal Democrats

TOM ELLIS, THE Labour MP who defected to the Social Democratic Party soon after its formation in 1981, played a prominent part in the creation of the Social and Liberal Democratic Alliance which became, in turn, the Liberal Democratic Party. His decision to turn his coat was prompted by a belief that the Labour Party had fallen prey to 'the loony left' and that a new party was needed to seize the centre ground of British politics.

Elected as the Labour member for Wrexham in 1970, Tom Ellis served that constituency well until 1983, latterly as a member of the SDP, but lost his seat at the general election of that year and was never again returned to office, despite contesting Clwyd South West and standing as an Alliance candidate in other parts of Wales. The nadir of his electoral fortunes was at the by-election in the Labour stronghold of Pontypridd in 1989 when he received a derisory 1,500 votes, about four per cent of the number cast.

From 1975 to 1979 he served as a nominated Labour member of the European Parliament, an institution of which he approved because, unlike Westminster, it was not in thrall to any hegemony and held out hope for such national communities as Wales, Brittany and Catalonia. In his thinking about the nation-state and the smaller nations of Western Europe Ellis was influenced by the French anthropologist Yves Person and the Scottish writer Tom Nairn, author of *The Break-Up of Britain* (1977).

He found it hard to stomach the 'ideological delusion'

which he detected in the Labour Party's dithering over whether Britain should join the European Economic Community. At the heart of its dilemma, he believed, was the unitary, centralist, British State and the two-party system that is one of its buttresses. His rigorous critique of the Labour Party and its failure to put people and community before pragmatic skulduggery was based on his profound scepticism towards the British State and his desire to see new, democratic institutions taking its place in the life of the peoples of Britain.

Tom Ellis had become unhappy with the Labour Party almost as soon as he entered Parliament in 1970, mainly on account of its adherence to outmoded economic theories, its Euroscepticism and what he saw as its English/British nationalism, and had found himself in hot water with his constituency party over more than one issue, particularly after it was infiltrated by the Militant Tendency. The cynicism of some Labour members and the simplistic dogma of others awakened doubts which had hitherto lain dormant. Labour, he thought, had become 'a doctrinal party without a doctrine'.

The final blow came in 1979 when some Labour MPs, with Leo Abse and Neil Kinnock foremost among them, declared themselves against the measure of devolution which their government was proposing for Wales and Scotland. Tom Ellis was one of the seven Welsh Labour MPs who voted (with Liberals and Nationalists) in favour of the Bill and campaigned for a Yes vote in the referendum that followed. He was appalled that so many of his fellow MPs sat on their hands and allowed the government's proposal to be roundly defeated in Wales.

Neil Kinnock's failure to lead the Labour Party to victory later in the year confirmed Tom Ellis in his view that a new radicalism was needed. He took a decision to leave Labour during the week of the party's annual conference in the autumn of 1980, an occasion marred by bitter altercations between rival factions that led even to a display of fisticuffs on the floor of the hall. He resigned from the Labour Party in the year following, shortly after his father, a party stalwart since the 1920s, had done the same.

Tom Ellis's contribution to John Osmond's symposium *The National Question Again: Welsh Political Identity in the 1980s* (1985) describes his disillusion with Labour and his conversion to Social Democracy. Few MPs could set down with such clarity of conviction the principles by which they claim to function. The chapter is also a document of uncommon percipience, wide in its references and still uncannily relevant to the governance of the United Kingdom today

Ellis was prepared to sacrifice his career as a Labour MP for his vision of a decentralized Britain. In the autumn of 1980 he attended meetings called by 'the Gang of Four' – David Owen, Bill Rodgers, Roy Jenkins and Shirley Williams – who drew upon his memorandum on the creation of a social democratic party when writing 'the Limehouse Declaration' of January 1981. By that time Ellis was perhaps nearer to the Liberals than to the Social Democrats, particularly in his insistence that whatever the new arrangements might be, they would have to allow for a federal approach to party organization and policy in Wales. He also found it difficult to work with the fractious David Owen, though he was elected President of the Social Democratic Party's Council in Wales.

At the General Election of June 1983 the fledgling Alliance won 25 per cent of the votes and 23 seats, two of which were in Wales, but Ellis lost his seat to a Conservative, whose party was returned to power under Margaret Thatcher – the worst of all outcomes in his judgement. He was cast down by this result, and not only for personal reasons, but – describing himself modestly as a man 'of mildly contemplative temperament' – he continued to think, write and speak eloquently about what he wanted for Wales and Britain. Why he was never attracted to Plaid Cymru remains a matter to which only a few of his close associates were privy.

Tom Ellis had enjoyed a strong personal following in Wrexham, based largely on his genial, attentive, earnest manner and his close identification with the coal-mining villages of north-east Wales, an area known as Maelor. He had been born, the son and grandson of miners, in Pant, a village that is now part of Rhosllannerchrugog and within five miles of the border with England.

Rhos was a close-knit, hillside community of some ten thousand people, the majority Welsh-speaking, but the boy attended an Anglican Church school which dispensed instruction through the medium of English and his parents were told to discourage the speaking of Welsh at home. The consequent loss of his native language left a deep scar in his personality which started to heal only as he began relearning the language at Ruabon Grammar School. Years later he was to write that he was still struggling 'to resist the potentially corrosive quality of that experience'.

The boy was familiar with strike, lockout and explosion: the infamous Gresford Disaster, one of the worst in the annals of British mining, occurred in a neighbouring village when he was ten years old and his father had been a member of the rescue brigade that searched for survivors. Whenever Tom Ellis and I met we would discuss the evergreen mystery of who wrote the ballad that begins: 'You've heard of the Gresford Disaster, / The terrible price that was paid, / Two hundred and sixty-two colliers were lost / And three of the rescue brigade.' The other interest we had in common was contemporary Welsh and English poetry, from which he could quote with ease and understanding. He wrote a perceptive study of R.S. Thomas in Welsh which appeared in 2008.

Even as a boy his ambition had been to become a colliery manager. He had trained as a chemist, having taken a degree in the subject at the University College of North Wales, Bangor, but his heart had always been in the coal industry. In 1947, the year the mines were nationalized, he joined his father underground and continued to work at the coal-face for another eight years, leaving only so that he could study mining engineering at Nottingham University.

He achieved his boyhood ambition when, at the age of 33 in 1957, he was put in charge of Bersham, a colliery not far from his home. A popular manager, mainly because he knew how to handle his men in good times and bad, he gave the impression that he loved working in the coal industry and would swop his job for no other. Pit safety and good working relations were always at the top of his list of priorities, as he demonstrated in his book *Mines and Men* (1971).

His autobiography, *Dan Loriau Maelor* ('Under the floors of Maelor', 2003), is an insider's account of the coal industry of north-east Wales and the largely Welsh-speaking culture of the mining villages which depended on it until the pit-closures of the 1980s. The book, an English version of which appeared as *After the Dust Has Settled*, ends with a revealing sketch of how the SDP/Liberal Alliance was conceived and eventually brought to birth and of his part in its travails. His rare flashes of animus were reserved for irresponsible NCB officials and politicians who put personal ambition before service to their electors. But there was something of Dr Pangloss in Tom Ellis's sunny temperament: in his book, all was for the best in the best of all possible worlds.

Robert Thomas Ellis, colliery manager and politician; born Pant, Rhosllannerchrugog, Denbighshire 15 March 1924; married 1949 Nona Harcourt Williams (deceased; three sons, one daughter); MP for Wrexham (Labour, 1970–81; SDP, 1981–3); MEP (Labour, 1975–9); died 14 April 2010.

The Independent (20 April 2010)

EMRYS EVANS

'Emrys Midland Bank'

EMRYS EVANS WAS the public face of the Midland Bank in Wales. He joined its staff in 1941, shortly before war service with the Royal Navy, returning in 1946 to resume a career which ended only with his retirement in 1984, by which time he had been Senior Regional Director for eight years. So closely was he associated with the bank that he was affectionately known in Wales, where there is a dire shortage of surnames, as Emrys Midland Bank, the title of a programme about him shown on S4C, by a sad coincidence, on the day of his death and which he did not live to see.

His passing on the very eve of the Royal Welsh Agricultural Show, which is celebrating its centenary year at Builth this week, was a further blow to the public life of Wales, for Evans had served as chairman of the show's board of management since 1999 and its prestige as the premier event in the agricultural community's calendar was one that was close to his heart.

He was not only a banker but also a man devoted to charitable work in a variety of fields. He held more than 50 senior appointments ranging from the chairmanship of the Tenovus Centre of Cancer Research and the Kidney Research Unit for Wales to the presidency of the National Eisteddfod and trusteeship of the Children's Hospice for Wales Appeal. There is a hardly a charity with which he was not associated, sometimes from behind the scenes, and for this selfless work he was held in the highest regard in many quarters. He had the ability to concentrate minds and lead from the front whenever money was needed for a good cause. In 1994, when he was 70, he walked from Holyhead to Cardiff in a bid to raise £100,000 for Tenovus.

Emrys Evans was born at Maes-glas, a small farm at Y Foel, on the earthwork that marks the border between the old counties of Montgomeryshire and Merioneth, in 1924. He spoke Welsh with the attractive accent of his native place and the language was always a matter of the utmost importance to him. As Regional Director for Wales of 'the listening bank', he was attentive to those who, in the early 1960s, were calling for the wider use of Welsh in banking and was proud to think that the Midland was among the first to introduce bilingual cheques, now accepted by all banks as the norm, before the campaign had started. Such a policy, he had successfully argued, was 'good for the bottom line'.

After schooling at Llanfair Caereinion, he was called up in 1942 and, two years later, at the age of 20, took part in the D-Day landings, during which he was mentioned in despatches. He and two other radio operators were dropped off the Normandy coast near Arromanches from a motor torpedo boat, a day in advance of the invasion, with orders to report back on enemy troop movements. Hiding on the cliffs, they watched as an armada of boats unloaded their men, vehicles and equipment and the first soldiers fought their way up the beaches. Out of his group of 58, only 10 men survived, an experience that Evans admitted left a permanent scar; he was loath to speak about it and not even his family heard the full story.

His rise in the world of banking was rapid: from working behind the counter at branches in Wales and then in London, where he was posted to Head Office at Poultry, he became Regional Director for South Wales in 1972, then for Wales in 1974, and in 1976 Senior Regional Director. Hand in hand with his professional career went his work with myriad organizations prominent in the business and economic life of Wales. From 1979 to 1981 he was Chairman of the CBI in Wales and from 1982 to 1990 of the Welsh Committee for

Economic and Industrial Affairs. Among the projects that gave him most satisfaction was the setting up of business initiative schemes working through the medium of the Welsh language to regenerate areas of industrial and social decline.

His services as a dependable and knowledgeable public servant who never wore his political colours on his sleeve were enlisted by numerous bodies such as Barnardo's, the Welsh Sports Aid Trust, Llandovery College, the Council for the Protection of Rural Wales, the National Playing Fields Association, the Welsh Language Board, the Design Council for Wales and the Prince of Wales Committee. At a local level he found great delight in meetings of the Cardiff Business Club, in regular worship at Ebeneser, a bastion of the Welsh Congregationalist Church in Cardiff which he served as Secretary, and as High Sheriff of Glamorgan in 1985–86. He also played an important role in the affairs of the University of Wales, as Treasurer, and as Chairman of the Council of Swansea University. From 1988 to 1996 he was Treasurer of Mansfield College, Oxford.

Emrys Evans was an approachable man with a sunny temperament who usually regretted having to turn down a request for financial help. In a country where support for things cultural from the commercial sector is uncommon, difficult to secure and not often renewable, he made the Midland Bank (now HSBC) a by-word for an enlightened, generous attitude to the public life of Wales, from which thousands have benefited.

William Emrys Evans, banker: born Y Foel, Montgomeryshire 4 April 1924; staff, Midland Bank 1941–67, Assistant General Manager (Agriculture) 1967–72, Regional Director, South Wales 1972–4, Regional Director, Wales 1974–76, Senior Regional Director, Wales 1976–84; CBE 1981; married 1946 Mair Thomas (one daughter); died Dinas Powis, Vale of Glamorgan 18 July 2004.

The Independent (21 July 2004)

LYN EVANS

Chief Executive of the Independent Television Authority in Wales

THE EARLY 1960s were turbulent times in the development of independent broadcasting in Wales. The first commercial television company, Television Wales and the West (TWW), founded in 1958, shared its territory with Granada. When in 1962 a new consortium, Teledu Cymru, was launched under the leadership of Dr Haydn Williams, Director of Education for Flintshire, its main rival was TWW. Unable for technical reasons to reach its target audience – its signal was too weak for the mountainous terrain – Teledu Cymru ran almost immediately into financial difficulty and, amid bitter acrimony, folded less than a year later.

That TWW was able to take over the assets and function of Teledu Cymru, including the provision of seven hours of Welsh-language programmes a week, a crucial consideration, was in large measure facilitated by Lyn Evans, the Independent Television Authority's Chief Executive in Wales. The eyes and ears of the ITA (later the Independent Broadcasting Authority, or IBA, and now the Independent Television Commission, or ITC), Evans brought to his post a profound understanding of the politics of broadcasting, as well as managerial skills of a high order, which ensured that the takeover and subsequent course of independent broadcasting in Wales would be as smooth as possible.

Although he avoided the limelight, preferring to play the discreet civil servant, it was generally known that Evans was at the heart of the decision-making process. He provided, moreover, a persuasive voice in the committees of the ITA in London. At home, although the most genial of men, he was not averse to speaking plainly if he thought the interests of programme-makers and television executives were in jeopardy. Television, he believed, was a vital sector of the nation's cultural life and needed the most favourable circumstances if it was to flourish.

The same commitment to high standards was demonstrated by Evans after the establishment of Harlech Television (later HTV), which he oversaw with his usual percipience. One of his extra-office duties, which he accepted with alacrity, was to undertake public engagements the length and breadth of Wales, in which he was able to speak with great eloquence to lay audiences about the complexities of broadcasting policy and practice.

Born in Cardiff in 1914, Lyn Evans was the son of Howell T. Evans, headmaster of the County School at Aberaeron in Cardiganshire, where he was brought up from the age of four. He was inordinately proud of his father's reputation as the author of a number of books on the history of Wales, some of which were widely used as secondary school textbooks during the inter-war years, and wrote an affectionate biography of him, *Portrait of a Pioneer* (1982).

Although his father was a major influence on his cultural attitudes, it was a matter of regret for Evans that, typical of the time and class to which he belonged, he had not been brought up Welsh-speaking, something he put right when, as a young adult he learnt the language. It was a source of pride to him that his three children were able to speak Welsh.

Nor did he emulate his father's distinguished academic career, but left school at the age of 15 to become a cub reporter on the staff of the *South Wales Journal of Commerce* in Cardiff's docklands, then as a staff reporter for the *Western Mail* and *The South Wales Echo*.

After war service with the RAF he joined *The Daily Herald* (in south Wales and London), and finally the *News Chronicle* as editor of its Welsh pages, a post he held until the late 1950s. He moved from journalism into the Civil Service on his appointment as Senior Information Officer of the Central Office of Information in Cardiff.

In 1959 his experience as an administrator and journalist covering Welsh affairs helped him secure the new post of Officer for Wales and the West of England in the Cardiff office of the ITA where he remained until his retirement in 1979. For his services to broadcasting in Wales he was appointed OBE in 1969.

A private man, as much by instinct as by the exigencies of his professional status, Lyn Evans nevertheless played an active role in the social life of Cardiff. He was for many years President of Cardiff East Rotary Club and a member of the Cardiff Welsh Dining Club, a select and influential group which meets in the capital. He was also, as a staunch Baptist, a trustee of Tabernacl, the chapel in the heart of the city's shopping centre, and a member of several choirs.

Llywelyn (Lyn) John Evans, journalist and television executive: born Cardiff 16 July 1914; Officer for Wales and the West of England, Independent Television Authority, 1959–79; OBE 1969; married 1939 Edna Evans (one son, two daughters); died Cardiff 3 December 2001.

The Independent (7 December 2001)

YANN FOUÉRÉ

Breton militant and European federalist

YANN FOUÉRÉ SET out on a collision course with the centralist, unitary French State from the moment he began taking an interest in Breton affairs as a schoolboy during the inter-war years.

The crash came in 1945 when he had to leave Brittany in a hurry, first for Wales and then Ireland, to escape a sentence of 20 years' hard labour handed down for his part in the Emsav (as the Breton movement is known).

He was accused of collaboration with the Germans when all he had done was take part in the activities of Breton cultural circles in Paris. Before the war, however, he had been one of the founders of *Ar Brezhoneg er Skol*, a society for the teaching of Breton and Breton history, and Vice-President of *L'Union Régionale Bretonne*. He also launched, in 1942, two newspapers, *La Bretagne* and *La Dépêche de Brest*, in which he argued for a greater degree of autonomy for Brittany.

It was this latter activity, partly funded by the collaborationist Vichy regime, that was held against him: to have questioned the concept of the Republic as *'une et indivisible'* was enough to condemn him. He was tarred with the same brush as nationalist leaders who had actively collaborated with the Nazis and who, as the Allies advanced, had returned with them to Germany.

In Wales, where he assumed the alias Dr Moger, suggested by his wife's maiden name, he was given refuge at the home of Gwynfor Evans, the leader of Plaid Cymru. After being deprived of his job as a French tutor at University College, Swansea, and at a Catholic College in Llandeilo, he moved to Ireland to avoid arrest, and there settled with his wife and young children, taking the name Sean Mauger. In Connemara he set up a successful lobster farm, and continued writing, editing and organising for the Breton cause. The French Government exonerated him of all charges in 1958, after which he was allowed to return to Brittany.

A prolific writer, he wrote an influential book, *L'Europe aux Cents Drapeaux* (1968), translated as *Towards a Federal Europe: Nations or States?* (1980). He argued eloquently in favour of 'a third Europe' or 'a Europe of the peoples', in which Bretons, Basques, Catalans, Occitans, Galicians, Flemings, Frisians, Scots and Welsh would be among the minorities granted self-determination in a federal Europe.

Jean-Adolphe Fouéré, as he was known to the French civil state, was born in 1910 at Aignan, in Gascony, the son of a Breton senior civil servant. He was educated in St Brieuc and the Lycée Montaigne and Lycée Louis-le-Grand, two of the best secondary schools in Paris, later taking degrees in Law, the Humanities and Political Science at the Sorbonne. His passion for all things Breton was awakened when, as a schoolboy, he read *Breiz Atao* ('Brittany for ever'), the newspaper of the *Parti National Breton* which commanded the support of many nationalists and was later to be accused of collaboration. He followed his father into the Ministry of the Interior but, with his political opinions constrained, soon opted for the life of a journalist in Brittany.

After the war he was Secretary General of the *Comité Consultatif de Bretagne* and edited its newspaper, *La Bretagne*, which later became *L'Avenir de la Bretagne*, the organ of the Mouvement pour l'Organisation de la Bretagne (MOB). I first met him in 1961 shortly after he had co-founded the Breton branch of the Celtic League. Innocuous though this initiative was, he still had a reputation as a militant and, in the eyes of the authorities, he was a dangerous separatist. In October 1975, together with some 50 others, he was arrested on suspicion of involvement in preparations by the *Front de Libération de la Bretagne* (FLB) for a bombing campaign against building nuclear power stations in Brittany. He spent 105 days in La Santé prison in Paris but was released under a general amnesty.

In 1972 he founded *Strollad ar Vro* (SAV) and in 1981 led the formation of *Parti pour l'Organisation d'une Bretagne Libre* (POBL), both groups on the right of the political spectrum, neither of which met with any electoral success. His autobiography, one of a dozen books he wrote over the years, appeared in two parts: *La Patrie Interdite* in 1987 and *La Maison de Connemara* in 1995. But his most important initiative was the creation in 1999 of *Institut de Documentation Bretonne et Européenne*, which now houses his invaluable archive of material relating to the history and social life of Brittany. In the absence of a Breton national library it will serve as his monument.

Yann Fouéré (Jean-Adolphe Fouéré), Breton activist and European federalist: born Aignan, Gers, France 26 July 1910; married 1939 Marie-Magdeleine Mauger (two sons, three daughters); died Saint Brieuc, Brittany 21 October 2011.

The Independent (14 November 2011)

CHARLEZ AR GALL

Pioneer broadcaster in the Breton language

BECAUSE THE BRETON national movement had been compromised by the collaboration of a few individuals who went over to the German side during the Second World War, it took a special kind of courage to support any manifestation of the regional identity in the years immediately after the conflict. Taking up the cause of the language and its culture was most dangerous of all. Merely to have belonged to a folk dancing group or having taught Breton in evening classes was enough to invite the most vicious hostility from representatives of the French state. Charlez ar Gall was one of those who strove to rekindle the flame of Breton patriotism in such difficult circumstances.

A teacher of mathematics, he was educated at the *École Normale des Instituteurs* in Quimper where, in 1959, I first heard his name mentioned along with that of Per-Jakez Hélias, author of the best-selling memoir *Le cheval d'orgueil* ('The horse of pride'), with whom he worked closely. He married Jeanne-Marie Guillamet in 1942 and joined *Ar Falz* ('The sickle'), an organization for Socialist members of his profession, immediately after the end of hostilities in 1945. His first teaching post was in his native commune of L'Hôpital-Camfrout in the extreme west of Finistère, and then in Brest, and he soon became involved in teaching Breton to adults. His command of the language, in which he had been brought up by farming parents, was widely admired because he spoke it with precision and a high regard for its euphony and rich vocabulary.

It was as a broadcaster that he came into his own. In 1959 he succeeded Hélias on Radio Quimerc'h, the only station broadcasting in Breton at that time. Over the next seventeen years, on a part-time basis, he made more than 800 broadcasts from his office (there was no studio as such), pioneering the use of the language on the air-waves and promoting its status as a medium fit for civilized discourse in defiance of its detractors, who were legion. In 1964 he became the first speaker on Breton regional television, responsible for introducing the infamous one and a half minutes of daily news in the language. His fortnightly magazine programme *Breiz o Veva* ('Living Brittany'), beginning in 1971, was of twenty minutes duration. The situation has improved somewhat since then but it is generally agreed that Ar Gall, ably assisted by his wife Chanig, paved the way for whatever progress has been made.

His career as 'the voice of Brittany' was interrupted by two events which affected him deeply. In 1962 he was suspended for a month by the Minister of Information for having broadcast a ballad, *Emgann Montroulez* ('The battle of Morlaix'), which was thought 'seditious' because it challenged the authority of the French state. It celebrated the occupation of the Sous-Préfecture by farmers demonstrating against rising prices in agriculture. Again, in 1974, he was prevented from including in a news bulletin an item about the setting up of a committee for the defence of prisoners gaoled for their part in the campaigns of the *Front de Libération de la Bretagne* ('Front for the liberation of Brittany'). He resigned from his post as a matter of principle. A few days later there was an explosion at a television mast near Roc-Trédudon that was said to be the work of the *FLB*.

Outside broadcasting Ar Gall had literary interests of a high order. His booklet *Breizh hor bro* ('Brittany our country'), written with Job Jaffré in 1955, introduced many Bretons to the cultural traditions of a country about which they had been brought up in ignorance; it was translated as *Toutes les Cultures de Bretagne* in 2005. Thoroughly immersed in the history and literature of Brittany, he also wrote verse, short stories and essays for the magazine *Brud Nevez* and was one of the co-founders of the influential cultural federation *Emgleo Breiz* which, in 1967, collected 150,000 signatures on a petition calling for the teaching of Breton in schools, to no avail. The failure of this major initiative served the purpose of demonstrating to Breton activists what to expect from an unsympathetic state and how steep was the hill they would have to climb.

Revered for his broadcasting skills and the tenacity with which he furthered the cause of Breton, Ar Gall was appointed *Commandeur des Palmes Académiques* and he and his wife received the *Ordre de l'Hermine*, Brittany's highest honour, in 1990. At his death the world-famous singer Alan Stivell, whose records he had often played on air, described him as '*un homme vraiment bien, vraiment bon*'.

Charles Le Gall (Charlez ar Gall), broadcaster and writer: born L'Hôpital-Camfrout, Finistère 5 March 1921; married 1942 Jeanne-Marie (Chanig) Guillamet (two daughters); died Brest 3 November 2010.

The Independent (10 December 2010)

RAYMOND GARLICK

English writer who made the history of Wales his principal subject

RAYMOND GARLICK WAS one of a handful of Englishmen who, without renouncing their own nationality, are so closely associated with Wales, its language and literature, that they are generally taken to be Welsh writers, at least by affiliation and sympathies. Edward Thomas, John Cowper Powys and Alexander Cordell are, to a lesser or greater extent, other examples of this small but gallant band.

In Garlick's case, his identification with Wales went deeper, for he not only chose to live here but made the country's history and present condition the main theme of his work, learning the language and, during the 1970s, becoming embroiled in the struggle to win for it a measure of official status.

At the same time, he argued in favour of Wales's 'other language', English, as one of the languages of a fully bilingual Wales, teaching the literature written in it and, as poet, editor and critic, making a major contribution to its development. He was the most important critic of what he insisted on calling Anglo-Welsh literature long before it became known to a younger generation, in the 1990s, as Welsh Writing in English. Welsh literature, for him, was written in Welsh, in Tolkien's phrase 'the senior language of the men of Britain', and he always stuck to his guns on this cardinal point.

In his view, 'the problem language' in Wales was English: 'For Anglo-Welsh writers,' he wrote in my symposium *Artists in Wales* in 1973, 'it is not a provincialising, alienating, London patois, the sleazy dialect of admass, the insolent cant of the courts; for them it is one of the mother-tongues of Wales, a classical language of beauty and precision, used for literary purposes by some Welshmen for many centuries, a part of the double richness of Welsh civilization. The problem is how to make it a language of integration, of reconciliation, of justice.'

Raymond Garlick's major work of criticism, *An Introduction to Anglo-Welsh Literature*, long meditated and published in the *Writers of Wales* series in 1970, demonstrated that from the late 15th century there has existed a tradition of writing by Welshmen in English which deserves wider recognition, not least in the country's schools. Even today, despite a groundswell of support among teachers, it is still taught only patchily and usually from a narrow syllabus comprising Dylan Thomas and R.S. Thomas for the most part.

To those illustrious names he added many others, including George Herbert, Henry Vaughan and John Dyer, and beginning with Ieuan ap Hywel Swrdwal, a student at Oxford in about 1470 who, challenged by his friends to show that verse could be written in English according to the traditional rules of Welsh prosody and orthography, wrote the *englynion* of 'Hymn to the Virgin':

O michti ladi, owr leding – tw haf
   at hefn owr abeiding,
yntw ddy ffest efrlasting
I set a braents ws tw bring.

Raymond Garlick was born in the London suburb of Harlesden in 1926, the elder son of a clerk in the National Bank, and was brought up on a new estate in North Harrow, a place he detested for its snobbishness and philistinism. At the age of four he contracted a mysterious disease, thought to be septicaemia but never diagnosed, and spent a year in hospital, from which he was discharged, as the result of botched surgery, with a severely damaged foot. Having to accept that he was physically disabled made this handsome man all the more determined to achieve in art what was denied him in life – hence the formal elegance of many of his poems.

Sent to convalesce with his grandparents who had settled at Degannwy on the coast of north Wales, he discovered a rugged landscape and egalitarian people with whom he felt such an immediate affinity that he asked to be transferred from Harrow Boys' County School to the sixth form of the John Bright County School in Llandudno.

After matriculation, he was sent to work in the laboratories of the Kodak factory in Wealdstone but, having felt a call to the Anglican priesthood, left after six months to join the Community of the Resurrection in Leeds, only to fail his university examination in Latin a year later. This result gave him an opportunity to realise an ambition, hitherto concealed from his parents, to read English and History at the University College of North Wales at Bangor, where he enrolled in 1944.

At Bangor, then a ghostly place of elderly academics and medically unfit students, he began studying the history of Wales under the distinguished medievalist Sir John Edward Lloyd and its literature under the Professor of Welsh, Sir Ifor Williams. But the greatest influence on him as a poet was a Dutch refugee named Louis Soeterboek who, under the pseudonym Louis Olav Leroi, wrote verse in English and had published a novel in Welsh; they collaborated in bringing out a slim, privately printed volume of their own work.

Ever of independent mind, Garlick lived as an undergraduate at Tŷ'r Mynydd, a cottage above the slate-quarrying village of Rachub, insisting that he could fend for himself even in that hilly terrain. It was there, in conversation with the artist-writer Brenda Chamberlain and the artist-craftsman John Petts, that he knew himself to be a poet.

He was received into the Roman Catholic Church in 1948, the night before he married Elin Hughes, a fellow-student, a Welsh-speaker and already a convert to Catholicism. She was a fiery ultra-nationalist whose forthright political opinions, much in line with those of Saunders Lewis, the right-wing founder of Plaid Cymru, contrasted sharply with Raymond's eirenic, democratic and gentlemanly nature.

His appointment to a teaching post at Pembroke Dock County School in 1949 proved decisive because it brought him into contact with its headmaster, Roland Mathias, also a poet and historian, with whom he was to do much of his early work in the field of Anglo-Welsh literature. Together, and with the help of a small literary circle, they launched the magazine *Dock Leaves*, later retitled *The Anglo-Welsh Review*, which Garlick was to edit from 1949 to 1961.

The only English-language literary journal in Wales at the time, it took as its aim the closing of the breach between writers in the two languages of Wales and the critical study of what has been written by Welsh writers in English, but also carried articles about music and the visual arts.

From 1954 to 1960 Garlick lived in Blaenau Ffestiniog in Merioneth, where he had taken up a teaching post at the County School and where he enjoyed the warm friendship of John Cowper Powys, his neighbour. During these years he published three books: *Poems from the Mountain House* (1950), *The Welsh-Speaking Sea* (1954) and *Blaenau Observed* (1957), a long poem for radio. Well-shaped, technically meticulous, civilised in the deepest sense of having to do with the higher values, these poems struck a new note in Anglo-Welsh poetry, especially among readers more used to the windy abstractions of Dylan Thomas.

Leaving Wales early in 1961, Garlick took up a post at an international school at Eerde in the Netherlands. Although they spent only six years there, the Garlicks were so happy at Eerde that they seriously considered taking Dutch citizenship. By 1967, however, they were ready to return to Wales, partly so that their children could have a Welsh-language education and partly because Raymond saw signs that there might yet be a role for Anglo-Welsh literature.

Among the signs he had detected were the launching of

Poetry Wales in 1965 and, two years later, the Arts Council's setting up of a Literature Department charged with responsibility for supporting creative writing in both Welsh and English. He was to contribute regularly to my magazine and was a hard-working member of the Literature Committee during its inaugural years.

From 1967 until his retirement in 1986 he taught English at Trinity College, Carmarthen, where he became Principal Lecturer and Director of the Welsh Studies course. He also helped establish a link with the Central University of Iowa, teaching a module in Anglo-Welsh literature to American students.

His time at Trinity coincided with the campaigns of the Welsh Language Society, in which his wife, son, sister-in-law, and some of his friends and colleagues were arrested. The strict policy of non-violent civil disobedience espoused by the Society chimed with Garlick's own pacifism: 'For some of us, you see, Wales is another word for peace'.

He was a staunch supporter of those who were imprisoned for their stand against the intransigence of Whitehall and Westminster over such matters as bilingual road-signs and the establishment of a Welsh fourth television channel, employing his *saeva indignatio* to best effect against judges who handed down sentences out of all proportion to the offences committed.

The anguish he felt at seeing idealistic young people hauled before the courts proved a powerful stimulus to his poetry and he published three substantial collections in rapid succession: *A Sense of Europe* (1968), which looks back at the years in the forest of Eerde, *A Sense of Time* (1972), which includes the radio poem 'Acclamation', about the Forty Martyrs of England and Wales who were canonized by the Pope in 1970, and *Incense* (1976), a nicely ambiguous title for a book largely concerned with a Catholic's faith and his rage at the denial of civil rights.

Two political events took their toll on him. The Welsh

people's rejection of the Labour government's offer of administrative devolution at referendum in 1979 deeply disappointed him and he castigated 'certain Welsh electors / Who (the empire dead) chose to become / Colonials by referendum.'

He was also angered by the jingoism of the Malvinas adventure, writing in an essay published in *Authors Take Sides on the Falklands* (1982): 'I am appalled at the sanctimoniousness and violence of British nationalism, the warmongering of most of the English tabloid newspapers, the attacks on free and reasoned speech and the BBC, and the virtual collapse of democratic opposition in Parliament.'

Shortly afterwards, there occurred a double crisis in his life: his wife left him to live with another woman in the Netherlands (where she became a translator of Dutch literature into Welsh), and he came to the realization that he had never believed in God and, in Dr Johnson's phrase, must 'clear his mind of cant'. He left the Catholic Church and was divorced in 1982.

The poetic impulse also failed him at this time and it seemed as if he would write no more verse. He therefore put together his *Collected Poems 1946–86* (1987), though not before editing with Roland Mathias *Anglo-Welsh Poetry 1480–1980* (1984; revised edn 1993), still the most authoritative anthology of its kind.

The muse revisited him in March 1989 when a radio programme on W.B. Yeats prompted him to write nine poems in a month, and he was further stimulated by the birth of his grandchild Alys, in whom he found unbounded delight. The forty poems of this late flowering are to be found in *Travel Notes* (1992), which also recounts his own visit to Byzantium during a cruise in the Mediterranean, and recalls other journeys, including that of Dutch Jews to their terrible destinations. His last book, *R.S. Thomas: letters to Raymond Garlick*, was published in 2009.

Raymond Garlick has an assured place in the republic

of Welsh letters. He wrote a number of finely turned poems which are included in all the major anthologies. His political and cultural influence is more disputable. If some zealots remain suspicious and perplexed by his defence of English, still seen as an intrusive language in some quarters, it is a measure of how far a schismatic people still have to go before achieving the reconciliation which was the goal of all his work.

Raymond Garlick, poet, critic and teacher; born Harlesden, London 21 September 1926; married 1948 Elin Hughes (marriage dissolved, one adopted son and one adopted daughter); Lecturer in English and Director of Welsh Studies, Trinity College, Carmarthen, 1967–86; died Cardiff 19 March 2011.

The Independent (17 June 2011)

ARTHUR GIARDELLI

Painter who used found objects to evoke the forces of nature

THE PAINTER ARTHUR Giardelli was steeped in the work of the European avant-garde and brought to his adopted Wales, where he settled in 1947, a passionate belief that art transcends national boundaries, however firmly rooted it may be in the local and particular. He did more than any other artist to promote the work of his contemporaries, among whom were David Jones, Josef Herman and Ceri Richards, largely in his capacity as chairman of the influential 56 Group, which transformed the public perception of art in Wales with its many exhibitions and tireless lobbying of such bodies as the Arts Council and the National Museum.

His own work, to which he was utterly devoted during a long career as a maker, consisted mainly of relief constructions, abstract in form and fashioned from a variety of materials, both man-made and natural, such as slate, brassware, cork, wood, glass, timepieces, string, sacking, shells and paper from old books. These 'found objects' were arranged and embellished so as to evoke the passing of the seasons, the wind's energy and the movements of the tide. They bring to mind the Dadaists and the collages of Kurt Schwitters, and belong to a tradition that flowered in the 1950s with the Arte Povera movement in Spain and Italy.

Like Antoni Tàpies in Barcelona and Alberto Burri in Italy, both younger than he, Giardelli found his inspiration in what he could pick up on the beach or in secondhand shops. The result is often breathtaking in its formal elegance, revealing not only the innate beauty of flotsam and jetsam but also a metaphysical delight in discarded objects which has to do with time, space and the mystery of human life. The film made about him by BBC Wales in 1967 was aptly entitled *See What the Next Tide Brings*.

Although closely identified with art in Wales, Giardelli was born in Stockwell, London, in 1911, and brought up in Surrey, the son of an English mother and a father of Italian extraction, both schoolteachers. His grandfather had fought with Garibaldi for the liberation of Italy before emigrating to Britain; his father, mocked at school on account of his surname, had chosen to become 'more English than the English' and detested all thought of Italy, much to his son's chagrin.

At Hertford College, Oxford, Giardelli took a degree in Modern Languages and, at the Ruskin School of Art, where he received his only training, wrote a paper on Botticelli's illustrations for *The Divine Comedy* with the help of a book lent him by Kenneth Clark. His love of Dante, Villon, Racine and Ronsard made him (despite his dyslexia) the most literary of painters and, macaronic in his conversation, he never tired of quoting such lines as Phèdre's *'C'est Vénus toute entière à sa proie attachée'* ('It is Venus completely attached to her prey') or Francesca's description of how she and Paolo had come to commit adultery: *'E caddi come corpo morto cade'* ('And like a corpse fell to the ground').

The cosmopolitan-minded Giardelli had first discovered Wales in 1928 when his parents leased a cottage at Amroth in Pembrokeshire. The beaches, estuaries, coves, rock-pools and seascapes of the Dyfed coast held a deep fascination for the young man, preparing his mind for that subtly poetic observation of the natural scene which was to surface years later in his paintings and collages. But it was in Merthyr Tydfil, confronted by a very different, industrially ravaged though visually exciting landscape, that he decided to commit himself fully to his art. 'When the train finally pulled into Merthyr,' he once told me, 'I felt I'd come home'.

The Harvey Grammar School at Folkestone, where Giardelli taught French and English, had been evacuated to Merthyr in 1940. In the same year he registered as a conscientious objector and lost his job as a consequence. He had been a pacifist ever since hearing Gandhi speak in Oxford some years before. This crisis in his personal affairs was to be the making of him as an artist. Befriended by Quakers, he and his wife and their two small children were given accommodation at Trewern House, the Friends' Settlement in Dowlais, and work was found for them as lecturers and musicians – she played the piano well and he the viola. Shortly afterwards Giardelli took up a post as music teacher at Cyfarthfa Castle, one of the town's grammar schools. Even more importantly, it was in Dowlais, the old iron township high on the hill above Merthyr, that he made the acquaintance of Sir Cedric Morris and Heinz Koppel, both of whom encouraged him to concentrate on his painting.

After the war the Giardellis moved to Pendine in Carmarthenshire, where Arthur began a long and fruitful career as a lecturer with the Workers' Educational Association and tutor in the Department of Extra Mural Studies at the University College of Wales, Aberystwyth. Never neglecting his own work as a painter, he now threw himself into the politics of the art scene in Wales, displaying an altruism rare among practising artists.

He was one of the founders of the 56 Group and was elected its chairman in 1959, a position he held until 1998, after which he was made Life President. From 1965 to 1975 he served on the Art Committee of the Welsh Arts Council and became a leading member of the Contemporary Art Society for Wales. Lecturing took him on extended tours of the Netherlands, Egypt, Russia, China, the United States and Nepal, and between 1977 and 1980 he served as a member of the Calouste Gulbenkian inquiry into the economic situation of visual artists in the UK. It was in Holland that he first saw the work of Mondrian and, on his return to Pendine in 1955, had begun making abstract collages from found materials.

For his work on behalf of the arts in Wales Giardelli was

awarded an MBE in 1973 and made an Honorary Fellow of University College, Aberystwyth, six years later. In 1986 he was awarded the Silver Medal of the Czechoslovak Society for International Relations. His work was bought by the Tate Gallery, the National Museum of Wales and private collectors on both sides of the Atlantic. Among his most supportive patrons was the collector Eric Estorick of the Grosvenor Gallery in Dover Street, London, who in 1965 gave him a one-man exhibition and promptly bought everything in it, followed by another at his new premises in South Molton Street in 1987. A final accolade was the publication of a lavishly illustrated book containing the text of Giardelli's conversations with the art critic Derek Shiel, which served as a precursor to a retrospective exhibition of his work at Penarth's Washington Gallery in the summer of 2002.

Arthur Giardelli was an accomplished conversationalist and also a good listener. A religious man, he was generally eirenic in his attitude to other artists but could deliver some caustic opinions about public bodies in Wales when he thought their policies were not generous or effective enough. What he lacked in inches he made up in intelligence, enthusiasm, energy, wide knowledge, modesty and a delicious sense of humour. He had a great gift for hospitality and friendship, liking nothing better in his latter years than to receive visitors, whether old acquaintances or casual callers, at his home, The Golden Plover, near Warren in Pembrokeshire, a former schoolhouse which he and his second wife, whom he called Bim, had made into a studio and exhibition space for their collection of modern art.

The house is set in a district which will for long be closely associated with his art. 'We in Pembrokeshire', he told Tony Curtis in *Welsh Painters Talking* (1997), 'look into the setting sun. And when you look into the setting sun across the sea you are looking into a magic and a mystery – your eyes are dazzled by it... we watch the sea swallow that ball of fire, the sun.' It was Arthur Giardelli's achievement to have revealed for us something of that magic, that mystery, and to have allowed us a glimpse of the complexity of his own inner landscape.

Vincent Charles Arthur Giardelli, painter and teacher: born London 11 April 1911; Tutor in Art, University College of Wales, Aberystwyth, 1958–78; Chairman of the 56 Group Wales, 1959–98 and thereafter Life President; MBE 1973; married 1937 Phillis (Judy) Evelyn Berry (marriage dissolved, one son, one daughter), 1976 Beryl (Bim) Mary Butler; died Haverfordwest, Pembrokeshire 2 November 2009.

The Independent (6 November 2009)

IRIS GOWER

Bestselling author of historical romances

'THE TOWN OF Swansea disputes alone with Cardiff the title of Metropolis of Wales,' wrote Wirt Sykes, folklorist and United States Consul at Cardiff in 1883. 'Its situation is very fine, between lofty hills, on a bay so lovely that it has often been compared to that of Naples.' The compliment might well have served as epigraph to the novels of Iris Gower who took the town's topography, rich history and seafaring traditions as inexhaustible material for all her work.

Few novelists have enjoyed commercial success and worldwide fame as much as Iris Gower, unless it be Catherine Cookson, to whom she was often compared. Her books appeared regularly in the PLR lists of the hundred books most frequently borrowed from public libraries, sometimes at the rate of nine or ten titles a year, and they sold in their hundreds of thousands to a loyal readership throughout the English-speaking world. She published in all some 45 books, including about 30 novels, all of which were inspired by the town, later a city, where she had been born in 1939 and had lived all her life, or else by Gower, the nearby peninsula from which she took her pen-name. She once told me she had also considered Iris Langland and Iris Caswell as pseudonyms, after two of the best-known resorts in Gower.

Educated at the College of Art in her hometown, and working as a barmaid, she began writing for financial reasons, contributing articles and short stories to women's magazines. Her first two novels, *Tudor Tapestry* (1974) and *Bride of the Thirteenth Summer* (1975), caught the then current vogue for light historical fiction about the Tudor period. But it was in her next books, *The Copper Cloud* (1976) and *Return to Tip Row* (1977), that she began using the 19th and early 20th-century industrial Swansea setting that she was to make her own. The often grim condition of the working class pitted against local capitalists might have made for novels with a social message, a genre fully explored by other Welsh prose-writers, but she was able to strike a sunnier note and create characters and scenes that were convincing and memorable without recourse to ideology.

Once the taste for things Tudor had faded, she turned to writing about more exotic climes, but it was *Copper Kingdom* (1983), combining the romance of the earlier books with the meticulously-researched history of Swansea as 'the Copper Capital of the World', that established her in the international best-seller lists. Swansea is recognisable in these books as 'Sweyn's Eye', a reference to the town's Viking origins; the name denotes 'Sweyn's Island'. She was particularly good at conveying the bustle of commerce, the noise of heavy machinery and the perils of working and living in one of the most unhealthy milieux created by the Industrial Revolution. Several titles appeared in a linked sequence under the title 'Sweyn's Eye': *Proud Mary* (1984), *Spinners' Wharf* (1985), *Morgan's Woman* (1986), *Fiddler's Ferry* (1987) and *Black Gold* (1988).

That she was able to produce a novel a year, and usually with huge commercial success, is testimony to the tenacity of this most professional of writers and the readership she nurtured and strove to please. Even after her husband's sudden death, she carried on writing, putting in eight hours a day at her desk. Although some of her books are family sagas, they have considerably more substance than the average novel in this genre, their historical veracity and strong female characters having earned them a place on school syllabuses. Her heroines, in particular, are often complex and highly spirited, who rise above the passion and pain of their lot in life eventually to triumph against the odds and thereby find happiness, usually in the arms of the men they love. They run farms singlehandedly, take over pottery businesses and refurbish rundown hotels with no help from the men in their lives.

In *The Rowan Tree* (2003), set in 1831 and perhaps the most accomplished of her later work, drovers bring their cattle on the hoof from west Wales to London's Smithfield, working out their destinies as they go. It was followed by *Halfpenny Field* (2004), the second in the 'Drovers' series: when Iris Gower had a resounding success with a book she was always canny enough to follow it up with a sequel. With *Act of Love* (2006) she began a sequence set in Swansea's Palace Theatre and in *Bargain Bride* (2007) she introduced a new heroine, Charlotte Mortimer, who has to agree to a marriage proposal that looks more like a business contract.

Inevitably, academic critics looked down their noses at Iris Gower's novels, paying them no more attention than that reserved for bodice-rippers. That is to overlook their racy plots and vivid characters and to take a somewhat snooty attitude to books which are meant to afford pleasure to large numbers of readers. Modest and unassuming, she cared not one jot for the academics' put-down, intent only on entertaining her large readership. Described by one journalist as 'a cross between a sensible grandmother and the feisty heroine of one of her own novels' – her hair was the colour of flame – she had the advantage neither of a teaching post nor the patronage on which many writers rely, winning no major prizes and needing no subsidy for her writing. She did, however, earn an MA in Creative Writing at Cardiff University and, in 1999, was awarded an Honorary Fellowship by the University of Swansea.

Iris Richardson (Iris Gower), novelist: born Swansea 1939; married 1958 Tudor Davies (died 2002; four children); died Swansea 20 July 2010.

The Independent (28 July 2010)

RAY GRAVELL

Wales and British Lions rugby player
who won new admirers as an actor and broadcaster

RAY GRAVELL PLAYED rugby for Wales on 23 occasions
between 1975 and 1982. He was a member of the Welsh team
that won the Grand Slam and Triple Crown, and of the British
Lions team which toured South Africa in 1980. He was in
the Welsh side that beat Australia in 1975 and Fiji in 1985.
A powerful centre, he began his career with Llanelli RFC in
1969 and in 1980–82 was the team's captain. He was also in
the Scarlets' side that beat the All Blacks in 1972.

As a player he showed great respect for his opponents and
made many friendships which continued long after he hung up
his boots. His genial personality and exuberant commentaries
on radio and television brought him many admirers, though
he was more fluent in Welsh than in English. With Huw
Llewelyn Davies he broadcast the first Welsh commentary on
Welsh-language television in 1982.

His touch-line and half-time observations were witty,
knowledgeable and highly partisan, for there was no more
patriotic player than Ray Gravell. There was a boyish quality
to him that endeared him to thousands. Such was the esteem
in which he was held that the road where he lived in the
village of Mynydd-y-garreg was renamed Heol Gravell.

Born in Cydweli, Carmarthenshire in 1951, the son of
a collier, but brought up in Mynydd-y-garreg, Ray Gravell
was educated at the Queen Elisabeth Grammar School in
Carmarthen, where his talent for rugby was soon noticed.
For many years he was a youth officer employed by the
Manpower Services Commission.

A straight runner and hard tackler, he played his debut

game with Lampeter in 1970 and his final appearance was with Llandovery on 26 January 1985. After playing 485 games for Llanelli and scoring 120 tries, he decided to retire and thereafter concentrated on his career in broadcasting.

He took the leading role in *Bonner* in 1985 on S4C and had a walk-on part in Louis Malle's 1992 film *Damage*, which starred Jeremy Irons and Juliette Binoche, as well as presenting chat shows on BBC Wales and BBC Cymru. With Frank Hennessy he presented a weekly programme called *I'll Show You Mine* in which his humour and wealth of anecdote from his rugby days were put to good use.

So wide was his appeal that when he had a small part in the nightly soap *Pobol y Cwm*, it boosted the programme's ratings overnight. He also played a farmer in Peter O'Toole's production of Dylan Thomas's *Rebecca's Daughters* (1992).

His catchphrase 'Tip top!' (also the name of a programme he compered for BBC Cymru) became the hallmark of his television and radio appearances. Among the memorable moments associated with him was when he tried to teach the words of 'Sospan Fach', the Llanelli rugby-song, to Simon Weston, the Falklands War survivor, on the TV show *The Big Welsh Challenge*.

In his autobiography, *Grav* (1986), he described how as a young man he had discovered the body of his father near their home and what effect this suicide had on him. He was nevertheless of a jovial disposition, and even after the amputation of his right leg earlier this year – he suffered from diabetes – he remained cheerful and grateful for the love he had been shown by friends and strangers alike.

Although cast down, he was cheered by messages of support that came in from all over the world. He even appeared on Max Boyce's chat-show on BBC Wales and proudly displayed the artificial limb he had been given. Typically altruistic, he toured Britain giving talks about diabetes and organizing fund-raising events such as golf tournaments.

His first public appearance after his operation was at the

Eisteddfod organized by *Urdd Gobaith Cymru* (the Welsh League of Youth), whose activities were always near his heart. To thunderous applause he presented the BBC Cymru Talent Award.

The amputation of his leg interrupted his appearance as the Grand Sword Bearer in the ceremonies of the Gorsedd of Bards, a role he undertook with great enthusiasm. When the Archdruid cried *'A oes Heddwch?'* ('Is there Peace?'), Gravell, or Ray o'r Mynydd as he was known in bardic circles, held the enormous weapon aloft with pride and dignity, and always to tremendous dramatic effect. His place was taken by the formidable figure of Robyn McBride, the former Lions and Wales player, at this year's Eisteddfod and at the proclamation of next year's festival to be held in Cardiff, where there will be a gap hard to fill.

Raymond William Robert Gravell, rugby player, actor and broadcaster: born Cydweli, Carmarthenshire 12 September 1951; married 1991 Mari Roberts (two daughters); died 31 October 2007.

The Independent (2 November 2007)

SELWYN GRIFFITH

Archdruid of Wales and children's writer

THE DISMAY WITH which the audience greeted the news that the Deputy Archdruid, Selwyn Iolen, could not be present on the stage of this year's National Eisteddfod was a mark of the esteem and affection in which he was held in Welsh-speaking Wales. A popular figure, he represented the very type of cultured countryman who remains close to his roots and never seeks advancement beyond the community into which he is born. Selwyn lived almost all of his 83 years not far from his native place, the village of Bethel in the slate-quarrying district of north-west Wales. He served it well in various capacities and, an unambitious man, sought no wider stage for his talents.

He was in the public gaze for the first time when he won the Crown at the National Eisteddfod of 1989 with a long poem in the free metres on the subject *Arwyr* ('Heroes'). Besides describing his upbringing as a quarryman's son, he chose to write about some of the sportsmen whom he had admired as a boy, footballers such as Stanley Mathews and boxers like Jimmy Wilde and Tommy Farr. What few knew at the time was that he had once played in goal for Caernarfon Town and had had a test with Bolton Wanderers. The beautiful game's loss was Welsh literature's gain. Having won the Crown, he was now able to style himself *Prifardd* ('Chief poet') and, in due course, to stand for election to the role of Archdruid.

The public saw him again after he was elected in 2004. Using his bardic name Selwyn Iolen, which chimed with his origins in the parish of Llanddeiniolen, he carried out the role with great dignity and a mischievous grin that many thought typical of the man. Unlike some who hold the office, he refrained from making political statements but he nevertheless refused to be interviewed in English, though this was as much to do with his shyness in that language as anything else.

He was also seen on the Eisteddfod stage five years later when, as Deputy Archdruid, he stood in for Dic Jones, who was unwell. The present Archdruid, T. James Jones (Jim Parcnest), has paid tribute to his predecessor for his stage presence and, in particular, for the way in which he deflected the public gaze from himself onto the poet who was being chaired or crowned. He had no taste for hogging the limelight and was impervious to the adulation which Archdruids have habitually to suffer in Wales, both on and off the stage.

After schooling at Ysgol Syr Hugh Owen in Caernarfon, and military service with the RAF between 1948 and 1950, he worked for eighteen years as a rates collector with Gwyrfai Community Council, and later spent forty-six years as clerk to its counterpart in Llanddeiniolen. After training as a primary school teacher at the Normal College in Bangor, he taught at various schools and eventually became headmaster at Rhiwlas.

It was as a teacher of children of primary age that he came into his own. A gifted story-teller and rhymester, he wrote prolifically for children and was the Children's Poet of Wales long before that title became official and established in the country's literary life. He was particularly adept at composing pieces for recitation and took a special interest in encouraging young people to recite and read aloud. This he was able to do as an adjudicator at more than 450 country eisteddfodau up and down Wales, at which he was often to be seen delighting in the accomplishments of children whose talents he had spotted early on. He was the author of eight books of poems for young people.

He published a volume of verse for adults, *C'narfon a Cherddi Eraill* ('Caernarfon and other poems', 1979) and gave a typically modest account of his life in a volume of autobiography, *O Barc y Wern i Barc y Faenol* (2007). The first of the place names in the book's title was the *nom de plume* he had used when submitting his winning poems in 1989. The second refers to the location of the National Eisteddfod in the grounds of Y Faenol, a mansion on the shores of the Menai Straits where Bryn Terfel has put on his concerts, in 2005. It filled him with the better part of pride that a quarryman's son had become a national figure in the premier cultural event of Wales.

Selwyn Griffith (Selwyn Iolen), Archdruid of Wales (2005–08): born Bethel, Caernarfonshire 19 May 1928; married Myra Humphreys (one son); died Penisarwaun, Gwynedd 10 August 2011.

Previously unpublished

BRUCE GRIFFITHS

A distinguished member of the judiciary in Wales

BRUCE GRIFFITHS HAD a reputation as a hard-working, fair-minded judge on the Wales and Chester circuit where he sat from 1972 until his retirement in 1986. He also played a prominent part in the cultural affairs of Wales.

His greatest passion was for the visual arts. He was particularly enthusiastic about modern Welsh art, filling his home at Whitchurch, a suburb of north Cardiff, with canvases and busts by contemporary practitioners, many of whom became friends.

He was appointed to the Welsh Arts Council in 1972 and to chairmanship of its Art Committee three years later. He spoke with authority and eloquence on behalf of visual artists, summoning all his barrister's skills to argue his committee's case for a greater allocation of the council's funds and taking every opportunity of ensuring that Welsh art was promoted at home and abroad. From 1981 to 1992 he was Chairman of the Welsh Sculpture Trust and did much to encourage an art-form which many regarded as still, in Wales, in its infancy.

But it was as a leading member of the Contemporary Art Society for Wales that he left the most lasting impression. Chairman from 1987 to 1992, and Vice-Chairman thereafter, he led the society in its task of commissioning and exhibiting the work of living painters with inspirational panache. He was instrumental in bringing a number of European artists to Wales. His only public reward for this selfless work was a silver medal presented to him, somewhat incongruously, on behalf of the Czechoslovak Republic in 1986.

Griffiths was born in 1924 in Barry in the old county of

Glamorgan, although his family had strong connections with Aberdare. Educated at Whitchurch Grammar School in Cardiff and at King's College London, he served with the RAF until 1947 and, after demobilisation, was called to the Bar at Gray's Inn in 1952. He was a founder-member of the Bow Group, which was intended to be an effective counter to the Fabian Society, and served as its first chairman.

Although not Welsh-speaking, Griffiths thought of himself as a patriot, but one concerned with the highest standards and having no truck with the merely parochial or the second-rate, and he chose to follow a legal career in Wales. From 1964 to 1970 he was Chairman of the Local Appeals Tribunal of the Ministry of Social Security in Cardiff and from 1968 to 1972 Vice-Chairman of the Mental Health Tribunal, Wales. He was appointed Assistant Recorder of Birkenhead in 1965 and served in the same capacity in Cardiff, Swansea and Merthyr Tydfil from 1966 to 1971. Before taking silk in 1970, he was Deputy Chairman of Glamorgan Quarter Sessions and Commissioner of the Assize Roll Courts of Justice in London.

He was also well-read in English poetry. Every Christmas he would make a small anthology of his favourite poems which he sent to a select number of his friends. He suffered from asthma and spent part of the year in Mallorca, where one of his sons lives. During our last conversation, he told me with great pride that his grandchildren spoke four languages: English, Welsh, Catalan and Castilian. His wife, Mary, herself the daughter of a judge, has learned Welsh, as has their son David.

Central to Bruce Griffiths's work as a judge and his support for the visual and plastic arts in Wales was his Christian faith, which he expressed in his devotion to the Anglican Church. A regular communicant at St Mary's in Whitchurch, he was a member of the Governing Body of the Church in Wales from 1978 to 1992 and President of its Provincial Court from 1979 to 1992. He was also Chancellor to the Diocese of Monmouth until ill-health forced him to give up many of his public offices.

Bruce Fletcher Griffiths, judge: born Barry, Glamorgan 28 April 1924; called to the Bar, Gray's Inn 1952; QC 1970; judge on the Wales and Chester circuit 1972–86; married 1952 Mary Jenkins (two sons, one daughter); died Cardiff 17 January 1999.

The Independent (30 January 1999)

W.J. GRUFFYDD

Writer who helped keep alive
the Welsh tradition of 'country poets'

WHAT REMAINS OF the ancient bardic tradition of Wales is still to be found in certain parts of the western counties of Gwynedd and Ceredigion, where the writing of verse in traditional forms has survived the demise of the native aristocracy and gentry and now depends for its audience and vitality on its social function as the medium for recording such occasions as births, marriages and deaths, and for recounting incidents in the life of the neighbourhood.

Ffair-rhos, a village a little to the north of Pontrhydfendigaid in Ceredigion, is one of several such vicinities renowned for the clusters of *beirdd gwlad* or 'country poets' to be found there, and indeed is known as *pentref y beirdd* ('the poets' village') for that very reason. If Dafydd Jones is perhaps the better known, W.J. Gruffydd enjoyed a reputation as one of the most accomplished writers associated with the district, if only by the range of his literary interests and achievements.

Born in Ffair-rhos in 1916, William John Gruffydd first came to prominence as a poet at the National Eisteddfod held at Pwllheli in 1955 when he won the Crown for a poem in the free metres – that is to say, not in traditional Welsh prosody. He repeated this feat when he won again at Cardiff five years later, thus earning the honorific title *Prifardd* ('Chief poet'). Among the 40-odd eisteddfodic chairs which he collected in the way that some farmers collect rosettes, was the Chair of the Powys Eisteddfod, one of the most prestigious of the regional festivals in Wales.

From 1984 to 1987 he served as Archdruid of Wales, a role in which his genial personality and dignified stage presence made him a popular figure among those attending the National Festival. His bardic name was Elerydd and he used it to distinguish himself from others of the same name, not least the W.J. Gruffydd who was Professor of Welsh at Cardiff University for many years.

Educated at the Grammar School in Tregaron, he did not have the benefit of higher education but trained for the Baptist ministry in Swansea before working in ordinance factories for six years as part of the war effort. Ordained in 1946, he served his ministry at various chapels in Cardiganshire and Pembrokeshire, latterly at Y Glog, a place with which his name came to be generally associated.

In 1968 he won the coveted Sir Ifor Williams Memorial Prize, which enabled him to spend a term at the University College of North Wales, Bangor, and in the year following he was awarded a bursary by the Welsh Arts Council with the help of which he wrote a novel, *Angel heb Adenydd* ('Angel without wings', 1971).

His poems were published under the titles *Ffenestri* ('Windows', 1961) and *Cerddi'r Llygad* ('Poems for the Eye', 1973), and collected under the editorship of D. Islwyn Edwards in 1990. Many are in Cardiganshire dialect, for which he had a finely tuned ear, and most bring satire and a gentle humour to bear on people and local events, thus fulfilling his function as *bardd gwlad*. One of his most poignant poems is about the candlesticks made from corned beef tins by Italian prisoners of war for their chapel at Henllan, Carmarthenshire.

His novels and short stories are even more remarkable for the gallery of country characters who inhabit them, especially those featuring Tomos and Marged, two lovable old people who look out from deep in the Cardiganshire countryside on a changing world with wit and wisdom. Seven volumes of these stories were published to great acclaim. He also wrote detective novels.

His most unusual work is the novel *Hers a Cheffyl* ('Hearse and horse', 1967), one of the very few which attempt to bring the verbal fireworks of *Under Milk Wood* into the writing of Welsh prose. It observes the rituals of death and burial in the Welsh countryside, as well as the family tensions that follow, with deliciously black humour. The influence of Dylan Thomas on the literature of Wales has been, on the whole, detrimental but W.J. Gruffydd used a muscular style to produce his own effects.

He published his autobiography in two parts: *Meddylu* ('Contemplating', 1986) and *O Ffair Rhos i'r Maen Llog* ('From Ffair-rhos to the logan stone', 2003); the latter title refers to the large stone from which the Archdruid conducts the open-air ceremonies of the Gorsedd of Bards. He also wrote a good deal for the local and denominational press, and was for a while a correspondent for *The Times*, writing on country matters.

William John Gruffydd, Baptist minister and poet: born Ffair-rhos, Cardiganshire 24 September 1916; Archdruid of Wales 1984–87; married Jane Mary Owen (died 2010; one son, one daughter); died Llanelli, Carmarthenshire 21 April 2011.

The Independent (20 July 2011)

LOWRI GWILYM

Editor for Factual Programmes with S4C

LOWRI GWILYM WAS one of the most influential television executives in Wales. Appointed in 2004 as Editor for Factual Programmes and Co-productions by S4C, the fourth channel now broadcasting entirely in Welsh, she was associated with many of the best programmes put out by the channel, winning several international prizes for her work.

She also made programmes for radio. One of the most admired to be produced by her for BBC Cymru, where she worked for many years as a freelance prior to joining S4C, was *Beti a'i Phobol* ('Beti and her people'), the Welsh counterpart of *Desert Island Discs*, in which the matchless Beti George asks guests to talk about themselves and then request music which has special significance for them. One of the most popular long-running programmes ever to be broadcast in the language, its accolade is said to be the equivalent of an OBE in Welsh-speaking Wales. When, earlier this year, it celebrated its twenty-fifth year, there was no hesitation in asking Lowri Gwilym to be Beti George's guest.

Lowri Gwilym was one of the daughters of the late Gwyn Williams, sometime Professor of English at Universities in the Middle East, whose forefathers had farmed the bleak uplands of Mynydd Bach near Trefenter in Cardiganshire; she changed her surname when she was eighteen.The family took all their summer holidays at Trefenter, partly so that the girls and their brother Gwydion would speak Welsh, and this they all did to their father's satisfaction. The summer of 1951 which Gwyn and his second wife, Daisy, spent on the mountain, before Lowri was born, was lovingly recalled by their father in *Summer Journal* (2004) which she and her sister edited.

On his retirement and return to Wales in 1969 he set about renovating the family's old home, and lived there until 1983, so that the children had a strong identification with the area which lasts to this day. It was his daughter's intention to settle in the village later this year with her partner, the journalist Meic Birtwistle, and their two teenaged sons, a plan cruelly thwarted by her unexpected death, after a brief illness, on 21 July.

Lowri Gwilym was admired by all who knew her. A vegetarian *avant la lettre*, she led by example and never pressed her opinions on her family, friends, neighbours and colleagues, all of whom have spoken warmly of her. Having thrown herself into country ways with passion and understanding, she made a lasting contribution to the cultural life of Mynydd Bach, especially to Bethel chapel and Cofadail, a community initiative in Trefenter.

Educated at primary schools in Libya and Turkey, she took her first degree in Welsh at Bangor, and went on to do an MLitt at Linacre College, Oxford. She brought to her work as a producer for radio and television a rare intelligence and an academic regard for textual precision but also bore in mind the popular demands made by these media. In documentaries and current affairs programmes such as *O Flaen dy Lygaid* ('Before your very eyes'), the six-part series *Women in Politics*, *Wynebau Newydd* ('New faces'), *Cefn Gwlad* ('Countryside') and *O'r Galon* ('From the heart'), public service broadcasting was heard and seen at its very best.

High standards were important to her and she consistently achieved them by applying an analytical mind and a quietly determined streak in her character to everything she undertook. Her stint on the nightly feature programme *Wedi 7* ('After 7') taught her a great deal about the pressures of working to a deadline. Until recently she was content editor for the long-running current affairs series *Y Byd ar*

Bedwar ('The world on four'). One of her last triumphs, the documentary *Dwy Wraig Lloyd George* ('Lloyd George's two wives'), won a Bafta Cymru award earlier this year.

Her father, a poet and translator, had known Lawrence Durrell and moved in his literary circle in Alexandria between 1942 and 1951. Shortly after Lowri's birth he moved to a chair in Benghazi and then to Istanbul; it was for Durrell that Gwyn Williams made his first attempts at translating Welsh poetry into English. His pioneer, widely acclaimed selection of 'poems from the first thousand years of Welsh verse', entitled *The Burning Tree* (1956) and with a bilingual text, was dedicated to 'my daughters Teleri and Lowri in the hope that they may grow up to read both sides of the book'. In both cases their father's hope was realized: Lowri has been called 'the best-read person in broadcasting', and in both Welsh and English.

Given her cosmopolitan background, it was not surprising that Lowri also wrote verse and spoke several languages, which made her a *rara avis* in the studios of Broadcasting House, Llandaf. But there was also something warm and homely in her nature that endeared her to all her colleagues.

Lowri Gwilym, television executive: born Aberystwyth, Cardiganshire 14 October 1954; Editor for Factual Programmes and Co-productions, S4C; two sons with Meic Birtwistle; died Cardiff 21 July 2010.

The Independent (31 July 2010)

PATRICK HANNAN

Talented and witty commentator on Welsh affairs

THE JOURNALIST AND broadcaster Patrick Hannan, who has died aged 68, kept his finger on the pulse of public life in Wales for more than forty years. As industrial editor of the *Western Mail* and political correspondent at BBC Wales, and later as host of a myriad radio programmes, he won a reputation as an incisive interviewer and witty commentator on Welsh affairs during a period of rapid economic and social change.

He also broadcast regularly on BBC Radio Four, presenting the popular discussion programmes *Out of Order* and *Tea Junction*. He had a well-furnished mind that was both disciplined and wide-ranging in its grasp of what makes contemporary culture and of the personalities involved in it. Last week he and fellow-contestant Peter Stead won the *Round Britain Quiz*, their fifth triumph in ten years.

Pat Hannan was a journalist to his fingertips and cared passionately for the independence of what he called his 'trade'. He saw Wales not through rose-tinted spectacles but through the prism of his own learning and experience, bringing erudition and personal commitment to the task of tracking the country's industrial and political transformation during a turbulent period of its history.

Not once did he take sides in any dispute and if his sardonic manner sometimes had a touch of the sarcastic, there was never any doubt that he was speaking the truth as he saw it. Provocative, yes, and often striking sparks off those he interviewed, he nevertheless earned the respect of captains of industry, politicians and mandarins of public bodies alike, many of whom paid him tribute in the days after his sudden death. They include Rhodri Morgan, First Minister of Wales, who referred to him as 'an extraordinarily talented and witty journalist and broadcaster'.

Despite having been born in 'the posh part of Aberaman', a mining village in the Cynon Valley, where he was the doctor's son, he saw at first hand how a working-class community holds itself together in bad times and good, even if he was not quite of it, especially after receiving his secondary education at Cowbridge Grammar School, a fee-paying establishment in the leafy Vale of Glamorgan.

From there, in 1959, he went up to the University College of Wales, Aberystwyth, where he read History and first tasted newsprint as a contributor to *The Courier*, the College newspaper. As a contemporary of his, I remember him in Debates and in the Students' Union, where undergraduates intent on joining the fourth estate in the real world often gathered over their coffee-cups and the morning's papers. His was the most laid-back manner of them all.

Pat's first job was as a reporter with the *Western Mail* in Cardiff where he quickly learned the rudiments of journalism and made contact with the political life of Wales at every level. He was particularly good at unravelling the tribalist Labour politics of the south Wales valleys, and this became one of the themes of his first book, *The Welsh Illusion* (1999), which explored the persistence of myth in the face of incontrovertible evidence that, with the demise of heavy industry, the social fabric of Wales had changed utterly.

After his move to BBC Wales in 1970 Pat fronted the daily news programme *Good Evening Wales* and, more recently, the Sunday talk show, *Something Else* and the weekly political programme, *Called to Order*. His last documentary was about the reformist back-bencher Leo Abse. The same urge to examine what politicians get up to informed all the programmes he made for BBC Wales, BBC Two and HTV Wales, to which he brought a rigorous manner and a verbal dexterity that were second to none.

He published three more books. *Wales Off Message* (2000) traces the difficult birth of the National Assembly for Wales, in which he managed to bring out the comic side of things while making serious points about the nature of Wales's fledgeling democracy. His book *2001: A Year in Wales* (2002) is a diary reflecting on the obsessions, feuds and ambitions of those who try to climb the greasy pole of politics. Among the many *bons mots* one must suffice: 'In Wales we particularly resent strangers telling us what we already know and we are often willing to go to some lengths to prove them wrong, even if they're right.' *When Arthur Met Maggie* (2006), is about the miners' strike of 1984/85 and the clash of rival ideologies that have shaped our domestic world ever since. His last book, *A Useful Fiction: Adventures in British Democracy*, published in 2009, takes a wider view of the post-Thatcher years and the problems besetting the governments of Tony Blair and Gordon Brown.

He leaves a widow, Menna Richards, now Director of BBC Cymru/Wales, whom he married in 1985, and two sons and a daughter by his first marriage.

Patrick Hannan, journalist and broadcaster, born Aberaman, Glamorgan 26 September 1941; married secondly 1985 Menna Richards; died Cardiff 10 October 2009.

The Guardian (13 October 2009)

KEN HOPKINS

Labour Party stalwart converted to the cause of devolution

KEN HOPKINS SPENT decades hammering Welsh Nationalism in all its manifestations and was among the most implacable of Plaid Cymru's opponents.

As a Rhondda man he was in a long line of anti-Nat politicians who included the militant atheist Iori Thomas, long-serving MP for Rhondda West, and George Thomas, Viscount Tonypandy and Secretary of State for Wales, though he did not share their pathological hatred and vitriolic vocabulary.

He was nevertheless thoroughly in accord with the Labour Party's lukewarm outlook towards the Welsh language during the long years of its hegemony from 'the hungry Thirties' to the 1960s. It could hardly have been otherwise for a man whose career as teacher, headmaster and director of education must have owed something to party loyalties. He admitted this to me but saw nothing untoward in it.

Brought up on a poor estate in Ely, on the south-west side of Cardiff, the son of a Congregational minister, he recalled his earliest experience, of being thrust from a Welsh-speaking home into a playground where no other child spoke his language. Only one sympathetic teacher, remembering some Welsh from her own childhood, made a special effort by talking to him in his native language. He never forgot her kindness, but English soon became the language of his home – and by the time he reached adulthood he was no longer able to converse in Welsh.

He told me all this several times when we met in Cardiff's Civic Centre, where he was in the habit of taking a lunch-hour stroll in the company of George Askey, his deputy at

Mid Glamorgan County Council, where he was Director of Education during the 1970s. I always found him a warm-hearted and genial man with whom it was easy to exchange a yarn or two. He bore a passing resemblance to Eric Morecambe and the sight of him always raised a smile with me.

Educated at the Boys' County Grammar School in Porth, he was called up in 1943 and saw service as a submariner; he later read English at St Catherine's College, Oxford. He was a teacher and headmaster at Ferndale Grammar School in the Rhondda Fach before becoming Director of Education. He was already a member of the Labour Party and his allegiance never wavered. Twice secretary of the Rhondda Labour Party and chairman of Welsh Labour in 1991–92, he served on the party's Welsh and UK policy forums and was seen as a power behind the throne during Labour's incumbency at the Welsh Office. In 2009 he was given a Long Service Award and life membership of the Party. A highly literate man, he edited a lively symposium, *Rhondda Past and Future*, in 1975.

Like many in the post-industrial valleys of south Wales, he had been averse to devolution in the 1960s, especially as Plaid Cymru was making electoral gains that seemed to challenge one-party rule in the Labour heartlands. But after living under Thatcherism, and with a succession of Tories in the Welsh Office, he changed his mind after the No vote in the 1979 referendum. He became one of the keenest advocates of devolution leading up to Labour's landslide victory and the second referendum of 1997 and was influential in shaping Labour's policy, which was in favour of it. He took a leading role in the Yes campaign and was heartened when, two years later, the Welsh voted in favour of a National Assembly.

He remained, however, an ardent opponent of political nationalism and was horrified when his local seat at the first Assembly election was won by Plaid Cymru. It has since been regained for Labour.

Perhaps his most surprising initiative was a pamphlet,

Saving our Language, published by the Institute of Welsh Affairs in 2006. Drawing on his experience of losing his Welsh as a child, which he deeply regretted, he set out a number of proposals designed to restore the language as the birthright of every Welsh boy and girl. He called on the National Assembly to commit itself to transforming Wales into a truly bilingual country in which half the population would be able to speak Welsh by 2025. Among the sectors he identified were the school system, the media and popular support for a language manifesto to be drawn up by the Assembly. None of his recommendations was original, but some have already been implemented. Most remarkable was that his pamphlet signalled an apparent sea-change in the Labour Party's attitude to Welsh, the implications of which have still to be worked through.

Kenneth Samuel Hopkins, teacher, administrator and politician: born Pontycymer, Glamorgan 13 March 1925; married 1949 Margaret Lewis (one daughter); died Llantrisant, Rhondda Cynon Taf 23 July 2011.

The Independent (9 September 2011)

JOHN HOWELL

Staunch Welsh nationalist and Plaid Cymru stalwart

JOHN HOWELL WAS among those who contributed to the electoral progress of Plaid Cymru in the south-east of Wales during the 1960s. He stood twice as a parliamentary candidate in Caerffili, in 1959 and 1966, winning only about 4,000 votes on each occasion. But his charisma attracted many young people to the nationalist cause, among them Phil Williams, who joined the party after hearing him speak at a street meeting in the Rhymni Valley. At the by-election of 1968, two years after Gwynfor Evans' victory in Carmarthen and with Phil Williams the Plaid candidate, the vote in Caerffili increased to 14,274, some 40 per cent of the total votes, which placed the party very close to winning the seat.

Howell spent the rest of his life, until multiple sclerosis overcame him, working for Plaid Cymru in Caerffili, Merthyr Tydfil and Rhondda, devoting all his physical and mental energies to the nationalist cause. He worked as an engineer at the Llanwern steelworks but spent almost all his evenings and weekends working for Plaid. An original, not to say eccentric thinker, he was a frequent broadcaster with Radio Free Wales, the clandestine radio station designed to flout the ban on the party making political broadcasts. He believed passionately that the Welsh people should control the land, industry and resources of their country, as a first step towards independence.

To that end, Howell went to farm in Cardiganshire, not far from Cynog Dafis (later a Plaid MP) and Hywel ap Dafydd. This was his way of 'putting his shoulder to the wheel' (one of his favourite sayings). I first met him in 1959 and got to know him and his wife Janet while sharing a house with them and the poet Harri Webb in Merthyr in 1965. Soon afterwards, Howell went back to working in industry.

Given his upbringing, Howell's commitment to Wales was marvellously staunch. He had been born in 1928 in Lahore – in India in those days, but now in Pakistan. Although his parents were both Welsh-speakers, the language of his childhood was Urdu, which he learned from his *aya*, a remarkable young woman whose hero, Mahatma Gandhi, became his hero too. He was fond of speaking Urdu to Pakistanis while out canvassing for Plaid Cymru and with the nurse who looked after him towards the end of his life. He never learned much of his parents' language, but saw to it that his three children attended Welsh schools.

Howell had had a wholly English education at Aitchison College, 'the Eton of India', where he excelled at boxing, rugby and hockey. Although his father was one of the pillars of the Raj in the Punjab, Howell began taking an interest in the independence movement, and this led in 1938 to his being hastily sent back to England to finish his education at Clifton College. During the holidays he lived with an aunt at Llancaiach in east Glamorgan, his people's home. He later enrolled at Bristol University, where he graduated in mechanical engineering shortly before emigrating to Canada. Once there, he worked in civil aviation and witnessed the growing tension between French and English-speakers in that country. Now thinking of himself as a Welshman, he returned to Wales in 1957, almost immediately joining Plaid Cymru.

Even towards the end of his life, Howell was fond of discussing the fate of Wales. 'What's the situation, then?' he would ask anyone willing to stay up all night with him. He visited the National Assembly in his wheelchair with a mixture of pride and dissatisfaction. 'Wales deserves better than this,' he would say with a broad grin, 'but it's only a matter of time.'

John Dawkin Arnold Howell, engineer and Welsh nationalist: born Lahore, India 5 October 1928; married 1960 Janet Serman (one son, one daughter and one son deceased); died Cardiff 14 May 2009.

The Independent (30 July 2009)

RONAN HUON

Defender of the Breton language and literature

THE FORTUNES OF the Breton language and its contemporary literature depend largely on individuals devoted to its cause, there being few public bodies to lend their support, and what is achieved by these *animateurs* is often done in the face of stiff opposition from the French government and its local representatives.

Ronan Huon was one such, a man who from childhood into old age was in love with *brezhoneg*, the Breton language, and who served it in practical ways with a passion and tenacity which seemed to negate the very idea that it might be in danger of dying out. He wrote in it, published books in it, spoke it to his children and fought on its behalf, quietly but effectively, without bitterness but with a resolute application to solving the problems that beset it on every side. His death is a severe blow to the Breton movement but the many initiatives he put in hand are sure to bear fruit as other individuals come to take his place.

Born in Saint-Omer in the Pas-de-Calais in 1922, to parents who were both fluent speakers of Breton, Huon returned to their native town of Lannion when he was two years old, and it was there he was brought up. He was educated at the University of Rennes, where he took a degree in English and a diploma in Celtic Studies, a course which included a year in Swansea. On his return to Brittany in 1949 he was appointed English teacher at the lycée in Brest and spent the rest of his career there. His time in Wales was put to good use: he had learnt the rudiments of Welsh and found much to admire in the education system which, unlike that of France, made provision for the teaching of Welsh, and in the field of broadcasting, already well developed by the late 1940s.

It was a difficult time to be an activist in the Breton movement. Those who worked for the Breton language were tarred with the brush of collaboration with the Germans and progress was slow in restoring to Breton the conditions that were needed if it was to flourish as it had in the years between the wars. Like his great friend Per Denez, Huon managed to steer a course between the warring factions and never wore his political colours on his sleeve, preferring to make his mark in the cultural sector alone. The struggle continues to the present in a constant and often heated argument over whether Breton-language schools are entitled to financial support.

Huon was much given to launching literary magazines, beginning as a student in Rennes with *Tir-na-nog* ('Land of the Young'), which merged with two others in 1949 to form *Al Liamm* ('The link'), a review which he edited and published for more than 50 years. This bi-monthly magazine became the principal platform for just about every Breton writer of note to emerge during the post-war period. With a wide purview and familiar with the latest critical theories, it had sophistication and driving energy, and a circulation that was the envy of many periodicals in the other Celtic lands. Today, having run to 339 numbers, it is managed by the founder's son Tudual who, like his father, teaches English in a secondary school and is the author of several books in Breton.

The magazine's immediate success prompted Huon and his wife Elen to found a publishing imprint of the same name and together they published some 200 titles, without subsidy from any public source and with no distribution network other than what they and their friends were able to set up. The importance of this venture for the Breton cultural movement cannot be overestimated: without *Al Liamm* the writing and reading of Breton would have gone into terminal decline among the small literate community and the future of the language as the medium for creative writing and intellectual debate would have been put in jeopardy.

Above all, the magazine saved Breton from degenerating into the patois of a folk culture fit only for tourist consumption. There is nothing folksy about the contents of *Al Liamm*: its standards might be compared with those of the *London Review of Books*. The Huons produced books of poetry, plays, essays, short stories, novels, memoirs and documentaries, but it was a series of dictionaries that sold best, in particular those compiled by Roparz Hemon, the great man of Breton letters, which sold more than 100,000 copies. The *Al Liamm* imprint was taken over by another publisher, *An Here*, in 2000 and is now run from Plougastel-Daoulas.

Huon would have written much more of his own poetry and prose if he had not been so selfless in publishing the work of others and taking up the cudgels on behalf of Breton publishers: from 1985 to 1997 he was President of the *Association des Editeurs de Bretagne*, in which capacity he worked indefatigably for the wider distribution of Breton books and the commissioning of new authors. I recall how, in 1969, on the occasion of the Taliesin Congress held in Cardiff, he expressed wonder and admiration for the work of the Welsh Books Council and the Welsh Arts Council, the two bodies charged with promoting the books of Wales in those days, and the Welsh experience continued to inspire him.

He was an important poet and writer of short stories, notably *An Irin Glas* ('The plums', 1966) and *Ur Vouezh er Vorenn* ('A voice in the mist', 1980), and his translations from Welsh and English have been much admired. In 1992, in recognition of his achievement as editor, publisher and writer, Huon was presented with the *Collier de l'Hermine* by Pierre LeTreut, Vice-President of the Regional Council of Brittany and President of the *Institut Culturel de Bretagne*, the only award he ever received for a lifetime's labours.

Ronan Huon would not have sought any honour outside

Brittany, for the deep satisfaction he found in serving the language and literature of his native land was reward enough for this modest, genial and unremittingly generous man.

René Huon (Ronan Huon), writer, editor and publisher: born Saint-Omer, France 3 August 1922; married Elin Ar Meliner (four sons); died Brest 17 October 2003.

The Independent (28 October 2003)

DAFYDD HUWS

Psychiatrist, Plaid Cymru stalwart and wind-farm pioneer

THE DISTINGUISHED PSYCHIATRIST Dafydd Huws was passionately devoted to the cause of Plaid Cymru from his schooldays in Aberystwyth and played a leading role in the party's affairs for more than 50 years. He spent all his adult life in Cardiff, where he was elected the first Plaid member of the City Council in 1969, and in the general election of the following year stood against George Thomas, Secretary of State for Wales and arch-enemy of the Welsh Nationalist Party, polling some 10 per cent of the votes and beating the Liberal candidate into fourth place.

His enthusiasm for self-government knew no bounds. He once told me that he had been born a Welsh Nationalist and that his conviction sprang from his heart, not his head. His zeal was infectious and he was able to bring out large numbers of supporters, drawn as much to the man as to his party's policies. Even in the working-class wards of Cardiff, unpromising ground for the seeds of nationalism, he had a personal following that he cultivated in all possible ways, despite the fact that he was not by nature a proletarian rabble-rouser. It was his elegant wit and mischievous sense of humour that attracted many.

As a consultant psychiatrist at Whitchurch Hospital, in north Cardiff, from 1970 until his retirement in 1996, he could explain what makes a person feel an attachment to his native patch and want only the best for it. He had an enormous admiration for his fellow-Welshman Ernest Jones, psychoanalyst and biographer of Sigmund Freud, and was fond of quoting from Jones's autobiography, *Free Associations* (1959), to the effect that, although he regretted

154

his inability to speak Welsh, he considered his nationality to be an essential element in his personality – a view with which Freud concurred. In multicultural Cardiff, Huws would tell voters, 'To be Welsh means to belong, or to feel that we belong, whatever our language, colour or religion.' His nationalism was all the more attractive for being inclusive, and it was spiced with anecdotes about his experiences in the midst of men in turbans who proudly told him they were Welsh.

After challenging 'Our George' in Cardiff West in 1970, Huws stood against him again at both general elections of 1974, put up in his native Cardiganshire in 1979, and returned to the capital in 1983. On this last occasion he polled fewer than a thousand votes. His fortunes were a little better in the South Wales constituency at the European elections of 1984, when 13,201 voters (6.8 per cent) cast their votes for him. His lack of electoral success did not dishearten him; indeed, he revelled in the campaign and took great solace from having spread Plaid Cymru's message among the electorate, firm in his conviction that Wales was moving towards self-government. His joy at the creation of the National Assembly in 1999 was tempered by the view that it was only a step in the process of devolution which would lead to full self-government in due course. The Lifetime Award for which he was nominated by Plaid Cymru earlier this year was accepted by his wife Rhian at the party's annual conference held in September.

During the late 1980s Huws served as Plaid's chairman and in that capacity he was a member of a working party set up to consider the problems caused by the in-migration of English-speakers into the traditional heartlands of western and northern Wales. The group's report was a model of common sense and its recommendations to local government were balanced and reasonable, but it did little to stem the flood. Most notably, it called for the integration of incomers by providing them with the means of learning about the culture in which they found themselves, though few of those who settle in Welsh-speaking districts seem prepared to avail themselves of such opportunities.

Dafydd Huws was born in Aberystwyth in 1935 and brought up at nearby Llandre, but spent some of his early years in Kenya, where his father worked as a mining geologist. Determined to bring their children up as Welsh-speakers, his parents employed a Welsh teacher who ensured that they did not lose the language. Huws chose to worship at Welsh chapels for the rest of his life.

After leaving Ardwyn Grammar School in Aberystwyth, where he was known as Danskit, he trained at the Welsh National School of Medicine in Cardiff and was employed by the Medical Research Council for five years before taking up a post as consultant psychiatrist at Whitchurch Hospital in 1970; there he was well-known and popular as one of the doctors who ran the Tegfan Day Hospital. Among the professional bodies with which he was associated was the psychiatry division of the South Glamorgan Health Authority, which he served as Chair. He was also a member of the Wales Medical Campaign against Nuclear Weapons.

It was on the hill known as Mynydd Gorddu, overlooking Tal-y-bont in Ceredigion, that he built a wind farm that was one of the first in Wales. Inspired by a visit to the Centre for Alternative Technology near Machynlleth, and a subsequent visit to Denmark, he was a keen advocate of wind energy and had a worldwide knowledge of the industry. His pioneering spirit was generally recognised by those who advocate the use of wind energy in Wales and his wind farm has been described by Eryl Vaughan, chief executive of Windpower Wales Ltd, as 'his legacy to the Welsh nation'.

I knew Huws in a more private capacity. Sharing my interest in the four-line poetic form known as the *triban*, popular among the poets of Glamorgan, we would exchange examples we had garnered from our reading and sometimes compose others with which to entertain ourselves. For those unfamiliar with Welsh, perhaps I should add that the bawdy song 'The Good Ship Venus' is made up entirely of *tribannau*. When I pointed this out to my friend, who was the most broad-minded of men, he laughed heartily and we agreed that the song must have been composed by a Welshman!

Dafydd John Lewys Huws, psychiatrist and wind-farm pioneer: born Aberystwyth, Cardiganshire 29 November 1935; consultant psychiatrist, Whitchurch Hospital, Cardiff 1970–1996; married 1976 Rhian Jones (two sons, three daughters); died Caerffili 3 July 2011.

The Independent (14 September 2011)

GLYN JAMES

Plaid Cymru leader in the Rhondda
and pioneer of Radio Free Wales

TELEVISION VIEWERS IN Wales during the late 1950s were able to tune in to an extra radio programme after the closedown of the BBC service around eleven o'clock. As the signal faded, they would hear: 'Do not switch off. Do not switch off. You are listening to the voice of Free Wales.' There followed a mix of news, interviews and folksongs that ended with the Welsh national anthem and sometimes 'Men of Harlech'. The man behind this daring initiative, which predated Radio Caroline, was Glyn James, a prominent Welsh Nationalist and stalwart of Plaid Cymru in the Rhondda Valley.

The pirate radio was started after Plaid Cymru was banned by Charles Hill, the Postmaster General, from making party political broadcasts and thus found itself at a disadvantage in the electoral fray that was just hotting up in Wales. The radio was run by a small group of Nationalists who had built their transmitter on advice from members of the Scottish National Party. This contraption had a range of only a few miles but the wheeze received widespread publicity and contributed to a sense of national resurgence. The transmitter was moved from place to place and none of the broadcasters, who included Plaid Cymru's President Gwynfor Evans, Carwyn James the rugby player, Rhydwen Williams the writer, Ray Smith the actor and Harri Webb the poet, was ever brought to book. Eventually, Plaid Cymru was allowed air-time, after which Radio Free Wales entered the annals of Welsh Nationalist legend.

I once played a small part in one of these clandestine broadcasts which took place in the attic of Garth Newydd, a rambling old house in Merthyr Tydfil where I lived in a commune with other Plaid activists. My job was to listen for any knock on the door and, sure enough, it came: it was the local bobby on his late-night beat, calling as he often did for a chat and cigarette. Fortunately, Glyn James and Harri Webb had also heard the knock, and down they came into the living-room to find me in nervous conversation with the caller. I made them all a pot of tea and the policeman was kept in pleasant conversation with Glyn and Harri for more than an hour while the conspirators upstairs made illegal use of the airwaves. None of us was cooler than Glyn James who used his immense charm to entertain the unexpected caller with an assortment of stories and jokes.

Within the year Glyn had become a part-time organizer for Plaid Cymru in south-east Wales, which was always the area in which he felt most at home, winning many adherents to the Nationalist cause. A little later, he was elected to Rhondda Borough Council and then the Mid-Glamorgan County Council on which he served two terms (1961–64 and 1967–69); he was elected Mayor of Rhondda in 1960 and Honorary Alderman in 1991. He also stood as the party's candidate at General Elections in Rhondda constituencies on seven occasions between 1955 and 1979, a tireless campaigner whose energies never flagged.

Glyn James was a native of Llangrannog in Cardiganshire, one of the eight children of a carpenter who had worked in the Rhondda coalmines. Educated at Cardigan Grammar School and the Glamorgan Technical College in Trefforest near Pontypridd, which later metamorphosed into the University of Glamorgan, he served his apprenticeship at a foundry in Cardigan before qualifying as a mining engineer in 1942. At the Tylorstown pit where he took his first job as a fitter he was given the task of adjusting the hooter so that local people could distinguish its wail from other pit-hooters in the Valley. He spent the rest of his life working at pits in the Rhondda, where he met Hawys Williams, daughter of a Ferndale minister, who was to become his wife. A talented guitarist, she was often to be heard singing folksongs on Radio Free Wales and was his helpmeet in all the electioneering to which he devoted his life.

Recruited by Kitchener Davies, the inspirational pioneer of Plaid's cause in the Rhondda, Glyn joined the party at the age of 19 in 1944 and spoke in public for the first time at the General Election of the year following. He took part in some of the earliest extra-parliamentary Nationalist campaigns such as the unsuccessful attempt to prevent the Army building a training camp at Trawsfynydd in Merioneth, where he sat down in the road with some of Plaid Cymru's leaders. On the day the mines were nationalized in 1947, he ran up a Red Dragon to replace the Union Flag which had hitherto been flown above the pit where he worked. He also took part in demonstrations against the monarchy during the run-up to the investiture of the Prince of Wales in 1969.

During the miners' strike of 1972 he and another county councillor were arrested for having hurled leaflets calling for '*Cyfiawnder i'r glowyr! Justice for the miners!*' into the debating chamber of the House of Commons, for which they spent a night in the cells and were assaulted by the police. After 1972, when the party began to disappoint those who had hoped for an outbreak of Nationalist feeling in the industrial valleys of the south-east, Glyn James was among those who grew ever more critical of its leaders, though he continued his political activities as vigorously as before.

Although Welsh was his first language, and that of his home in Ferndale in the Rhondda Fach, he was not aligned with the militant language movement *Cymdeithas yr Iaith Gymraeg*, preferring to fight for jobs and investment in the valleys of south Wales. He was nevertheless active in the Welsh Schools Movement for which he was awarded the T. H. Parry-Williams Medal at the National Eisteddfod of 1991, one of the most prestigious honours to which a Welsh-speaking patriot can aspire. He was also made an honorary member of the Gorsedd of Bards for his services to Welsh culture in the Rhondda.

Undoubtedly one of Plaid Cymru's most flamboyant characters, Glyn had a convivial personality, a sturdy physique, a mop of flame-red hair, bushy sideburns, and a sonorous voice – he had toyed with the idea of becoming a full-time actor for radio and was a popular lay-preacher – as well as a fine flow of rhetoric in both Welsh and English. He lived to see Plaid Cymru make electoral progress in the Rhondda in the persons of younger men and women who had been inspired by him and he expressed satisfaction when the party entered coalition with Labour in the National Assembly in 2007.

Glyndwr Powell James, mining engineer, Plaid Cymru activist and pioneer of Radio Free Wales; born Llangrannog, Cardiganshire 26 March 1925; married Hawys Williams (two children); died Llwynypia, Rhondda Cynon Taf 4 December 2010.

The Independent (18 Decemeber 2010)

Dafydd Jenkins

Barrister and authority on the laws of medieval Wales

HISTORIANS BELIEVE THAT Wales in the Dark Ages consisted of several warring kingdoms each of which had its own system of dispensing laws whose origins lay in some obscure tribal past before the Anglo-Saxon invasion of the island of Britain. Tradition has it that these laws were brought together under the aegis of Hywel ap Cadell, or Hywel Dda, the only king of Wales to be given the epithet 'Good', at a convention held at Whitland in what is now Carmarthenshire around the middle of the 10th century. The Law of Hywel Dda, a contemporary of Alfred of Wessex, whom he may have been emulating in this respect, survived the loss of Welsh political independence in 1282 and continued thereafter as what the Act of Union of 1536 called 'the sinister usages and customs' of Wales.

Dafydd Jenkins, a member of the Law Department at the University College of Wales, Aberystwyth, put together a composite text from manuscript sources dating from the early 13th century and threw a great deal of light on the complexities of its language and meanings. As well as a number of studies in Welsh, he published the fruit of his research in *Celtic Law Papers* (1973), *Hywel Dda and the Law of Medieval Wales* (1985), and *The Law of Hywel Dda* (1986), and (with Morfydd E. Owen) edited *The Welsh Law of Women* (1980), a Festschrift presented to Professor Daniel A. Binchy. These books demonstrated that the Laws, as well as being one of the chief glories of medieval Wales, are also valuable material for students of social history, anthropolgy, jurisprudence and comparative law.

Bringing to this work the expertise of a professional lawyer, Jenkins also made a lucid and, for the first time, an accurate translation of the texts which took into account the anonymous authorship and literary quality of medieval legal prose and pointed to the implications the Laws had for the literature of the period, notably the Welsh prose masterpiece known as *The Mabinogion*, through which Arthurian themes were taken into the literatures of Europe.

Above all, he demonstrated that one of the strongest features of the Welsh language was the technical vocabulary of the law-books, in particular its rich store of abstract nouns and its flexible syntax that was capable of expressing the most abstruse matters. The books, many of which were handed down from one generation of lawyers to the next, are an invaluable source of evidence about the nature of medieval Welsh society, from the king's court through the professional classes of priest, physician and poet to the rules governing marriage, divorce, property, theft and murder. Foremost among the laws were *perchentyaeth*, based on an ancient principle to do with a man's responsibilities towards his family, relatives and neighbours, and *galanas*, setting out the rules of redress for offences against the individual.

Dafydd Jenkins was born in London on St David's Day 1911 but brought up by Welsh-speaking parents from Cardiganshire, where he settled in 1938. After attending Merchant Taylors' School, he read Natural Sciences and Law at Sidney Sussex College, Cambridge, was called to the Bar at Gray's Inn in 1934 and was practising as a barrister on the South Wales circuit in Carmarthen at the time of 'the Fire in Llŷn' two years later.

The act of arson carried out by Saunders Lewis, D.J. Williams and Lewis Valentine, three leaders of the fledgeling Plaid Cymru, at Penrhos, near Pwllheli, was a protest against the building of an RAF bombing school on the land of Penyberth, a house significant in the history of Welsh Recusancy. All constitutional means of preventing the development, including the unanimous support of all the Welsh MPs and County Councils, had failed. On the night of 8 September 1936 huts and building materials were set alight by the three Nationalists, after which they reported themselves to the police. Their trial at Caernarfon Assizes, at which the jury failed to reach a verdict, and their retrial at the Old Bailey, where they were convicted and sentenced to a term of imprisonment, caused outrage in Wales and was to have a profound and lasting influence on the country's cultural and political ethos.

Dafydd Jenkins, although an active member of Plaid Cymru, was not directly involved in the incident at Penyberth but wrote an authoritative account of it in *Tân yn Llŷn* (1937), a book translated into English by Ann Corkett as *A Nation on Trial* (1998). He also worked unstintingly as Secretary of the National Language Petition of 1938 which, under the chairmanship of William George, Lloyd George's brother, collected 400,000 signatures in support of a request to the British Government that Welsh be granted a measure of official status in the public life of its own country, a concession that was not wrung from it until 1967.

As a literary journalist between 1936 and 1942 Jenkins was closely associated with the brothers Alun and Aneirin Talfan Davies in editing and publishing the magazine *Heddiw* ('Today'). Intended to be a Welsh counterpart to English journals such as the *New Statesman*, the magazine was rather more literary and provided an important platform for writers of the day. It discussed Welsh Nationalism from a left-of-centre point of view and in its editorials took the Republican side in the Spanish Civil War. Both before and during the world war it devoted a great deal of space to pacifist arguments based on the Catholic concept of 'the just war' which was greatly agitating many intellectuals in Wales, and its overall stance was liberal and progressive.

For a while during the 1930s, as the right-wing Saunders Lewis tightened his grip on Plaid Cymru's policies, Jenkins grew ever more uncomfortable. He believed the Party should make a direct approach to Welsh Socialists whom he believed might respond to the case for national self-determination: 'Wales cannot be won for Home Rule unless the Socialists of Wales are won over,' he wrote in *The Welsh Nationalist*, only to be told (in an unsigned article almost certainly by Lewis) that his description of Party policy as 'essentially socialist' was not correct because it was opposed to 'centralized bureaucracy'. He nevertheless remained a Plaid Cymru member and played an active role in its affairs in both Cardiganshire and nationally after the war when Lewis was replaced by a more democratically minded leader, Gwynfor Evans.

During the second world war Jenkins, a committed pacifist on Christian grounds, registered as a conscientious objector and was ordered to work on the land, his first experience of farming and his introduction to the tradition of agricultural co-operation which had long been practised in Cardiganshire. He was one of the contributors to a series of pamphlets published by *Cymdeithas Heddychwyr Cymru*, a Welsh equivalent of the Peace Pledge Union.

In the Parliament for Wales Campaign launched in 1951 on an all-party basis under the chairmanship of Megan Lloyd George, the Liberal MP for Anglesey, Dafydd Jenkins played a prominent part. A quarter of a million people declared themselves in favour of an elected, legislative Parliament but the initiative failed, largely because, of the 36 MPs representing constituencies in Wales, only six supported it, of whom five were Labour members in defiance of their Party's policy, but partly because the British political system cannot be changed by petition alone.

An accomplished writer in both Welsh and English, Jenkins won the Prose Medal at the National Eisteddfod in 1946 with a volume of literary criticism and published two books about Denmark and Sweden, where he was a frequent visitor. He also translated some of the stories of Kate Roberts, which appeared in 1946 as *A Summer's Day* with a foreword by Storm Jameson, and contributed a charming monograph on the life and work of D.J. Williams to the *Writers of Wales* series. Among his many local initiatives was the creation of *Cymdeithas Lyfrau Ceredigion*, a book society which specialized in the publication of books of Cardiganshire interest. He was also a keen member of the Welsh Academy, the national association of writers in Wales, and was contributing vigorously to its journal, *Taliesin*, in his ninetieth year.

Jenkins joined the staff of the Law Department at Aberystwyth in 1965 and held a personal Chair in Legal History and Welsh Law from 1975 until his retirement in 1978. For many years he was a leading member of the colloquia on Welsh medieval law held at the constituent Colleges of the University of Wales, and among his colleagues he was generally considered to be the doyen. A somewhat formal, perhaps shy man, without the homelier characteristics of many of his compatriots, he gave generously of his erudition to younger scholars working in the same field and found great satisfaction in their success.

Dafydd Arwyn Jenkins, barrister and scholar, born London 1 March 1911; Lecturer in Law at the University College of Wales, Aberystwyth, 1965–75, Professor of Legal History and Welsh Law, 1975–78 (and Emeritus); married Gwyneth Owen (one son); died Blaenpennal, Ceredigion 5 May 2012.

The Independent (28 May 2012)

J. GERAINT JENKINS

Maritime historian and authority on rural crafts

'SALT WATER FLOWS through my veins, as it did in many of my ancestors', though unlike them I have expressed it not by sailing to distant parts but in my books,' wrote J. Geraint Jenkins in his autobiography *Morwr Tir Sych* ('Dry land sailor', 2007).

As Curator of the Welsh Folk Museum (now the National History Museum) at St Fagans, on the outskirts of Cardiff, and of the Welsh Industrial and Maritime Museum, J. Geraint Jenkins played a leading role in the preservation and interpretation of the maritime history of Wales. He published more than fifty books, many to do with the seafaring traditions of west Wales, and was generally acknowledged as an authority on his subject.

He also made expert studies of other aspects of Welsh folk life, including traditional farm implements, rural crafts, the woollen industry and Cardiff shipowners. But his heart was in writing books about the sea and the communities that depend on it for their livelihood. His survey of coastal fishing, *The Inshore Fishermen of Wales* (1991), together with *Nets and Coracles* (1974) and *Welsh Ships and Sailing Men* (2005), reflect his lifelong fascination with those who go down to the sea in ships, doing business in great waters. He never tired of pointing out that Wales has six hundred miles of coast.

Born into a seafaring family at Llangrannog in Cardiganshire in 1929, J. Geraint Jenkins received a wholly English education at the village school and at Cardigan Grammar School. He first felt the romance of the sea while being taken to various ports in Wales and England to see his father, who worked on tramp steamers, and his first ambition was to become a sailor. The district was thoroughly Welsh-speaking and he retained a love of his first language throughout his career, writing in it such books as *Crefftwyr Gwlad* ('Country craftsmen', 1971), *Traddodiad y Môr* ('The maritime tradition', 2004), *Ar Lan Hen Afon* ('On the bank of an old river', 2005) and *Y Cwrwgl* ('The coracle', 2006); the last-named is a short study of the small, nearly square, keel-less boat made of wickerwork covered with water-proofed calico which was to be seen, until recent times, on the rivers Teifi, Tywi and Taf in west Wales. He also edited a history of his old school in the language by which he set great store.

He spent two years reading Welsh, Economics and Geography at University College, Swansea, before moving to the University College of Wales, Aberystwyth, where he graduated with a degree in Geography and Anthropology in 1950. He made the move in order to study under E.G. Bowen, who held the Gregynog Chair of Geography and Anthropology at Aberystwyth, and Alwyn J. Rees, the renowned sociologist, who supervised his master's degree. It was while at Aberystwyth that he first tasted strong drink, having been brought up in a strictly teetotal home, though he more than made up for this abstinence in later life. The chapel he attended, Penmorfa, was the subject of his monograph published in 1998.

His first proper job was that of Assistant Keeper in the Museum of English Rural Life housed at Reading University where he went in 1953. Among his responsibilities was the wardenship of Whiteknights Hall of Residence, which went with a part-time lectureship. But the salary was only £450, paid quarterly, and on being refused a rise he began writing articles for magazines such as *Country Life*, *The Countryman* and *Tatler* as a means of supplementing his meagre income. His first article was about a man named Owen Deane of Great Hampden in Buckinghamshire, a chair bodger or broom squire who made Windsor chairs for a living. Thus he became acquainted with English craftsmen and discovered an interest in an aspect of material culture that he was to write about for the rest of his life. His first book was the magisterial study *The English Farm Wagon* (1961), a detailed and comprehensive account which recorded information precariously held in the memories of the oldest members of the community.

Anxious for his sons to be educated through the medium of Welsh, he returned to Wales in 1960 to take up a post as Assistant Keeper in the Welsh Folk Museum at St Fagans, near Cardiff. The man who appointed him was Iorwerth C. Peate, the Museum's founder, a prickly character with whom Geraint Jenkins managed to get on well. Almost immediately he took on a miller, a blacksmith, a cowper, a saddler, a clogmaker and a baker, all of whom were set to work in the grounds of the open-air Museum. He was promoted Keeper of Material Culture in 1969. His interest in the woollen mills of west Wales resulted in *The Welsh Woollen Industry* (1969) and several lesser studies, all researched with meticulous care and written in an attractively lucid style in both Welsh and English. It also led in 1976 to the establishment of the National Wool Museum at Drefach Felindre in the Teifi Valley. During his time at St Fagans he began editing the magazine *Folk Life* and was to remain in that capacity for twenty years. His *Life and Tradition in Rural Wales* (1976), a useful survey, was also written at this time.

In 1977, drawn by his wish to be engaged in something to do with the sea, he moved to the Welsh Industrial and Maritime Museum in Cardiff's docklands. He was to spend nine happy years there but in 1987 was tempted back to St Fagans, this time as Curator. The move was a mistake, for it took place just as the National Museum, of which the Folk Museum is an outstation, was coming in for interference from the Conservative Government and its representatives in Wales. As a patriotic Welshman he often clashed with the English businessmen appointed to the quango, and fell out regularly with the Museum's Curator, Alistair Wilson, whom he detested because this dour Scot showed no sympathy with things Welsh. He was also disappointed in colleagues and Council members who were willing to put up with the non-Welsh ambience of the Museum and accept the financial limitations set on its work.

Taking early retirement in 1992, he and his wife Nansi went back to Penbryn in the district where he had grown up. There he found all changed. The predominantly Welsh culture of his boyhood had almost disappeared, English incomers with no interest in learning the language had settled in most of the farms, Llangrannog had become a holiday village deserted out of season, and most of his old friends had died. He nevertheless threw himself into politics – he had been a longstanding member of the Welsh Liberal Party – and was elected onto the County Council. He served as High Sheriff of the County in 1994 and took his turn as Chairman of Ceredigion County Council from 2002 to 2003. One of the things he accomplished, as a member of the Cadwgan Trust, was the purchase of Cardigan Castle, where the first National Eisteddfod was held in 1176, with a view to restoring it as a heritage centre.

A man of Pickwickian frame, J. Geraint Jenkins was excellent company late at night and liked nothing better than the company of the less abstemious among Welsh writers, wits and artists. He reserved his animus for the more sober-sided of his compatriots, especially those who put their patriotism after their own careers. This outspokenness sometimes landed him in hot water but, for the most part, did not interfere with his genial manner which was seen at its best when he was among country people in whose culture he found deep and lasting delight.

John Geraint Jenkins, historian: born Llangrannog, Cardiganshire 4 January 1929; Curator, Welsh Industrial and Maritime Museum (1979–87); Curator, Welsh Folk Museum (1987–91); High Sheriff of Ceredigion (1994–5); Chairman, Ceredigion County Council (2002–3); married 1954 Nansi Jarman (two sons and one son deceased); died Carmarthen 15 August 2009.

The Independent (25 September 2009)

MARGARET JOHN

Comic actress who starred in *Gavin and Stacey*

MARGARET JOHN CAME into her own as a comic actress in the part of Doris, the outrageously saucy, octogenarian neighbour in the hit BBC series *Gavin and Stacey* who propositions the embarrassed young man, newly married, with a lascivious wink and the words 'If you are interested in that sort of thing, you know, I'm very open-minded and discreet, okay?'

She appeared in every episode and made the part one of the most memorable in the series. If the romantic interest centred on Mathew Horne as Gavin and Joanna Page as Stacey, it was Margaret John who was given some of the funniest, not to say filthiest, one-liners by the show's co-writers, Ruth Jones and James Corden.

The show made her 'a national treasure' almost overnight. This was no thespian cliché: she was genuinely loved by her many fans for her sunny character both on and off screen, and among her fellow actors was held in the highest regard as a kind, generous woman who was admired by younger people for her professionalism, sense of humour and kind heart.

Viewers in Wales warmed to her as the typical Welsh Mam in all 38 episodes of the BBC Wales farce *High Hopes* (2002–8), written by Boyd Clack, in which she plays Mrs Elsie Hepplewhite, the ferociously protective head of a dysfunctional family living on a sink estate where petty crime is endemic. Again, she is given some of the raunchiest lines: having appalled her hypochondriac son Fagin (played by Robert Blythe) with the admission that in her younger days she was a stripper, he asks, 'How far did you go, Mam?', to which she replies, 'All over south Wales, son, all over south Wales'. Reminiscing about her libidinous youth, she says, 'Girls these days are too fussy, they are. I never turned any man down – as long as they were clean and tidy.'

She was able to use such unpromising material in an innocently deadpan manner that managed to maintain her dignity at the same time as it milked the humour for all its worth. The same talent was seen in *Little Britain*, in which she played a lesbian pensioner who shocks even Matt Lucas's militantly gay character, Dafydd. With such cameo appearances, Margaret John was to Welsh comedy what Liz Smith (Nanna in *The Royle Family*) was to English comedy, and she had a huge following: 'I get hugged by women and kissed by men in supermarkets. It's lovely!' she said in a television profile made of her in 2010. 'It's great to be a sex goddess at my age!'

For all her star status, she came late to comedy. Born in Swansea in 1926 (though she was always loth to divulge the date of her birth), she at first wanted to be a nurse or vet, but set her heart on a stage career after acting in chapel productions and with the Swansea Welsh Drama Society. Her first public appearances were at the town's Grand Theatre where she had small parts in weekly repertoire, so that by the time she enrolled at the London Academy of Music and Dramatic Art she had some acting experience on which to draw.

Her television career began in the 1950s, soon after leaving LAMDA, with small parts in series such as *Softly, Softly, Dixon of Dock Green* and *Z Cars*, in which she usually played working-class women exploited by petty criminals and thwarted by officialdom, her lilting Welsh accent apparent even when the episode was set in London's East End. She was more at home in the BBC adaptation of Richard Llewellyn's novel *How Green Was My Valley* in 1960, a rite of passage for most Welsh actors. Also in 1960, she was seen in Alun Owen's play, *After the Funeral*. She appeared in most of the soaps, including *Coronation Street*, *Last of the Summer Wine*, *Emmerdale*, *Crossroads* and *Blake's Seven*, and starred opposite Nerys Hughes in the long-running *District Nurse*. Her first comic role was with Mike Yarwood in 1977.

Shortly afterwards, she knew great sadness in her personal life: her musician husband Ben, first violinist with the London Symphony Orchestra, whom she had married in 1975, died suddenly.

Her later career took in *Doctor Who*, in which she had first appeared as early as 1968: she rejoined the cast in 2006 with David Tennant as the eponymous doctor, and also had parts in *Casualty*, *Doctors*, *Sherlock Holmes*, *Lovejoy*, and *The Ruth Rendell Mysteries*. She appeared with Paul O'Grady and Rosie Cavaliero in the Bingo! comedy, *Eyes Down*, in 2003. More substantial parts came her way with David Schwimmer's *Run Fatboy Run* (2007), *The Mighty Boosh* and *Framed*, a BBC Wales production in which Trevor Eve and Eve Myles had the leading parts. She kept up the comedy as a kinky Granny in the spoof *A Bit of Tom Jones*. Her last stage appearance was in 2009 when she took part in *The Vagina Monologues* at the Millennium Centre in Cardiff.

But none of these roles brought her the acclaim she enjoyed after appearing in *Gavin and Stacey* and *High Hopes*, and it is as the old lady who looked like a sweet pensioner but who could deliver a punch-line to hilarious effect that she will be fondly remembered.

In recognition of a career that had lasted sixty years she was awarded the Lifetime Achievement Award by Bafta Cymru in 2009.

Margaret John, actor: born Swansea 15 December 1926; married 1975 Ben Thomas (died 1978); died Swansea 2 February 2011.

The Independent (3 February 2011)

ANGHARAD JONES

Television executive and Welsh prose-writer

ANGHARAD JONES WAS the woman behind some of the most popular programmes ever seen on S4C, the fourth television channel in Wales, where from 1996 to 2007 she was Commissioning Editor for Drama and Film.

Among the soap-operas she commissioned were *Con Passionate*, about a male voice choir whose members are in and out of love with their conductor, played by the vivacious classical singer Shan Cothi; *Eldra*, a tale about a Welsh gypsy girl; and *Caerdydd*, which took the lid off the steamy affairs of those whose lives revolve around the National Assembly in Cardiff Bay. All had her hallmarks: a gripping story-line, dramatic scenes and racy dialogue.

Another soap with a political theme was *Llafur Cariad* ('A labour of love') which shone an unflinching light into the murky machinations of those who attempt to climb the greasy pole, often with poignant, even hilarious effects.

After leaving S4C in 2007 she worked as a consultant at the media production company Calon TV, one of the many enterprises which have won for Cardiff a reputation as 'Media City'. It has made some of the best children's programmes ever, including *Superted*, *Sali Mali* and *Sam Tân/Fireman Sam*. Many of its productions have been made back-to-back, that is to say in both Welsh and English, and have sold widely for dubbing into other languages.

She was widely respected among colleagues and those who control the purse-strings, bringing to her job a bright intelligence, an articulate approach to the industry's problems and a cheerful acceptance of the frustrations attendant on working in a milieu where some pretty monstrous egos are at play.

Her understanding of television and its requirements began at home, for she was the youngest of the four daughters of Gwyn Erfyl Jones, who spent a lifetime with HTV Wales, latterly as its North Wales representative.

She was also a prose-writer of extraordinary talent. In 1984 she won the Crown at the Urdd National Eisteddfod, the youth festival long regarded as a cradle for emerging literary talent, and in 1995 the Literature Medal at the National Eisteddfod, the premier festival of Wales, for a novel published as *Y Dylluan Wen* ('The white owl'), which was later adapted for television. It starred the folk-singer Siân James whose vibrant voice gave it a haunting folk quality well-suited to the original. The words of many of the singer's songs were written by Angharad Jones, who inherited her mother Lisa's musical gifts.

Her debut as a writer was made with a collection of stories and poems, *Datod Gwlwm* ('Undoing a knot') in 1990, after which she was regarded as one of the rising stars of contemporary Welsh letters. She was praised, *inter alia*, for the richness and fluency of her Welsh, which was not surprising because she had been raised in a cultured home and had read Welsh at the University College of North Wales in Bangor. Her first job was lecturing in Welsh at the Normal College in that city.

Although she wrote virtually nothing in English, a translation of one of her stories – a subtle and disturbing tale set in an 'ordinary' street – appeared in my anthology of new Welsh short fiction, *A White Afternoon*, in 1998.

She also wrote verse and took part in *Talwrn y Beirdd*, the traditional gatherings at which poets writing in the strict metres lock horns with one another in bardic contention, displaying wit and technical expertise.

Angharad's body was pulled from the sea by coastguards near the pier at Penarth, Cardiff's nearest coastal resort, on the morning of 9 January. South Wales Police investigating the circumstances of her death said it was not being treated as suspicious and the Coroner had been informed.

Meinir Angharad Jones, television executive and writer: born Dolgellau, Meirionnydd 12 May 1962; Commissioning Editor for Drama and Film, S4C (1996–2007); one daughter with Maredudd ab Iestyn; died Penarth, Vale of Glamorgan 8/9 January 2010.

The Independent (25 January 2010)

DIC JONES

Archdruid of Wales and master poet in the strict metres

WHEN DIC JONES won the Chair at the National Eisteddfod in 1966 he was hailed as a master of the traditional metres whose like had not been seen since medieval times. By this was meant he wrote *cynghanedd* – the intricate system of metrics, syllable counts and rhyme which Gerard Manley Hopkins called, somewhat inadequately, 'consonantal chiming' – and with such brilliance that he could be compared with poets like Dafydd ap Gwilym, a contemporary of Chaucer, whose work is one of the chief glories of Welsh literature.

The poem which brought him prominence on a national stage was entitled '*Cynhaeaf*' ('Harvest') and it was praised by one of the three adjudicators, Thomas Parry, the sternest of critics, for its consummate craftsmanship and rich imagery drawn from the poet's observation of the natural world and the passing of the seasons. When Dic Jones came to publish his second volume of verse three years later, it was natural that it should take the title of his magnificent poem, '*Caneuon Cynhaeaf*' ('Harvest songs'). His reputation as *Prifardd*, or Chief Poet, was now made and he took his place among the most accomplished Welsh poets of his day.

It would be a mistake to remember Dic Jones merely as a *bardd gwlad* or country poet, a rhymer on bucolic themes with straw behind his ears, for he was heir to a centuries-old tradition which is as sophisticated as, say, that of the *Jocs Florals* in Provence or the poetry of the great makars of Scotland such as Dunbar and Henryson. Technical virtuosity may be at its heart but it also has room for a world-view that is as much intellectual as it is lyrical. Dic Jones wrote poems in which he addressed famous politicians and commented on the wonders of technology such as the Telstar space satellite and the military base at Aber-porth.

Dic Jones farmed Yr Hendre at Blaenannerch near Aber-porth in lower Cardiganshire, as his people had done for centuries. He knew himself to be a poet while still a pupil at the Cardigan County School and was soon taken under the wing of Alun Cilie, a member of a famous family of poets who lived at nearby Llangrannog, and it was he who tutored the budding poet in the craft of Welsh prosody. It was not long before Dic Jones could turn out a perfect *englyn*, the four-line poem that is as precise as the haiku or tanka, except it has rules of alliteration, stress, consonant-count and rhyme that make the Japanese forms seem crass in comparison. One simple example, about the Christmas tree, must suffice:

Pren y plant a'r hen Santa – a'i wanwyn
   Yng nghanol y gaea',
   Ni ry' ffrwyth nes darffo'r ha',
   Nid yw'n ir nes daw'n eira.

('The children's tree and old Santa's, its springtime is in the middle of winter, it bears no fruit until summer is over, it flourishes only when snow has come.')

Like many poets who are devoted to the form, Dic Jones had hundreds of *englynion* by heart; make that thousands, for there seemed to be no bottom to the well from which he drew inspiration. So adept was he that his conversation sparkled with whole sentences in *cynghanedd* and witty couplets in seven-syllabled lines which he composed at the drop of a hat. There may be something mathematical about the requirements of the craft – it can be learned in a few years by a gifted amateur – but the master-poets, of whom Dic Jones was one, rise above the form's restrictions and makes their verses sing. Many of his shorter poems (he also wrote epigrams, limericks and topical ballads) rely for their effect on humour and satire and he could always be counted upon to cause laughter among his listeners.

For this reason he was in constant demand at weddings and parties, and when asked for a celebratory poem on any occasion, large or small, he would readily oblige, thus carrying out the function of the country poet that has for long enlivened the cultural ambience of rural Wales. On his own behalf, he wrote a poem requesting a loan from his bank, another greeting his fellow-poet T. Llew Jones, in hospital after an accident, and another protesting about a rise in water-rates, all in immaculate *cynghanedd* and to a high standard. One is hard put to think of any other language in which literary activity of this kind is the norm.

Dic Jones first came to public notice by winning the Chair in five consecutive years at the Eisteddfod held by *Urdd Gobaith Cymru* (Welsh League of Youth), but unlike many youngsters who carry off that prize he went on to fulfil his early promise by publishing his first collection, *Agor Grwn* ('Cutting a furrow'), in 1960. It was followed by *Storom Awst* ('August storm', 1978) and *Sgubo'r Storws* ('Clearing out the storehouse', 1986). Many of these poems celebrate the close-knit communities of Cardiganshire, giving the lie to the hate-writing of Caradoc Evans who, a generation or two before, had pilloried them for their grudging soil, brutish peasantry and perverted religion.

There is something joyous and uplifting about Dic Jones's portraits of his neighbours, their dogs and livestock, and even their machinery for he wrote poems extolling the Ffyrgi and the Jac Codi Baw – the Ferguson Massey tractor and the JCB that have brought such improvements to the ways the land is worked. His example reminds us that poetry is not always written out of a tortured or neurotic mind but is sometimes produced by a sunny temperament and an uncomplicated lifestyle close to the soil and the elements.

Two events cast a cloud over the serenity of Dic Jones's view of Wales and the world. The first was the death, at three months, of his daughter Esyllt, a Downs Syndrome child, and the controversy that followed a most unfortunate mix-up in the Chair competition at the National Eisteddfod of 1976, an important occasion since it was the eighth centenary of that venerable festival. The adjudicators chose his poem on the subject 'Gwanwyn' (Spring'), submitted under a pseudonym as usual, as the best in the competition but, because it turned out he was a member of the Literature Panel and had thus had fore-knowledge of the set subject, he was disqualified and, at the very last moment, the Chair was awarded to a reluctant and dark-browed Alan Llwyd.

Acrimony and controversy followed and opposing camps emerged, the incident doing considerable damage to the *amour-propre* of both poets and showing up a degree of administrative bungling on the Eisteddfod's part. Dic Jones took such setbacks with the dignity of the true poet: 'When a man manages to write a verse that is completely to his liking, or a couplet he can recite to himself as it brings a tear to his eye, he knows deep down that it makes no difference what any adjudicator, or anyone else, says of it... He has received his prize and will spend the rest of his life trying to savour again that fleeting moment.'

Dic Jones's last years were taken up in trying to find ways of maintaining Yr Hendre against the ravages of the foot-and-mouth epidemic and the myriad difficulties facing the farming industry. One of his initiatives was to hire out part of his land for summer visitors who were put up in teepees under the supervision of one of his sons, Brychan Llŷr, a well-known pop musician. A muscular man, with a handshake that made strangers wince, Dic Jones never lost his sense of humour, his delight in choral singing, his social obligations and his devotion to the craft of poetry. Many younger poets sought him out and he continued to take part in the popular poetry contests held annually in the Literature Pavilion at the National Eisteddfod. He became Archdruid of Wales in 2007 but officiated only once, at the Eisteddfod held in Cardiff in

2008, and was prevented by illness from taking part in the ceremonies at Bala in the following year.

He gave an account of his life up to 1973 in *Os Hoffech Wybod* ('If you'd like to know', 1989), and published a last collection of topical poems and articles, *Golwg Arall* ('Another view', 2001), which he had contributed to the weekly magazine *Golwg*. The title of his autobiography has resonance for Welsh readers for it is a quotation from Ceiriog's famous poem, 'Alun Mabon', which reads (in translation): 'If you'd like to know how a man like me lives: I learned from my father the first craft of humankind.' Dic Jones may have been, by his own admission, an indifferent farmer, but as a poet he takes his place among the finest practitioners of an art that rewards them with everlasting renown – everlasting, that is, for as long as Welsh remains a language in which literary genius can find expression.

Richard Lewis Jones (Dic Jones), farmer and poet: born Tre'r-ddôl, Cardiganshire 30 March 1934; married 1959 Siân Jones (three sons, two daughters and one daughter deceased); died Blaenannerch, Ceredigion 18 August 2009.

The Independent (21 August 2009)

GRENFELL JONES

Cartoonist and satirist of the south Wales valleys

THE FORMER MINING village of Aberflyarff is not to be found on any ordnance map of south Wales. Yet its steep terraces, dilapidated chapels, ubiquitous sheep, combative choirs, polluted rivers, hapless drunks and perilous coaltips are all part of how the people of the valleys have come to see, and laugh at, themselves in the years since the demise of the region's heavy industries.

Grenfell Jones, known only as Gren, who has died aged 72, created the legendary village in the pages of the *South Wales Echo*, to which he contributed a daily cartoon for some 40 years. He made readers smile with his send-up of valley types such as the corrupt councillor, the deranged rugby fan, and the anarchist sheep, Neville and Nigel, whose fleeces bore such slogans as 'Keep Wales tidy – dump your rubbish in England.'

He could sometimes be ribald. The promiscuous barmaid Bromide Lil complains that she's been unfaithful to her lover on only two occasions – 'once with the Male Voice Choir and once with the Aberflyarff seconds.' He could also turn a baleful eye on the use of the Welsh language in English-speaking areas: one of his proletarians says, 'I like bilingual signs – they make me feel I'm abroad.' Cultural pretension always came in for his grapeshot: the conductor of the Aberflyarff Male Voice Choir tells a posh audience, 'And if you feel like joining in the chorus – don't.'

There was nothing bitter or unkind about Gren's satire, though he could make acerbic comments on public bodies when the occasion demanded. He dipped his pen in gall only when some celebrity from beyond Offa's Dyke cast aspersions on the Welsh character, but then his compatriots knew he was laughing with, not at, them. To be featured in a Gren cartoon was an accolade that many sought, especially politicians craving publicity at all costs.

Jones knew south Wales from the inside: he had been born into a mining family at Hengoed in the Rhymney Valley. As a small boy he was given paper and pencils to keep him amused in chapel and soon he was filling the blank pages of hymn books with caricatures of the preachers and deacons. He learned early that drawing could be subversive.

He was educated locally, and after national service with the RAF, worked as an engineering draughtsman, but dreamt of becoming an illustrator. For five years he lived precariously by selling cartoons to *Whizzer* and *Chips*. His first big break came in 1968 when he joined the *South Wales Echo* in Cardiff. Every day for the rest of his life he would draw a cartoon reflecting current events in Wales and the world.

His early mentor was Jon of the *Daily Mail*, who advised him to draw what he knew best, and he soon realised he had material on his own doorstep that only a native could appreciate, such as the feral sheep that come down from the hills to forage in the valley streets: 'I stopped my car while driving with friends through Pontlottyn, so that a sheep could cross the road. My friends were amazed that I should be treating a sheep like one of the community, which of course in the valleys they are.'

In his strip *Ponty and Pop*, which appeared in the *Sports Echo* on a Saturday evening, he created wisecracking characters who expressed something of his long-suffering but indomitable people who have known only the rigours of de-industrialisation. It was their ability to grin at misfortune which endeared them to Gren. This is how he summed up Port Talbot on the occasion of its being voted 'the dirtiest town in Britain': an old lady sits in a garden, the sky dark with smoke from the steelworks and her daughter calls to her, 'Drink your tea, Mam – before it gets dirty.'

Official recognition of Gren's talents came when he was named Provincial Cartoonist of the Year four times during the 1980s and with an MBE for his services to the newspaper industry in 1989.

His second wife Ann, whom he married in 1993, died in 2006; he is survived by two sons from his first marriage.

Grenfell (Gren) Jones, cartoonist, born 13 June 1934; died 4 January 2007.

The Guardian (13 March 2007)

STEWART JONES

Actor and comedian who used English for comic effect

ONE OF THE stalwarts of Welsh-language television, in which he made a name for himself as an actor and comedian, Stewart Jones was unusual in that he was born in Edinburgh and named Stewart Whyte McEwan by his unmarried parents.

At the age of six months, he was given to a Welsh couple who brought him to Eifionydd, the district on the Llŷn peninsula which was then thoroughly Welsh-speaking. His adoptive father, aged 63, was employed as a carpenter on the Forth Bridge but had deep family roots in Gwynedd and resolved to bring up the boy as Welsh. Stewart Jones, as he chose to be known during a long and successful career, acknowledged the influence of the district of Rhoslan which went to the making of him as a performer who delighted in the spoken word.

At the age of 26, married with children of his own, he went looking for his birth parents, David and Adelaide McEwan, by then married and living in Old Scone, Perth. Arriving at their house unannounced, he was warmly received by his mother, a teacher whose maiden name had been Bremner, but when his father came home all the farmworker could say was, 'Well you do understand, we can't have you back. Socially it would not be acceptable.' He was given a lift to the station and never saw either of them ever again. When, many years later, he read his autobiography on the radio he burst into tears after recording this passage from it.

Stewart once said of the circumstances of his birth, 'I came in a straw basket on a train from Edinburgh to Eifionydd, like Moses, except I wasn't found in the rushes of the Nile but arrived on a station platform.' It was not until he was interviewed and made a television programme about it for S4C in 1995 that the full story became known.

Although the experience of having been given away left its mark on him, he did not allow it to trouble him unduly, at least not outwardly. The truth about his parentage had gradually dawned on him when he was in his teens because his adoptive parents had used to receive money from an address in Scotland. He was not legally adopted and his surname remained McEwan for official purposes for the rest of his life.

His *alter ego* was Ifas y Tryc, a character devised for him by his friend Wil Sam Jones for the BBC Cymru programme *Stiwdio B*. Ifas, in bowler hat and wing-collar, was a porter who would lean on his trolley while delivering his homespun philosophy in a lugubrious manner straight to camera. The horse sense and waspish one-liners were directed at officialdom, the pompous, the overbearing English visitor to rural Wales, and representatives of the London government, in particular 'the England Revenue' with whom he had a long-running feud. Many of his catch-phrases, such as *'sgersli belîf'* and *'Britannia rŵls ddy Wêls'*, used English for comic effect, and have entered the everyday language of Welsh-speakers. His autobiography, published in 2001, was entitled *Dwi'n deud dim, deud ydw i...* which may be rendered as 'I'm not saying anything, what I'm *saying* is... '

Stewart Jones was also a serious actor who performed in some of the plays of Saunders Lewis, generally considered to be the greatest Welsh playwright of the twentieth century. In the early days of Welsh radio he had parts in plays produced to a high standard by the Cegin company in Criccieth and by the little theatre at Llangefni in Anglesey. With the advent of Welsh television he was seen in plays by Wil Sam Jones, Emyr Humphreys, Eigra Lewis Roberts, Huw Lloyd Edwards, Meic Povey, Harold Pinter, and Bertold Brecht.

When not acting, he earned a living as a carpenter and later kept a shop and boarding house in Criccieth which he named *Pros Kairon* ('For the time being' in Greek), the title of a play by Huw Lloyd Edwards. When visitors asked what the name meant he would tell them it was Welsh for 'Bed and Breakfast'.

Having won the prestigious Llwyd o'r Bryn Prize at the National Eisteddfod on two occasions, he was in constant demand as a reader of poetry, which he enhanced with his rich voice and intelligent interpretation. Many consider him to be one of the best readers of Welsh poetry ever heard on radio.

His most-admired television performance, and one for which he won a Bafta Cymru award, was given as William Davies in Emlyn Williams's play *Oed yr Addewid* ('The promised age', 2000). The old man, trapped in a care home, is facing the possibility he will have to sell everything he owns to pay for it. A lifelong socialist, he feels resentful towards Margaret Thatcher's government for putting a price on everything he holds dear.

The play is a study of poverty, old age and dementia amid the beautiful scenery of the Llŷn peninsula. As *Do not go gentle* it was shown at the Commonwealth Film Festival and the Palm Springs International Film Festival of 2002 and was screened on S4C as a tribute to the actor in the week of his death.

Stewart Whyte McEwan (Stewart Jones), actor: born Edinburgh 3 June 1928; married 1950 Jean Roberts (died 2005, two sons, two daughters and one son deceased); died Bangor, Gwynedd 25 July 2011.

Previously unpublished

T. LLEW JONES

Poet and prolific writer of Welsh children's books

T. LLEW JONES wrote some of the best-loved children's books in the Welsh language. Long before Roald Dahl and J.K. Rowling, he enjoyed cult status among young readers in Wales, turning out some eighty books that were snapped up for their exciting yarns, thumping rhymes and sheer entertainment value. As both poet and prose-writer, he seemed to know instinctively what children like to read and, with no thought for adult taste or the approval of literary critics, provided them with their favourite reading, whether adventure stories, folk-tales, whodunits, magic realism, historical romances, ghost-stories or humorous verse. There is no school in Wales that does not have his books on its library shelves and hardly one he did not visit, often to the rapturous reception more usually reserved for pop-singers.

He set such store by the response of his young readers that on one famous occasion, having been awarded the prestigious Tir na n-Og Prize for his *Tân ar y Comin* ('Fire on the common', 1975), a story about gypsies, he was prepared to bite the hand of the adjudicators because they had announced that, in their opinion, the book was good only in parts. 'This prize has somewhat tarnished my reputation,' he told them pointedly. 'It was grudgingly given and I am accepting it in the same spirit. You are grown-up readers with jaded appetites, but the many thousands of children who have enjoyed my book have better judgement and theirs is the only one that matters.'

T. Llew Jones came to prominence as a children's writer in the early 1950s. Alun R. Edwards, the trail-blazing Librarian of Cardiganshire whose mission in life was to promote popular books in Welsh, had called a conference of teachers at which it was decided to commission fiction and light verse that would be bought in bulk for use in the county's schools, and Jones, already known as a poet, was expected to play his part in this initiative. Over the next ten years he produced as many books, including a schools anthology that remained in use for half a century and a retelling of Celtic folk-tales.

His interest in folklore provided him with themes for several of his best books, among them novels about the pirate Bartholmew Roberts, known in Welsh tradition as Black Bart, and Siôn Cwilt, a smuggler who kept his contraband in caves on the wild coast of Cardiganshire in the 18th century. But his prose masterpiece is a trilogy about Twm Siôn Catti, the real-life highwayman who has a place in the hearts of Welsh children similar to Dick Turpin's among young English readers: *Y Ffordd Beryglus* ('The dangerous road', 1963), *Ymysg Lladron* ('Among thieves', 1965) and *Dial o'r Diwedd* ('Revenge at last', 1968). These novels are enjoyed by adult readers for their polished style and gripping plots.

Born at Pentre-cwrt in Carmarthenshire in 1915, T. Llew Jones, a weaver's son, belonged to a hardy breed of small farmers and sailors who had worked the land and gone to sea for generations. His interest in story-telling was awoken when, at the age of seven, as reward for good behaviour, he was allowed to listen to his headmaster begin reading a tale about a man who left his infant child with the keeper of a toll-gate and then disappeared into the night. Since, on account of some misdemeanour, he was not allowed to hear the next episode, Jones never discovered what happened to man or child, and for years thereafter wondered what had become of them. The unfinished narrative troubled him until, in 1973, he was able to write the story from beginning to end as *Un Noson Dywyll* ('One dark night'), perhaps his finest novel.

A voracious reader by the time he entered the Grammar School at Llandysul (he once told me that, before leaving primary school, he had read everything in the classroom cupboard, including *The Life of Gladstone*), he began writing a novel in English about a hard-hearted squire whom he called Enoch Allstone, but abandoned it after a friend who had read the first few pages complained that he knew exactly how it would end. A second attempt at writing a story during an English lesson came to nought when the teacher thought it so good that he accused the boy of plagiarism and caned him for it; this incident persuaded him that it was more important for primary school children to read than it was for them to be given exercises in 'creative writing', and he often said so.

Having left school at the age of 16, but unable to train for Anglican orders on account of his father's death and the need to supplement the family income, Jones spent the next few years doing what manual work he could find in the vicinity of his home. His marriage in 1940 to one of the daughters of Cilie – a remarkable group of country poets renowned in Welsh literary circles – proved the making of him, for it brought him into close contact with poets like Isfoel, Alun Cilie and Dic Jones, with whom he learned his craft in bardic contention, though not before he was called up (on his wedding day) and sent to serve with the RAF, and later the Army, in Egypt and Italy. From camp he began sending home poems which his wife passed on to Dewi Emrys, editor of a poetry column in the weekly paper *Y Cymro*.

At the same time he began learning chess, a game at which he and his younger son, Iolo, represented Wales in the Chess Olympiads and about which they wrote a book together. His elder son, Emyr Llewelyn, born while his father was overseas in 1941, is among the most seasoned of Welsh-language militants. He has been fined many times and, in 1963, received a year's gaol sentence for his part in sabotage at the site of the Tryweryn reservoir in Merioneth. Again in 2000 he was imprisoned for a week after refusing to pay his licence fee as part of the campaign to persuade BBC Cymru and S4C to ban English in their programmes. T. Llew Jones backed his son in all his bruising confrontations with the law, sharing his determination to defend the Welsh-speaking communities of west Wales from the influx of English settlers.

On demobilization in 1946, T. Llew Jones underwent a year's fast-track training as a teacher in Cardiff and soon afterwards took up a headmaster's post at the primary school in Tre-groes in Cardiganshire. It was there he began publishing his short stories, most of which he had written in order to supplement his meagre salary. In 1958, having moved to Coed-y-bryn, near Llandysul, he won the Chair at the National Eisteddfod with a poem on the theme 'Caerleon-on-Usk', the reputed site of King Arthur's court. The poem was praised by the adjudicators for its mastery of traditional prosody and for its relevance to contemporary Wales; this feat he repeated in the year following with a poem entitled 'Y Dringwr' ('The climber'). The best of his poems for adults are to be found in *Sŵn y Malu* ('The sound of breaking', 1967) and *Canu'n Iach!* ('Farewell!', 1987).

Although he was never asked to become Archdruid, as he might have expected after winning the Chair twice, T. Llew Jones played a prominent part in maintaining the Welsh Rule at the National Eisteddfod against those who were calling for it to be slackened in the late 1970s so that some use could be made of English in competitions and concerts. He also proved a redoubtable champion of standard literary Welsh, deploring any attempt by the Welsh Books Council and the Welsh Joint Education Committee to promote a simplified version for the sake of those learning the language. For him, the vigorous speech of his boyhood would always be good enough as the medium for his writing.

In his literary precepts he was conservative, resisting any attempt to tinker with the traditional rules of prosody and, as Chairman of *Cymdeithas Cerdd Dafod*, the society for poets writing in the strict metres, was able to exert an avuncular influence on younger bloods calling for change. He preferred to contribute poems, reviews and articles to *Y Cardi*, the county's homespun magazine, than to the journals of Academe. In 1979 he caused a stir among more advanced bivouacs on the Welsh literary front by castigating, in a foreword to an anthology he had edited, what he considered to be 'difficult poetry', by which he meant writing that was 'capable of more than one interpretation'. In the same year he refused to become a member of the Welsh Academy, the national association of writers in Wales, on the grounds that he did not believe writers should form 'cliques' and, anyway, he thought the invitation had come too late. Ultra-sensitive to criticism, especially when it came from people who were not themselves writers, T. Llew could be prickly towards those who failed to pay him his full meed of praise. Nor was he very keen to see his work translated into English, relenting only once to let the poet Gillian Clarke make, under the title *One Moonlit Night*, a version of his book *Lleuad yn Olau* (1989), a collection of folk-tales. He gave a typically spirited account of his own life in his autobiography, *Fy Mhobl I* ('My people', 2002), deliberately borrowing the title of a notorious book by Caradoc Evans.

T. Llew Jones enjoyed his reputation as the foremost children's writer in Wales but only on his own terms. The University of Wales awarded him an honorary MA in 1977, but he took more pleasure in appearing as Day President at the Urdd's Eisteddfod in 1981. During his speech, to his great delight, children swarmed onto the stage with placards illustrating the titles of his many books, to thunderous applause and leaving not a dry eye in the pavilion. He, in turn, paid affectionate tribute to his young fans because 'they read with their hearts' and spoke of his belief that, like Peter Pan, he had inside him 'a child who refused to grow up or ever grow old'.

Thomas Llewelyn Jones, poet and children's writer: born Pentre-cwrt, Carmarthenshire 11 October 1915; married 1940 Margaret Jones (died 2002, two sons); died Pontgarreg, Ceredigion 9 January 2009.

The Independent (4 February 2009)

PETER LAW

Labour rebel who saw off the 'official'
candidate in the 2005 General Election at Blaenau Gwent

THE APPLECART OF Welsh Labour politics was well and truly upset when, on 5 May 2005, a former party stalwart in Blaenau Gwent – an upland, post-industrial, heavily populated, working-class constituency, with Ebbw Vale at its heart – was elected as its Independent MP. The shock was all the greater in that the parliamentary seat, a Labour bastion since the days of Aneurin Bevan, and more recently Michael Foot, was considered the safest in Wales and the fifth safest in Britain.

The local Member of the Welsh Assembly, Peter Law, had defied his party by standing against the official Labour candidate and had demonstrated, like S.O. Davies in Merthyr Tydfil some 35 years before, that grassroots loyalty can sometimes prevail over the party machine. Once again, Labour's control freaks had egg on their face.

Peter Law had been a member of the Labour Party since 1963. Born in Abergavenny in 1948 and educated at Llan-foist Primary School, King Henry School, Nantyglo Community College and the Open University, he first earned a living as a grocer and public relations consultant but was soon devoting more and more of his time to politics. He served as chair of Gwent Healthcare NHS Trust and as a member of the Blaenau Gwent Borough Council, where he earned a reputation as an intelligent, articulate and hard-working Labour activist; in 1988–89 he was the borough's Mayor. A gentle and cultured man, he learned Welsh and was a member of the consultative committee which preceded the establishment of the Welsh Language Board in 1988.

Standing down from local government in 1999 in order to seek election to the National Assembly, he became AM for Blaenau Gwent and was duly appointed to the first Labour cabinet in Cardiff Bay with a brief for Local Government, Environment and Planning, only to be dropped when the coalition with the Liberal Democrats was formed in October of the year following, in a move calculated to ensure the Labour Party would hang on to power. He subsequently proved a persistent critic of the coalition administration, voting on a number of occasions against the Welsh Assembly Government's proposals.

He was punished when, after the second Assembly election of 2003, he ran for the post of Deputy Presiding Officer and was defeated by a single vote – his fellow Labour AMs voting against him en bloc in favour of John Marek, another ex-Labour man, thus ensuring that with Marek's election a non-Labour member would, for procedural reasons, be removed from the voting process. By now Law had the reputation of being a loose cannon and his erstwhile comrades closed ranks against him with that special animus which is often reserved for family feuds.

When Llew Smith, MP for Blaenau Gwent, announced his intention of retiring from Parliament before the general election of 2005, a major row broke out as the National Executive of the Welsh Labour Party insisted that selection of new candidates be restricted to all-woman shortlists. Law and Smith argued passionately for the right of the local party to select a candidate in Blaenau Gwent from an open list but in this they were overruled by the party's central office.

Immediately after Peter Law's election as an Independent MP he was expelled from the Labour Party, together with all those who had publicly taken his side and worked for him. After an intense campaign which had brought many of Labour's big guns to Blaenau Gwent – a sight about as common as a butterfly on an iceberg – and a high turnout of 66 per cent, reflecting keen public interest in the contest, he had polled

20,505 votes (58 per cent of the votes cast), against 11,384 (32 per cent) for the Labour candidate. In his victory speech on polling night, he told the stony-faced Labour supporters, 'This is what you get when you don't listen to people.'

But the party, always unforgiving of its rebels, was vitriolic in its denunciation of him and the bad feeling in the constituency has persisted to this day. The flames were fanned again by the announcement this month that the defeated Labour candidate, Maggie Jones, had been made a life peer – the jiggery-pokery of which Law and Smith had complained seemed to be confirmed. The Labour Party has now changed its all-women rule in elections for the parliamentary seat but not for the Assembly.

The expulsion of Peter Law, who held a dual mandate as both MP and AM, had disastrous consequences for the Labour Party in Wales in that, after May 2005, it was deprived of its majority in the National Assembly and would henceforward suffer a series of defeats at the hands of the combined opposition parties who, when they could muster a degree of agreement, voted down a number of Labour initiatives, notably an attempt by the Arts Minister to strip the Arts Council of most of its powers and to fund five of its major clients directly, thus removing the arm's-length principle.

Peter Law, the first Independent Welsh MP for many years, was chosen as Welsh Politician of the Year 2005 by the *Wales Yearbook*, a manual much thumbed by the political class. Not least among the facts taken into consideration was that he had fought the Blaenau Gwent seat while recovering from surgery to remove a brain tumour, which he announced just before his electoral triumph.

The accolade also recognised that he had been spurred not by personal ambition but by what he perceived as gross interference in local Labour affairs by an overweening party headquarters. He nevertheless kept his sunny temperament throughout the bitter controversy and the opprobrium it brought him. To watch him work the busy streets of the old steel towns of Ebbw Vale, Tredegar and Abertyleri of a Saturday morning – he seemed to know everyone and everyone recognised him – was to see a genuinely popular politician among his own people.

Peter John Law, politician: born Abergavenny, Monmouthshire 1 April 1948; chairman, Gwent Healthcare NHS Trust 1999; AM (Labour) for Blaenau Gwent 1999–2005, (Independent) 2005–06; Environment and Local Government Secretary, National Assembly for Wales 1999–2000; MP (Independent) for Blaenau Gwent 2005–6; married 1976 Patricia Bolter (two sons, three daughters); died Nantyglo, Blaenau Gwent 25 April 2006.

The Independent (26 April 2006)

ANTHONY LEWIS

Militant Welsh Nationalist

THE NATIONALIST MOVEMENT in Wales, like its counterparts in Scotland and Ireland, has always had its share of colourful characters who have added a whiff of sulphur to the bland pottage of constitutional politics.

One such was Anthony Lewis, who spent some 40 years on the fringes of Plaid Cymru, a party that was highly embarrassed, in the 1960s, by the Free Wales Army, a small band of uniformed men who, as far as is known, never fired a shot in anger or caused physical injury to anyone. With Cayo Evans and Dennis Coslett, also now *hors de combat*, Tony Lewis was often to be seen carrying a flag in commemoration of some prince or martyr, or briefing gullible journalists down from London about the FWA's guerrilla strength up in the hills.

The FWA leaders – all nine of them – were brought to trial in Swansea on 1 July 1969, the very day the Queen invested her son Charles as Prince of Wales at Caernarfon Castle, a ceremony the militants had planned to disrupt. The nine had been kept in solitary confinement since their arrest on 26 February. Lewis, after a trial lasting 53 days, was found guilty of being a member of an illegal organization but, unlike Evans and Coslett, not guilty of managing the FWA, and so escaped a custodial sentence.

One of his favourite anecdotes recounted how, while they were awaiting trial, the prison governor, out of the goodness of his heart, had allowed the nine to watch an international rugby match. When the governor asked whether he had enjoyed it, Lewis replied that he wasn't really interested in rugby: the time had been spent in forming an escape committee.

The trial did not put a stop to violence, or the threat of it, and soon afterwards a much more shadowy and effective group calling itself MAC (*Mudiad Amddiffyn Cymru* or 'Movement for the Defence of Wales') began causing explosions at buildings associated with the Crown. The destruction of property continued into the 1970s with the arson campaign of *Meibion Glyndŵr* ('Sons of Glyndŵr') against second homes owned by English people in Welsh-speaking areas. By then the police were showing renewed interest in Lewis, and for a while he was on the run from the law, but eventually turned himself in and no charge was brought against him.

For Lewis, the trial was the culmination of several years of political activity which had run into the sand of electoral defeat. As a member of the Patriotic Front, a splinter-group of Plaid Cymru dissidents given to braggadocio and not very subtle innuendo, he had often had his home searched and been taken down to the police station for questioning. At the time he was working as a bus conductor and would sometimes arrive home at the end of his shift to find plain-clothes detectives waiting at his door.

Lewis had joined Plaid Cymru shortly after finishing his military service with the RAF in Germany. Brought up in a working-class home in Usk, a very anglicized town, and kept ignorant of things Welsh at school, he now grew aware that he had a country with its own history and language. He once told me he had suddenly realised the depth of his feelings as a Welshman after being called Taffy by English officers and taunted by other squaddies on account of his accent.

But he was attracted to a stronger brew than what constitutional nationalism had to offer: living in Cwmbran, a New Town in Monmouthshire not noted for its Welsh identity or the vigour of its cultural life, he formed a unit of like-minded friends and they called themselves the Patriotic Front. They even had their own social club, the 'Patriot's Rest', until

Plaid Cymru outlawed the group in 1966. Lewis designed the Front's uniforms, and its symbol, devised by the poet Harri Webb and based on the White Eagle of Snowdonia, he made into cap-badges. It was not long before slogans began appearing on walls the length and breadth of Wales that were accompanied by this potent piece of symbolism.

The Cwmbran group soon merged with others who were happy to march under the banner of the FWA. But there was always a touch of the comic about what Tony Lewis got up to. On one occasion he presented himself at the embassy of the United Arab Republic in London dressed in full uniform, only to be told that it was about to close and that he should come back next day; to his great chagrin, he was given even shorter shrift at the Cuban embassy.

Again, the charabanc which Lewis had booked to take the Cwmbran group to Bala for the opening in 1963 of the Tryweryn dam, which had drowned a village and valley to make a reservoir for Liverpool, failed to turn up, and so he was prevented from taking part in a protest against a project which had brought him, and many others, into the ranks of the nationalist movement a few years before.

After the FWA trial, Lewis was in no whit daunted and resumed his political activities, though was never taken to the bosom of mainstream nationalism. Fortunately, he was a gifted self-taught craftsman, especially in the working of silver, and he now began to receive commissions. While living on the Isle of Man, he made Celtic medals for the House of Keys and ran a jewellery shop. In 1982 he made an attractive medallion for the seventh centenary of the death of Llywelyn ap Gruffydd, the last prince of independent Wales, which has become something of a collector's item. He also made, for the National Eisteddfod, a number of silver crowns that are among the finest ever awarded at the festival, as well as an elegant silver gilt trophy, the World Wide Welsh Award, which was presented to Gwynfor Evans in 2000.

A highly intelligent autodidact, a mild-mannered man with

a splendid blond moustache, Lewis spoke fluent German and Dutch but not, oddly enough, given his patriotism, Welsh. He was also a talented musician, playing the harp, flute and fiddle for his own pleasure and for any late-night company that cared to listen. He remained staunch in his attachment to the cause of Welsh nationalism, and when I last met him at the National Eisteddfod he seemed as convinced as ever that Wales would, in due course, become a republic. He was also a good friend to the bi-monthly magazine *Cambria*, saving it from folding more than once.

There will be scores of people at his funeral carrying not only the Red Dragon but also the red-and-yellow standard of Owain Glyndŵr and the golden cross on a black ground which is the flag of St David. Tony Lewis, who was very keen on heraldic devices and symbolic pageantry, will be given a send-off with the ceremonial panache he always brought to his own public appearances.

Anthony Harold Lewis, political activist and craftsman: born Usk, Monmouthshire 15 April 1937; married 1958 Gillian Pewtner (one son, one daughter); died Barry, Vale of Glamorgan 8 November 2005.

The Independent (11 November 2005)

IWAN LLWYD

Poet and troubadour whose trademark was a trilby

ONE OF THE most accomplished poets of his generation, Iwan Llwyd explored all the media through which he might find a wider audience for his poetry, including radio and television, as well as public readings and musical performances in his native Wales and the Americas. He was particularly fond of marrying word and image, often in collaboration with such leading artists as Iwan Bala, Catrin Williams and Anthony Evans, the photographers Marian Delyth and Aled Rhys Hughes, and the television producer Michael Bayley Hughes for whose programmes he wrote poems that were an integral part of the script. He was tired of television that was 'merely wallpaper' and wanted to reclaim it as a medium for the creative writer.

One of his books, *Rhyw Deid yn Dod Miwn* ('A tide coming in', 2008), celebrates the coast of Wales, not the usual tourist spots but those where man intrudes on the natural scene. All his books were meant to have visual appeal and to show how verse and illustrations can complement one another, and this one, with stunning photographs by Aled Rhys Hughes, is among the most elegant.

At his happiest in troubadour mode, with his trademark trilby and toting his guitar, he wandered all over Europe and ventured into some pretty out-of-the-way places in South America. The skyscrapers and bright lights of the Big Apple are featured in his book *Hanner Cant* ('Fifty', 2007), which has photographs by Marian Delyth, but the west coasts of Wales and Ireland are featured too, for he was as much a poet of place as one who sang about the people he loved.

Born in the village of Carno, Montgomeryshire, in 1957,

Iwan Lloyd Williams – like many creative people in Wales he dropped his anglicized surnames – was a son of the manse. He grew up in the Conwy Valley and in Bangor, later making his home in nearby Tal-y-bont; he began writing verse while still at Friars School, Bangor. After taking a degree in Welsh at Aberystwyth, and in due course a master's for a thesis on the bardic patrons of north-west Wales, he worked with a theatre company and in public relations before resolving to live by his pen, which he did intermittently for the rest of his life.

He made his debut with *Sonedau Nos Sadwrn* ('Saturday night sonnets', 1981); the sonnet form, together with the rhyming couplets he learned from T.H. Parry-Williams, was a favourite of his and he returned to it in what was to be his last collection, *Sonedau Pnawn Sul* ('Sunday afternoon sonnets', 2009). There was nothing obscure in his work, and some of his poems have the plangent quality of folk song.

The most contemporary and freewheeling are to be found in *Dan Anesthetig* ('Under anæsthetic', 1987) and *Dan Ddylanwad* ('Under an influence', 1997), the latter volume the fruit of commissions from S4C, in which the full blast of the American experience is to be felt. Here are poems about Bob Dylan, Ellis Island, Woodstock, the Harley Davidson, Hiawatha, Memphis, Route 66, Native Americans, and Haight Ashbury. The collection, with artwork by Anthony Evans, was named Welsh Book of the Year in 1997.

The wide range of which he was capable is evident in *Be' di Blwyddyn rhwng Ffrindia?* ('What's a year between friends?', 2003), which brings together a substantial collection of 117 poems written between 1990 and 1999. The image of the open road and a world without boundaries, particularly in the arts, is central in these richly ironic poems.

Iwan Llwyd also played bass guitar in various bands, alongside other poets and musicians such as Myrddin ap Dafydd, Steve Eaves, Ifor ap Glyn, Twm Morys, Meirion MacIntyre Huws, and Geraint Løvgreen, thus reviving the ancient Welsh tradition of declaiming verse to musical accompaniment. The tour he made with Twm Morys (the son of travel-writer Jan Morris) in South America during the autumn of 1998, which produced the poems in *Eldorado* (1999), is the very stuff of legend among the poets of Wales.

He often visited schools, delighting pupils with his infectious love of the Welsh language and teaching them the rudiments of *cynghanedd*, the system of metrical prosody which has been the pride of Welsh poets down the ages. With Myrddin ap Dafydd he edited *Mae'n Gêm o Ddau Fileniwm* ('It's a game of two millennia', 2002), a handbook for use in schools about the Welsh literary tradition, in which ten contemporary poets introduce their own work and discuss the influences on it. In May 2006 he read at the United Nations building in New York as part of the People's Poetry Gathering.

The title *Prifardd* ('Chief poet') became his in 1990 after he had won the Crown at the National Eisteddfod with a collection of poems entitled '*Gwreichion*' ('Sparks'). He was to have been one of the competition's three adjudicators at the Festival which is to be held at Ebbw Vale in August, where his poetry will no doubt be given its full meed of praise.

Iwan Lloyd Williams (Iwan Llwyd), poet: born Carno, Montgomeryshire 15 November 1957; married 1985 Nia Lloyd (one daughter); died Bangor, Gwynedd 28 May 2010.

The Independent (27 July 2010)

PHILIP MADOC

Actor who played a U-boat captain in *Dad's Army*

WHEN THE ACTOR Philip Madoc was awarded an honorary degree by the University of Glamorgan in 2001 he told the congregation that, in his time, he had played many distinguished parts – Lloyd George, Hitler, Trotsky, Othello, Dr Faustus, the Master of the Universe – but that he considered the honour now conferred upon him to be the greatest of all. The rapt attention with which his acceptance speech was heard was a mark not only of his stage presence but of the man's wit, modesty and natural charm. After the ceremony, he was mobbed by the graduates, their parents and teaching staff alike.

Whatever fame his starring roles had brought him during a long and successful career in the theatre, the cinema, and on television, the reason why so many wanted to shake his hand and get his autograph was that here was the man who in 1973 had played the arrogant U-boat captain captured by the Walmington-on-Sea platoon of the Home Guard in the hugely popular television series, *Dad's Army*. Taking out his notebook to write down the names of his captors, the German helps to create one of the funniest moments in the series when he demands of the hapless Private Pike 'Vat iss your name?', at which Captain Mainwaring shouts, 'Don't tell him, Pike!' The scene, the only occasion on which Philip Madoc appeared in the series, was voted Number One in a Comedy Top Ten by the readers of the magazine *Classic Television* in 1999, and never fails to raise a smile.

The menacing persona of the U-boat captain was one Philip Madoc made his stock-in-trade. It owed a lot to his dark good looks, deep voice and slightly foreign air that lent itself to parts in which a touch of the alien and sinister was called for. One of his earliest roles was that of the relentless SS officer Lutzig in the World War II serial *Manhunt* (1969) and, three years later, he played the vicious Huron warrior Magua in *The Last of the Mohicans*. But he also appeared as German soldiers, often, it must be said, as stereotypes, in countless other productions. It was as if his very Welshness was enough to suggest that here was no English gentleman but an all-purpose foreigner with an exotic accent, a form of type-casting in which he delighted, since he was the most approachable and non-aggressive of men.

He was born Phillip Jones in Twynyrodyn, an old iron-making village high on the hill above Merthyr Tydfil, in 1934. He found himself interested in drama as a teenager at Cyfarthfa Castle School but trained as a linguist at the University College, Cardiff, and the University of Vienna, where he learned enough German to make his later appearances in Wehrmacht uniform utterly convincing and where he was the first foreign student to be awarded the Diploma of the Interpreters' Institute. But still drawn to the stage, he gave up an interpreter's job in occupied Vienna and spent three years at the Royal College of Dramatic Arts in London. Within a year of leaving RADA, now as Philip Madoc – he took his stage name from the twelfth-century prince who is reputed to have discovered America – he was treading the boards with the Royal Shakespeare Company in *Measure for Measure*. He later played Othello, Iago, Macbeth and Dr Faustus.

His television appearances were counted in the hundreds and all played with the same brooding intensity that he was so good at. He made five episodes of *The Avengers*, and four of *Doctor Who* in the days when Peter Cushing and later Tom Baker played the Doctor. More meaty roles came his way in *A Very British Coup*, *The Saint*, *Inspector Barlow*, *Porridge*, *The Sweeney*, *Maigret*, *A Bouquet of Barbed Wire*, *The Goodies*, *Brother Cadfael*, *Midsomer Murders* and *Casualty*, in the twelfth episode of which he played an uncooperative, disabled old man to memorable effect. Indeed, it sometimes seemed a cameo role had been reserved for Philip Madoc in just about every British television series and he was rarely out of work.

In his native Wales, Philip Madoc co-starred with Hywel Bennett during the 1990s as the formidable but world-weary Chief Inspector Noel Bain in the detective thriller *A Mind to Kill*, which also went out from S4C in a Welsh-language version, *Noson yr Heliwr* ('Night of the Hunter'). The actor had enough Welsh to learn his part well and often managed, for the sake of authenticity, to use words from the Merthyr idiom he had spoken as a youth. The English-language version led to a spin-off series shown on Channel Five. He also had a part in *A Light in the Valley*, starring Glyn Houston, Michael Bogdanov's nostalgic but moving film about life in the Rhondda Valley which was screened by BBC Wales in 1998.

But the performance that made him a household name in Wales and brought him fame in England was the part of the Welsh statesman Lloyd George. The drama-doc *The Life and Times of David Lloyd George*, which was broadcast in 1981, began with the politician's boyhood in Llanystumdwy, where he was baptized in the river from which, as Earl Lloyd-George of Dwyfor, he was to take his title, through his rapid rise to prominence as a Radical Liberal MP, to his Premiership during the Great War, and the subsequent decline in his influence and death in 1945. The actor was given the same mane of white hair, assumed the same pugnacious mien and used his gifts to convey the sonorous magic of Lloyd George's oratory.

Philip Madoc was a longstanding member of Plaid Cymru and, although he was never to live in Wales after his early successes, gave generously to the Welsh Nationalist cause. He served as Vice-President of the London Welsh Society and the London Welsh Male Voice Choir. He was a fine reader of Welsh poetry and a popular narrator of audio books for the visually impaired. Among the religious texts he recorded were certain Buddhist writings, to which he felt himself drawn in later life. Unlike his first wife, Ruth Madoc, who as the lovelorn Gladys Pugh put on a comic Welsh accent in the holiday-camp series *Hi-di-Hi!*, he had a naturally mellifluous voice that was able to convey the subtleties and emotional power of what he was reading with a rare intelligence and without histrionics.

Phillip Jones (Philip Madoc), actor: born Merthyr Tydfil, Glamorgan 5 July 1934; married firstly Ruth Llewellyn (one son, one daughter, marriage dissolved); secondly Diane (marriage dissolved); died Northwood 5 March 2012.

The Independent (7 March 2012)

JUDITH MARO

Writer and Jewish patriot who fought with Haganah in Palestine

JUDITH MARO TOOK part in the campaign to establish the state of Israel, fighting with Haganah against both Arabs and the British in what was then Palestine.

The state was born in 1948 but by then, appalled by the bloody conflict between Israelis and Arabs, who also claimed Palestine as their homeland, she had left the Middle East and settled in Britain with her husband, the sculptor Jonah Jones, whom she had married two years previously. After their move to Wales, she felt such an affinity with her 'new, old country' that she would allow her books to be published in English only after they had appeared in Welsh.

Born Ida Grossman in Dnepropetrovsk in the eastern Ukraine, she was brought up in Haifa, where her father was Professor of Mathematics in the Technology Institute. Her home was not religious and she did not attend the synagogue, though she was encouraged to read the Bible for the light it threw on the history of her people. At the age of three she and her parents witnessed the shooting of Jews by Arabs in the Old City of Jerusalem, an experience that left an indelible mark on her.

A precocious child, fluent in five languages including Hebrew and Arabic, she once told me she had read Stefan Zweig and Feuchtwanger by the time she was seven. The first shadow fell across her childhood when her best friend, a girl named Miriam, was taken back to France just before that country's fall in 1940 and was later killed in Auschwitz.

While still at the Montessori school she attended, she stumbled on some documents that were of interest to Haganah, the people's militia dedicated to defending Jews and resisting British rule, and soon she was sworn in as a member. The movement became the most important thing in her life and she was to cherish the training it gave her in self-reliance ever after.

During the Arab uprising of 1936–39, she learnt Morse code and taught it to others defending the Kibbutzim against attack by the Kaukaji. Like many Jews of the time, she was a great admirer of Orde Wingate, the British captain who championed the Zionist cause and taught it military tactics. By the time she was 16 (she claimed never to have been an adolescent) she was a member of Hashomer, a youth movement inspired by Marxist doctrines.

During the Second World War Grossman joined the Auxiliary Territorial Service and enrolled at the Hebrew University in Jerusalem to read Law, though she eventually took a degree in Eastern Studies. At war's end, like all citizens of Palestine under the British Mandate, she was dismissed from the ATS and thereafter, for her, Britain became the power that was standing in the way of a homeland for the Jews.

Among her activities was boarding the boats bringing Jews who had survived the Nazi camps and preparing them for their new life in what was not yet Israel. To a British civil servant who asked her what a Jewish homeland meant to these wretched people that they were so desperate to make landfall, she replied, 'It's quite simple: it's our country; it's ours, despite its conquerors, despite all the colonisers in times gone by and more recently.'

She met Jonah Jones at Mount Carmel College, a British Army education centre, and after a whirlwind courtship carried on under the nose of the military authorities, married him in 1946 in a clandestine ceremony and without official permission. She spent the seven-month War of Independence as an officer of the Palmach, the commando wing of Haganah, in the hills of Galilee. Only as the tension began to slacken did she think of joining her husband and then only with deep misgivings about leaving a country to which she was so passionately committed.

Her service with the ATS and her marriage to a Gentile caused difficulties for her on both sides of the political divide and she gradually realised there was no place for her in the new state of Israel. She had, moreover, seen enough of racial conflict and bloodshed. Even more critically, she despaired of seeing a unified, bi-national country in which Jew and Arab could live in harmony. She and her husband arrived in Britain in June 1947.

After several years on Tyneside, the Joneses settled on the Llŷn pensinsula of north-west Wales, where Jonah Jones began earning a precarious living as a sculptor and calligrapher. In the rugged landscape of Snowdonia Judith found similarities with her native land, particularly in its Biblical toponymy. She also took to the area's hardy people with real affection, though sometimes wishing they would show more backbone in their dealings with English incomers. The children soon learned Welsh and grew up to be fluent speakers of the language.

Assuming the pen-name Judith Maro, and having followed her husband into the Church of Rome, she described her early years in a volume of autobiography, *Atgofion Haganah* ('Haganah memories', 1972) and drew on her experiences in a novel, *Y Porth nid â'n Angof* (1974), which later appeared as *The Remembered Gate*.

A collection of essays, *Hen Wlad Newydd* (1974), took its title partly from 'Hen Wlad fy Nhadau', the Welsh national anthem, and partly from a novel, *Old-New Land* (1902), by the founder of Zionism, Theodor Herzl. Her novel *Y Carlwm* (1986) appeared in English as *The Stoat* in 2009. Extracts from her writings are to be found in Grahame Davies's anthology, *The Chosen People: Wales and the Jews* (2002).

A restless, vivacious woman who liked nothing better than an argument, Judith Maro was often to be met in the streets of north Cardiff, heavily scarfed against the rigours of the Welsh summer but always ready to stop for an animated chat about the latest political events in Wales and Israel.

She had found in her adopted country a peace which she had never known in the Holy Land. Shalom, Tangnefedd.

Ida (Yehudit Anastasia) Grossman (Judith Maro), Jewish patriot and writer: born Dnepropetrovsk, Ukraine 24 November 1919; married 1946 Jonah Jones (two sons, one daughter); died Swansea 16 November 2011.

The Independent (5 December 2011)

BERNEZ AN NAIL

Prolific author, administrator and publisher of Breton books

FEW BRETONS HAVE devoted their lives to promoting their culture with the flair and dogged determination shown by Bernez an Nail. A leading member of the cultural movement in Brittany which struggles to maintain its identity in the face of hostility on the part of the French State and often the indifference of its own people, he worked hard for more than thirty years to demonstrate the richness and beauty of Breton literature and, with a patriot's commitment to the Breton language, brought many gems into the light of day which otherwise might have been lost.

From 1979 to 1983, while based in Paris, where he had decided to learn Breton after reading of the appalling loss of some 250,000 Bretons in the Great War, he was Secretary General of the *Comité d'Etude et de Liaison des Intérêts Bretons (CELIB)*, a consultative body created by the journalist Joseph Martray which was concerned primarily with the modernization of agriculture in Brittany and in the forefront of the rural unrest of 1961 when Breton farmers came out to demonstrate on their tractors.

Other organizations with which he worked were groups aiming to bring together the disparate (and often competing) bodies that were trying to put back together the culture that had been shattered during and immediately after the Second World War, especially during *l'épuration* when Breton patriots and sympathizers were killed or jailed on charges of having collaborated with the German occupiers.

The centre known as *Ker Vreizh* (House of Brittany) in Paris served as a base for most Breton activity at that time and it was there Bernez an Nail – his unusual surname deriving perhaps from An Ael (The Angel) – came into his own as an activist who was willing to put his shoulder to the wheel and learn administrative skills which were to serve him in good stead for the rest of his career.

When he moved to become Director of *l'Institut Cuturel de Bretagne/ Skol Uhel ar Vro* in 1983 he already had a reputation as a dedicated and highly competent administrator whose talents were at the service of the Breton language and its literature. He remained in that post for fourteen years after which, in 2001, he founded the publishing imprint *Les portes du large*, where he brought out beautifully produced books relating to Brittany and its people. Many he wrote himself, often in collaboration with his wife Jacqueline, a reference librarian in Rennes, notably *Dictionnaire des auteurs de jeunesse de Bretagne*, *Dictionnaire des femmes de Bretagne* and *Dictionnaire des romanciers de Bretagne*, all three very useful works of reference and all produced to the highest possible standard.

He was also very active with *L'association des éditeurs de Bretagne*, which represents the publishers of Brittany, and in the work of *Le centre régional du livre en Bretagne*, which promotes reading and literacy, both of which were very close to his heart. He was a longstanding member of the International Celtic Congress which facilitates contacts between the Celtic peoples at the cultural level.

Bernez an Nail, known to the French authorities as Bernard Le Nail, was born in Paris in1946; his father was French Consul in Mexico and he spent a large part of his adolescence in South America. Educated at *Hautes Etudes Commerciales* in Paris, for which entry is extremely competitive and where he was awarded the coveted Diploma, he took his first job with the Chamber of Trade and Industry in Nantes. But he was from the first attracted to cultural questions and soon switched tack.

He was to spend the rest of his life in the Breton movement, never indicating his political views lest he be charged with wishing to impair the unity of the Hexagon (*La république une et indivisible* by which French Jacobinism maintains its grip on its 'regions') but working hard and single-mindedly to restore in Breton eyes the worth of the language and culture.

He wrote about 250 articles for the website of *Agence Bretagne Presse* and a number of books for visitors to Brittany, including the prestigious *Guide Bleue* (1991) and the *Guide Gallimard* (1997). One of his many interests was toponymy as demonstrated in his masterly books *Les noms de lieu bretons* (2001) and *Dictionnaire de la Loire-Atlantique* (2010). He was a man who happily accepted an extraordinarily heavy workload, often writing several books concurrently and sometimes under the pseudonym Joseph Bréhier, and his encyclopaedic knowledge of Brittany was put at the service of anyone who requested it. Described on the day of his death as 'part of our collective memory', he was a historian of uncommon ability, unearthing episodes and personalities in Breton history that had been overlooked by other historians and becoming an expert on the Breton diaspora.

Although he was not politically active, lest it jeopardize his life's work, he was nevertheless a man of the Centre Left, and a practising Catholic. When in 1999 the French Communist paper *L'Humanité* accused him of having been a member of a clandestine separatist group he strenuously denied it but made no apology for his defence of Breton culture.

He refused the award of the *Collier de l'Hermine*, the greatest honour Brittany can bestow on those who have served her well, saying it was his patriotic duty to research and publish his findings for the sake of Brittany's survival as a *bro* (country/ region) with its own ancient and distinctive identity.

Bernez an Nail / Bernard Le Nail, Breton patriot, publisher and historian: born Paris 1946; Secretary-General CELIB (1979–83), Director Institut Culturel de Bretagne / Skol Uhel ar Vro (1983–2000); married Jacqueline Hérault (three children); died Rennes 5 January 2010.

The Independent (26 February 2010)

GORDON PARRY

Affable Chairman of the Wales Tourist Board

GORDON PARRY WAS the very epitome of Christian Socialism, whose principles he endeavoured to put into practice during a lifetime of public service. He held high office with a variety of national bodies in his native Wales, but it was his attachment to the Baptist faith of his youth and his passionate love of the county of Pembrokeshire that distinguished him from many politicos of his generation.

Born near the small town of Narberth in 1925, he never moved very far from his native patch, delighting in the people and landscapes of the westernmost county of Wales and content to put his talents at the service of the local community. He spoke with that striking burr, half-Welsh and half-Irish, that seemed to have grown out of the legendary past of Dyfed, land of *The Mabinogion*, which has seen countless waves of immigration from across the water.

Educated at Neyland in the south of the county and below the Landsker line that marks the Englishry from the Welshry in these parts, he was brought up English-speaking but had great affection for the Welsh language and regretted that he was unable to speak it with any fluency. The last time I saw him he had just been to a Welsh chapel in Cardiff, 'because I love the sound of the language'; he had taught himself enough to hold conversations in it.

He was by profession a teacher, trained at Trinity College, Carmarthen, and holding posts at primary schools in Pembroke Dock, Neyland and Haverfordwest before becoming, in 1952, Librarian and Housemaster at the County

Secondary School in Haverfordwest. From 1969 to 1978 he was Warden of the Pembrokeshire Teachers' Centre.

He once told me that he had been born a socialist and had imbibed its philosophy with his mother's milk and that was confirmed in his autobiography, *A Legacy for Life* (1996). A lifelong and largely contented member of the Labour Party, he stood as its candidate on four occasions: in Monmouth (against the Conservative Peter Thorneycroft) in 1959 and in Pembroke in 1970 and at the two general elections of 1974. In the last three of these the seat was held, by a margin of about two per cent, by Nicholas Edwards, who was to become Secretary of State for Wales.

It was during the campaign of October 1974 that, according to local folklore, he won his spurs as a Labour stalwart. Harold Wilson, the Labour leader, was expected to speak at a public meeting, but was several hours late reaching the hall and so, knowing his people as he did, Gordon Parry stood in the breach and entertained the audience with his considerable skills as a public speaker until Wilson eventually arrived. For this sterling service, it is said, Parry was made a life peer by James Callaghan in 1975.

Be that as it may, Parry's career blossomed soon afterwards. He was appointed to the Open University's Advisory Committee on Studies in Education, which he served as Chairman from 1978 to 1984, and to the British Tourist Authority. Tourism, and its special environmental requirements in the coastal and rural areas of Pembrokeshire, was given high priority in his long list of public appointments. He served with the Keep Wales Tidy Committee, the Keep Britain Beautiful Campaign, and Clean World International.

But it was as Chairman of the Wales Tourist Board from 1978 to 1984 that he came to prominence as a public figure. He led the board during a critical phase of its development, always with acumen and the affable style which became his trademark. He was an approachable, cheerful and genuinely friendly man who never lost the common touch, and who could initiate projects, often from behind the scenes, making sure they would be well funded and supported by the rich and famous, whose arms he was not averse to twisting if he thought they would lend their names to his schemes.

A regular visitor to Georgia in the United States, where he was made Grand Marshal of the Cherry Blossom Festival at Macon, he made a friend of President Jimmy Carter, who was duly informed about the attractions of Pembrokeshire.

Parry also had a fine regard for the handicapped, serving as a President of the Spastics Society, the South Wales Region of the National Society for Mentally Handicapped Children and the Society of Handicapped Drivers in Wales. This interest arose after he was involved in a horrific road accident in which a friend was killed; he was left with serious facial scars, which he camouflaged with a beard, and a permanent injury to his leg. One of his nicest anecdotes related how he was pulled out of the wreckage by a passing rugby team.

With typically droll humour, he gave as one of his recreations in *Who's Who* 'watching the Welsh rugby XV win the Grand Slam'.

Gordon Samuel David Parry, teacher and public servant: born Narberth, Pembrokeshire 30 November 1925; Librarian and Housemaster, County Secondary School, Haverfordwest 1952–62, 1963–8; Warden, Pembrokeshire Teachers' Centre 1969–78; created 1975 Baron Parry; Chairman, Wales Tourist Board 1978–84; Chairman, Keep Wales Tidy Committee 1979–86; Chairman, British Cleaning Council 1983–7; Chairman, Milford Docks Company 1984–91, President 1991–2004; Chairman, Keep Britain Beautiful Campaign 1986–96; Chairman, Keep Britain Tidy Group (later Tidy Britain) 1986–91; Chairman, Clean World International 1991–6; married 1948 Glenys Incledon (died 2004; one daughter); died Llangwm, Pembrokeshire 1 September 2004.

The Independent (6 September 2004)

MEIRION PENNAR

Poet who challenged readers to understand his cerebral verse

POETRY IN THE Welsh language, even in its Modernist phase, tends to be conservative in the forms it chooses and the modes it adopts, as if the weight of fifteen centuries' tradition, as well as enriching the poet's armature, bears down on those who write experimentally or in a fundamentally different way. A minority culture under threat from its more powerful neighbour is generally hostile to its avant-garde and that has certainly been true in Wales.

Meirion Pennar burst on to the literary scene in 1971, at the age of 26, like a trumpet blast during a chapel service. Born in Cardiff, one of the five children of the polymath Pennar Davies, he had what he described as 'an unliterary upbringing' in Bangor and Brecon until he reached the sixth form at Dynevor Grammar School in Swansea, when he began writing verse of such complexity that not even his father, a highly accomplished poet and distinguished theologian, could make much of it.

As an undergraduate at University College, Swansea, where he took a degree in Welsh, and a research student at Jesus College, Oxford, he mixed his literary interests with taking part in the campaigns of *Cymdeithas yr Iaith Gymraeg*, the society that works for greater use of the Welsh language. He was a staunch Welsh Nationalist and stood as the Plaid Cymru candidate in Swansea West at the General Election of 1983. He also wrote a lively column in *Y Ddraig Goch* ('The red dragon'), one of the party's papers.

His first academic post was teaching Welsh at University College, Dublin, where he met his future wife, Carmel Gahan. He then spent nineteen years in the Welsh Department at St David's University College, Lampeter, where he specialized in medieval poetry and the 19th-century novel. He was a popular lecturer but, dogged by ill health, he retired in 1994.

Most of the poems in his first collection, *Syndod y Sêr* ('The stars' surprise', 1971), were written after he had discovered the poets of the Expressionismus group, whom he was able to read in their own language because his mother was German and she had passed the language on to him. Thus the work of Stadler, Stramm, Werfel, Benn, Heym and Trakl was introduced to readers of Welsh poetry, to the consternation of many, especially those critics ensconced in the eisteddfodic culture who thought his work had little more than curiosity value. As if to proclaim its contemporaneity, the book also included two poems about the war in Vietnam.

What most readers found disconcerting in Meirion Pennar's verse was the complete lack of traditional punctuation, as in the poems of Arp, the Dadaists and Surrealists, and Apollinaire, though not the 'acrobatic audiovisuals' of e.e. cummings about whose methods he had reservations. They had also to get used to what he called 'rhythmic spasms', his name for arranging words not in lines or stanzas but in 'clusters', as if they had been drawn 'from his own entrails'. For readers more used to the sedate 'consonantal chiming' of traditional Welsh prosody, this was hard to take.

Meirion Pennar's poems bristle with allusions to the earliest Welsh poetry. For example, a famous line from *Y Gododdin*, which tells of the defeat of a British warband at Catraeth (thought to be modern-day Catterick) by Mercian forces in about the year 600, reads in English: 'His sword rang in the heads of mothers'. This changes to 'let my typewriter sound forth in the heads of mothers' in one of the poems by which he is represented in *The Bloodaxe Book of Modern Welsh Poetry* (2003).

Spotting the echoes affords a modicum of pleasure for the literate Welsh reader but, at the same time, many of his images are hermetically sealed. The only concession the poet makes to our understanding are the notes on such topics as Odin, Athena, Gaul, Eustache Deschamps, Croce, and the Odyssey.

His second collection, *Pair Dadeni* ('Cauldron of rebirth', 1977), is a long poem of 28 pages which deconstructs and re-assembles the story of Efnisien and Bendigeidfran in *The Mabinogion*, the great collection of stories from the medieval period. Although it has mythic resonance, the poem has a good deal to say about modern Ireland, but it demands more than one reading before its 'meaning' starts to become clear. He also published the long poems *Saga* (1972) and *Y Gadwyn* (1976), and another book, *Peredur* (1991).

The same preoccupation with medieval texts informed Meirion Pennar's academic interests. He translated the poems of Taliesin, the late 6th-century poet living in 'the Old North' (today the north of England and the south of Scotland) and *The Black Book of Carmarthen*, the oldest manuscript collection of poetry in the Welsh language which dates from the 12th and early 13th centuries. The latter work includes the verses said to have been written by Myrddin (Merlin) after the battle of Arfderydd in the year 573 while he was hiding in the wood of Celyddon (the Caledonian forest), where he lived as a wild man, lost his reason and received the gift of prophecy.

A quotation from Meirion Pennar's version of the Black Book can be seen on the wall of the new market in Carmarthen town. He will be remembered as a poet who, while still a young man, made a valiant attempt to take Welsh poetry in new directions without its having to renounce its illustrious past.

Andreas Meirion Pennar, poet and scholar: born Cardiff 24 December 1944; lecturer in Welsh, St David's University College, Lampeter (1975–94); married Carmel Gahan (marriage dissolved, one son); died Swansea 9 December 2010.

The Independent (28 December 2010)

ELUNED PHILLIPS

The only woman poet to have won
the National Eisteddfod's Crown twice

ELUNED PHILLIPS WAS unusual among Welsh writers of her
generation in that she embraced a bohemian lifestyle which
took her to pre-war London and Paris, where she made the
acquaintance of such major artists as Augustus John, Dylan
Thomas, Edith Piaf, Jean Cocteau, Maurice Chevalier and
Pablo Picasso, the last of whom showed her the unfinished
'Guernica' with the paint still wet on the canvas. She even
made it to Casablanca, where she might easily have fitted
in among the habitués of Rick's Bar. Nearer home, she was
only the second woman to win the Crown, one of the major
literary prizes awarded at the National Eisteddfod, and this
she achieved on two occasions: first in 1967 and again in 1983.
It was for this remarkable feat rather than her picaresque
adventures in foreign parts that she was most admired in her
native Wales.

Famously reticent about the details of her life, even in
her memoir, *The Reluctant Redhead* (2007), she was always
loth to reveal so much as the year of her birth. In the *Oxford
Companion to the Literature of Wales* (1986) it was given as
1915?, whereas in fact she had been born on 27 October
1914 – the same day as Dylan Thomas, whom she heartily
disliked because of his fecklessness and scrounging habits.
Nor does her book provide much information about the time
she spent in the company of Picasso, Cocteau and Chevalier,
though about Piaf, with whom she seems to have had more
of a rapport, she wrote movingly. Disappointingly, the book is
largely the record (without many facts that can be checked)
of the adventures this 'topsy-turvy' but independently-minded

woman had whenever she could shake off the confines of her native patch. Many of her escapades and her short-fuse temper she attributed to the red hair she had as a young woman.

Her introduction to the raffish milieu of London's Fitzrovia was made possible in the late 1930s by Dewi Emrys (Dewi Emrys James), the dissolute ex-preacher and talented poet whose life she treated in a biography published in 1971. Once described as 'the Welsh Dylan Thomas', as if Thomas were not Welsh because he wrote in English, Dewi Emrys was so tormented by the alcoholism that eventually killed him in 1952 that he immediately pawned the silver Crown he had won at the National Eisteddfod in order to buy more drink. Her biography went some way to correcting Dewi Emrys's image as a *poète maudit* by debunking many of the apocryphal stories told about him and pointing to the very considerable qualities of his intricate verse.

Eluned Phillips was born at Cenarth in southern Cardiganshire, a village famous for its coracles from which men fished the Teifi. Her father was killed in the First World War while she was still a child and she never knew him, but she was brought up in a warm-hearted extended family, which included the aunt to whom she was devoted, and a grandmother who encouraged her to take up every challenge with the admonition, 'Go for it, girl! Give it your best shot!'. From primary school at Abercych, a district renowned for its associations with the *Mabinogion*, she went to Cardigan Grammar School where, a dreamy child, she did not distinguish herself academically but began competing in local eisteddfodau.

She drew more sustenance from the Congregationalist chapel in Cenarth and from hearing folk-stories about the poet Dafydd ap Gwilym and the Princess Nest, known as 'The Helen of Wales' on account of her abduction by a Prince of the royal house of Powys in 1109. It was at Sunday school she learned to read in Welsh, became a fine public speaker and learned the rules of *cynghanedd*, the complex system of traditional prosody used by many Welsh poets to this day. She was admitted into the Gorsedd of Bards as Luned Teifi at the age of twenty-two, the blue robe being exchanged for the white, decorated with laurel leaves, after she had won her first Crown.

Eluned's fascination with the life of the Left Bank was facilitated by a friend at her London boarding school whose mother worked in Paris: the two girls were exploring Montparnasse when hardly out of school uniform. As she was fond of pointing out, Paris was nearer London than west Wales, and she went there often. In 1939 she entered the University of London with the intention of becoming a journalist, an ambition in which she was encouraged by Hannen Swaffer, then at the height of his fame in Fleet Street, but her studies there were interrupted by the outbreak of war. The war also put paid to her love-affair with a Breton nationalist she had met in Paris, the only romance she was prepared to write about in her memoirs but over which she nevertheless drew a discreet veil, except to say she knew him as Per and that, although rescued from a French gaol, he had later died of the injuries he had sustained while a prisoner.

After several years living as a pseudonymous writer for women's magazines in London, and penning a number of Mills and Boon-type romances to keep the wolf from her door, she returned to Newcastle Emlyn, where she took a job in a solicitor's office and served as a court translator. At about the same time she began writing scripts for the BBC in Wales and working as a roving reporter, but her thirst for adventure also took her to eastern Europe before the demise of the Soviet Union, to Ireland, where she became a friend of the folk-singer Seamus Ennis, to Australia and the United States, particularly to Los Angeles where, despite two serious car-crashes in 1997, she celebrated her ninetieth birthday. She had a close connection with several of the leading Welsh male voice choirs that visit California regularly and was usually to be seen taking full advantage of the hospitality extended on those occasions.

Her only book of poems was *Cerddi Glyn-y-Mêl* ('Glyn-y-mêl poems', 1985), which takes its title from the house in Cenarth she shared for many years with her aged aunt. Very few of her poems appeared in magazines and anthologies because she claimed never to send them off unless invited, which she seldom was. In her memoirs she provided an English translation of the long poem 'Clymau' ('Bonds') with which she had won her second Crown in 1983. An exploration of the ancestral links between Wales and the Welsh colony in Patagonia, the poem focusses on two soldiers, one a Welshman in the British Army and the other a Patagonian in the Argentinian, and on the tragedy involved in their having to fight each other.

She explained that she had written her memoirs in English (and on a computer acquired in her ninetieth year) so that her many friends all over the world could read about the life of 'a simple country girl with itchy feet'. The book ends with her standing mischievously in the wet concrete of the Millennium Centre then under construction in Cardiff Bay and the typically spirited advice she gave to many a young writer, 'Try to make as many footprints in the concrete as you can – and treasure them.'

Sara Adeline Eluned Phillips, poet: born Cenarth, Cardiganshire 27 October 1914; winner of the Crown at the National Eisteddfod, 1967 and 1983; died Carmarthen 10 January 2009.

The Independent (13 February 2009)

PETER PRENDERGAST

One of Britain's foremost landscape painters,
inspired by his native Wales

THE WELSH ARTIST Peter Prendergast, who has died aged
60, was one of Britain's foremost landscape painters. He
is best-known for his large expressionist paintings of the
old quarrying districts of north-west Wales, executed with
bold brushstrokes and, unlike Sir Kyffin Williams, from a
palette of many colours held between thick black lines.

Another difference between them is that Prendergast's
canvases have human traces in them, whereas Williams
usually found inspiration in the unpeopled grandeur of
Snowdonia. Some critics consider Prendergast the more
accomplished painter of the two, a view which underpins
many of the contributions made to a book about his life
and work, *The Painter's Quarry* (2006).

He was born in Abertridwr, a mining village in
Glamorgan. His father, an Irishman who had left Ireland
after the 1916 Easter Rising, worked underground for
36 years and instilled in him a love of nature and beautiful
things. Having failed the 11+ examination, a fact that was
to pain him as a grown man, he went to the local secondary
modern school where he was encouraged by Gomer Lewis,
an inspirational art master.

The boy began drawing the Aber valley, where he had
enjoyed an idyllic childhood in its fields and streams. He
also found subjects in the valley's people and relished a
sense of community – 'doors were always open' – and,
although he steered clear of party politics, he was always
to be a man of the Left. 'That's what Gomer Lewis did – he

made us start from our own lives and find out who we were and where we were coming from, and to have pride in it.'

Having won a county art scholarship at the age of 15, without any O levels, he did a two-year foundation course at the Cardiff School of Art in 1961 and two years later went up to the Slade in London. There he was allocated Frank Auerbach as his tutor, who was to become the second influence on him: 'Auerbach's teaching was objective and constructive. It was not about expressionism or any other label. It was more concerned with integrity, structure, geometry and drawing, painting things more convincingly and inventively. It certainly wasn't about copying or mirroring nature.' He won the Nettleship prize for figure drawing at the Slade in 1967 and became a superb colourist.

After two years doing an MA at Reading University, with a view to teaching should his painting not bring in enough money, Prendergast decided he needed to live and work in Wales and he settled in Bethesda, a quarrying village a few miles from Bangor. For a while he taught at Liverpool College of Art but was then made redundant, since drawing was no longer to be taught there; he later found work at Coleg Menai, where one of his sons now teaches an art foundation course.

Prendergast often pointed out that the terraces of Bethesda were not unlike those of industrial villages in south Wales, but with tips of waste slate instead of coal. For the next seven years he painted the Penrhyn quarry – 'the biggest man-made hole in Europe, like Breughel's *Tower of Babel*, but in reverse' – finding in this working environment the fascination which the pits and workings of the Aber valley had held for him as a child. Like Mont Sainte-Victoire for Cézanne, the Penrhyn was for Prendergast an inexhaustible source of inspiration and he painted it in all seasons, especially winter, and with an exuberance that was often breathtaking. It was as if he was determined to reveal how the very planet was formed.

Even in New York he drew on his experiences of Bethesda. In 1993, given the use of a 31st-floor apartment on West 53rd

Street by his London dealers, Agnew's, he drew the view looking towards the Hudson river as if it were a canyon, like the Penrhyn quarry, except that what concerned him now was the bustle of Manhattan. He would get up in the early hours and observe the yellow cabs hurtling up the street, trying to get something of the city's energy into his paintings.

By the early 1980s Prendergast had established himself as a painter in Wales, England, America and Australia: his work was being shown at London galleries and beginning to be taken seriously by metropolitan art critics. He had already won prizes at the 1975 and 1977 National Eisteddfod and had been included in the major Welsh Arts Council exhibition *The Dark Hills the Heavy Clouds* (1981). His decision to live in north Wales, latterly in another quarry village, Deiniolen, above Caernarfon, was not simply a matter of returning to his roots but the expression of a commitment to the concept of Welsh identity, a preoccupation he shared with Kyffin Williams, whom he had met at the Slade. His children were brought up Welsh-speaking and he took the patriotic view that Welsh artists should be promoted by the public bodies of Wales.

Part of that identity for Prendergast was his Catholic upbringing. Although he always dismissed the suggestion that his pictures were religious, he acknowledged that having gone to church had helped him make sense of his life, had given him a structure, a way of seeing the world. 'From when I was a kid I was going into Catholic churches which were full of colour, blues and gold. But I've never painted a picture with anything else in mind other than to try and paint the most ambitious and inventive image that I could.' Even so, many have detected spiritual references in his work, if only in the small bent church spires he managed to include in some of his later canvases. It was Sister Wendy Beckett who wrote in the catalogue to his 1993–94 touring exhibition, 'It is very tempting to ask viewers just to stand in silence and let the music "sing to the spirit".'

He is survived by Lesley, whom he married in 1968 and with whom he was out walking near their home in Deiniolen when he suffered a heart attack, and their two sons and two daughters.

Peter Prendergast, painter, born Abertridwr, Glamorgan 27 October 1946; died Bethesda, Gwynedd 14 January 2007.

The Guardian (22 January 2007)

EMYR PRICE

Historian of the early career of David Lloyd George

THE WELSH HISTORIAN and journalist Emyr Price was an authority on the early life and career of David Lloyd George. He was engaged in research into the work of the Liberal statesman, his family and party, for more than forty years, beginning with a thesis on his pre-parliamentary career which earned him an MA in 1964. His fascination with 'the little Celt from Cricieth' was rooted in his conviction that Lloyd George had a strong commitment to Home Rule for Wales, and was leader of the first modern Welsh nationalist movement, namely *Cymru Fydd* or Young Wales.

Whereas most English historians have tended to view Lloyd George's early career up to 1896 as irrelevant or, at best, merely the precursor to his successes at Westminster, Price took an altogether different view. His research showed that he was passionately concerned with winning a measure of official status for Welsh, in a country where the great majority of the people still spoke the language, and with legislating in favour of the working class, and that he campaigned fearlessly, often against entrenched opinion within his own party, to bring these measures about. His decision to become a careerist politician after the failure of Young Wales in 1896 was, Price argued, the only way Welsh aspirations – for Disestablishment of the Church, for example – could be realized.

Price also examined afresh Lloyd George's perception, as a Welshman, of some of the major issues that dominated his period of power at Westminster from 1908 to 1922, including the Irish Question, and the way in which Welsh values, particularly the Nonconformist ones of his youth, determined his actions. He had the immense advantage over historians such as John Grigg in being able to read the Welsh sources, including the family's papers and the many Welsh-language newspapers of the last two decades of the nineteenth century. Price saw Lloyd George as a visionary and Radical reformer, the first devolutionist of modern times.

He published extensively in his chosen field, including a study of Megan Lloyd George, the politician's daughter, in 1983. Besides many articles in the *Transactions of the Caernarfonshire Historical Society* (which he edited between 1981 and 1984) and the *Welsh History Review*, he wrote knowledgeably and attractively about the winning of universal suffrage and the welfare state, in both of which Lloyd George played a prominent role. One of the questions which exercised him was whether, from a Welsh point of view, Lloyd George should be considered a traitor or a hero – the controversy still inflames debate about him in the pubs of north Wales. His last book on the subject was in English: *David Lloyd George*, published by the University of Wales Press as the first volume in its *Celtic Radicals* series in 2006.

Emyr Price was born in Bangor in 1944, the year before Lloyd George died, and brought up in Pwllheli and Porthmadog. His family was staunchly radical, supporters on the distaff side of the Liberal Party and, on the spear, of the Independent Labour Party. Educated at the University College of North Wales, Bangor, he took his first job as head of the History Department at Ysgol Brynrefail in Llanrug, staying there until 1973 when he was appointed to a lecturer's post at the Normal College in Bangor. He was given sabbatical leave in 1979 so that he could follow a postgraduate course in Social Administration at the London School of Economics, during which he wrote a thesis on the office of the Welsh Ombudsman.

In 1983 he was appointed editor of *Y Faner* ('The flag'), the most venerable and radical of all Welsh-language newspapers, though he continued to hold classes under the auspices of the Workers' Education Association and the Extra-mural

Department at Bangor. In 1984 the paper took a lead in collecting money for the Welsh Language Centre at Nant Gwrtheyrn, on the tip of the Llŷn peninsula, an inititaive with which he remained associated for many years, and for the striking miners of south Wales. His editorship of *Y Faner*, however, coincided with the nadir in the paper's fortunes: he stayed only three years and, losing readers, the weekly folded shortly after the Arts Council withdrew its subsidy. He then found work as a producer and scriptwriter of current affairs programmes for HTV, notably *Canrif y Werin* ('The people's century') and – with typical evenhandedness – documentaries about such luminaries as Gwynfor Evans and Cledwyn Hughes, leaders of Plaid Cymru and the Labour Party in Wales, both of whom he admired greatly.

The cause of the Welsh language, which Price spoke fluently and elegantly, was always near his heart, and it was one of the springs of his nationalism. He stood unsuccessfully as the Plaid Cymru candidate in the Conwy constituency at the General Election of 1979 and was otherwise active for the party in north-west Wales, but found himself sympathizing with the Labour Party too. A percipient critic of the nationalists from a left-wing point of view, and of Labour for its reluctance to deliver devolution, he deplored the fact that Plaid Cymru had consistently failed to make common cause with the quarrymen of north Wales and the miners and steelworkers of the south, a common front which, he believed, would have brought forward self-government for Wales by decades.

A somewhat pugnacious mien and dry manner belied a sense of humour and a warm-hearted approach to both journalism and history, both of which he managed to write with integrity and in the tradition that one is 'the first draft' of the other. He gave an entertaining and trenchant account of his own life, with many insights into the motives of some of his more ambitious friends, in *Fy Hanner Ganrif I* ('My half-century', 2002). The title is a reference to his chief leisure activity, cricket, which he played with panache, at county level as a schoolboy and for the Bontnewydd side, one of the best in north Wales. He was also a trustee of the Lloyd George Museum, situated not far from the statesman's old home at Llanystumdwy, near Cricieth.

Of his three children, his daughter Angharad Price is a distinguished prose-writer and literary theorist: in 2002 she won the Prose Medal at the National Eisteddfod, a triumph which filled him with the better part of pride.

Emyr Price, historian and journalist; born Bangor, Caernarfonshire 7 May 1944; married 1969, Mair Jones (two sons, one daughter); died Bangor, Gwynedd 22 March 2009.

The Independent (1 April 2009)

DENNIS REES

Publisher and pioneer of the Welsh record industry

DENNIS REES PLAYED a major role in the recording of Welsh popular music and the publishing of Welsh books at a crucial point in their histories – the 1960s, when political pressure was being brought to bear on local and central government by *Cymdeithas yr Iaith Gymraeg* (Welsh Language Society) and Plaid Cymru. As the call for devolved governance gathered pace, there was a blossoming in the country's cultural life which urgently required new forms of expression. The vinyl record joined the book and periodical as a medium for young Welsh-speakers impatient with the bearded orthodoxies of their elders and they found a sympathetic ally in Dennis Rees.

At the time, Rees was employed by Alun Talfan Davies QC as managing director of Llyfrau'r Dryw ('Wren books'), publisher of the influential monthly magazine *Barn* ('Opinion') and a plethora of books in the Welsh language on which the health of the country's literature largely relied. He was also in charge of Recordiau'r Dryw ('Wren records'), the company's other arm. For this reason, Rees was jocularly known as 'Den the Wren', a sobriquet in which he delighted in his usual genial manner. A former cinema manager and employee of the Rank Organisation, he was an astute businessman but had cultural interests of his own that were now given full rein.

He also understood the niceties of the publishing industry, and the even more complex processes of publishing books in the Welsh language, though I always had the impression his heart was really in the production of vinyl records for the popular market. He excelled in spotting and encouraging young musicians and bringing them to the company's recording studios in Alexandra Road, Swansea.

Always well turned out, he cut a trim, wholesome figure in the company of the trendy, not to say hippy musicians whom he was keen to record for the Dryw label. Although old enough to be the father of most of them, he was always respected, and liked, for his open mind and willingness to keep abreast of the new. If some of the youngsters thought they knew all about making records because they had read the *NME*, he would take them aside and put them right in his quiet way.

Undoubtedly the most important singer to be discovered by Rees was my near-namesake Meic Stevens. Not the easiest artiste to have to deal with, Stevens nevertheless gave the company some of his best performances. Among the songs he recorded were *Cân Walter* ('Walter's song'), *Mwg* ('Smoke') and *Yr Eryr a'r Golomen* ('The eagle and the dove'), and they remain among the all-time classics of Welsh popular music, beloved of audiences of all ages. Original copies of his LP *Gwymon* ('Seaweed') are known to have changed hands for hundreds of pounds.

Among other singers who signed up to the Dryw label were Endaf Emlyn, Y Diliau and Hogia'r Wyddfa. With Stevens came Heather Jones and Geraint Jarman and so Rees began to build up a catalogue that represented the best of the Welsh pop scene between 1962 and 1972. Rees also recorded live performances of the comedy duo Ryan and Ronnie which are some of the funniest acts ever staged in Welsh. One of his marketing ploys was to hire Swansea's Brangwyn Hall to promote his company's records in front of invited audiences who then undertook to buy the records as they appeared.

But by the mid-1970s a new record company had arrived on the Welsh pop scene, namely Sain, run by the singers and language activists Dafydd Iwan and Huw Jones (recently appointed chairman of S4C). For a while Recordiau'r Dryw struggled to bring out spoken-word records about the history and literature of Wales, but soon afterwards gave up its Swansea studios. Sain bought its catalogue and has dominated the industry ever since.

Rees went back to being a publisher of books and periodicals, including my magazine *Poetry Wales*. I dealt with him in my capacity as the Welsh Arts Council's literature director, always finding him jovial, straightforward and willing to consider publishing books, with subsidy, that might not otherwise have come his way. He also played a prominent part in the affairs of Côr Meibion Dyfnant, the Dunvant Male Choir, and served as chairman of Dunvant Rugby Club. He was very much a man for whom the local was the real and his delight in the triumphs of both choir and club knew no bounds.

Dennis Charles Rees, publisher and promoter of Welsh pop music: born Llanelli, Carmarthenshire 25 January 1927; married 1952 Madge Lodwig (two daughters); died Swansea 9 July 2011.

The Independent (1 September 2011)

HYWEL HEULYN ROBERTS

Veteran Welsh Nationalist and County Councillor

HYWEL HEULYN ROBERTS traced his commitment to the cause of Plaid Cymru to the night of 8 September 1936 when some huts and contractors' materials belonging to an RAF bombing school then being built at Penyberth on the Llŷn peninsula were set on fire by three of the party's leaders. He was staying at the time with his grandmother in Pwllheli and was among the first to inspect the damage caused by this symbolic act of arson. The excitement caused by 'the Fire in Llŷn', as the incident came to be known, affected him deeply for this was the first time in centuries a blow had been struck against a London government riding roughshod over local sensibilities.

When the three perpetrators – Saunders Lewis, D.J. Williams and Lewis Valentine – stood trial at Caernarfon Assizes the jury failed to reach a verdict, but at the Old Bailey in the following January they were each sentenced to nine months' imprisonment. Hywel Heulyn Roberts felt the sense of outrage more than most, drawing from the incident much of his pacifism and his conviction that Wales should no longer be governed from London. When, in 2007, he published his autobiography, he called it *Tân yn fy Nghalon* ('Fire in my heart').

A sense of Welsh patriotism had been nurtured in him as a boy growing up in Aigburth, a suburb of Liverpool, where he had been born in 1919. The city in those days had a thriving Welsh-language culture based on the chapel, Sunday school and eisteddfod, and on close family links with North Wales, for which it served *faute de mieux* as a capital. Educated at the Liverpool Institute High School

240

for Boys, he proudly wore a leek in his lapel on St David's Day and sang, to the tune 'Jerusalem', 'In Wales's green and pleasant land', while his parents saw to it that he spent every holiday with his grandparents in Pwllheli. When the time came for him to leave the Institute, his father having lost his job as an engineer with the White Star shipping company, he began work with Martins Bank in its Brunswick Street branch, Liverpool, in September 1936, barely a fortnight after the Fire in Llŷn.

He remained at the bank throughout the Second World War, having registered as a conscientious objector on Christian pacifist grounds: 'I base my objection to military service,' he told the tribunal, 'on the Christian religion which I profess and in whose teaching I have been brought up from my earliest days.' He had first-hand experience of the bombing of the city and, in 1942, joined the Royal Army Medical Corps in Denbigh, where he undertook non-combatant duties and learned to box. Tall, lantern-jawed, and broad-shouldered, he had handsome features marred only by a flat nose which many thought he had acquired in the ring, though in fact it had been broken during a cricket-match in Pwllheli. The rest of the war he spent at a camp for Italian and German prisoners in Hampton Lovett near Droitwich in Worcestershire, in some of whom he detected those human qualities which made him love his fellow-men. He was especially fond of Liverpudlians among whom he had been brought up and, as a Welsh Nationalist, was never anti-English in his outlook.

Even before the end of hostilities, he had begun the political activity to which he was to devote the rest of his life. In July 1945 he was given leave to work for Plaid Cymru in the Caernarfon Boroughs, Lloyd George's old seat, where he put into practice the financial skills he had learned at Martins Bank. Soon afterwards he was transferred to the bank's branch in Newport, Monmouthshire, but stayed there only two years before finding employment as a district manager with Silcocks, the animal foodstuffs company, which promptly sent him to work in Cardiganshire.

It was not long before 'Roberts Silcocks' was asked to stand as a candidate in the County Election of 1952, in which he was duly elected. Although he made no secret of his Nationalist affiliations, starting branches of Plaid Cymru up and down the County, he sat as an Independent member in the Cardiganshire tradition which was abandoned only in the 1970s. At the age of 33 he joined a Council where the average age was 65, thus coming up against some of the more entrenched members of the Dinosaur Tendency in the ruling Labour and Liberal Parties. He nevertheless succeeded in introducing important initiatives in the public use of Welsh in the Council's business and in the teaching of the language in the County's schools.

So began a distinguished career in local government which was to last unbroken for more than forty years. He served on the Cardiganshire County Council from 1952 to 1974 and, after the reorganization of county boundaries, on Dyfed County Council, of which he was Chairman from 1973 to 1976. Having left Silcocks in 1966, he and his wife Margaret kept a café and crafts shop in the small village of Synod Inn, a few miles south of Aberystwyth, which served not only as a petrol-pump station but as a meeting-place for Plaid Cymru members travelling up and down Cardigan Bay. He also played a part at a national level, standing as the party's candidate against Labour's Megan Lloyd George at Carmarthen in 1959, serving on its National Executive for many years, and helping to organize its campaigns in the by-elections in the Rhondda and Caerffili in 1967 and 1968 at which Plaid Cymru came near to winning those Labour seats.

Such was his reputation as a sensible, capable and good-humoured man, he was asked to serve on many public bodies – more than forty in all. They included the Welsh Folk Museum, Dyfed-Powys Police Authority, the Welsh Joint Education

Committee, the Court and Council of the University of Wales, the Welsh Theatre Company, the Welsh National School of Music and Drama, the National Museum of Wales, the Wales Tourist Board, the Sports Council for Wales, the Welsh National Opera Company and the Welsh Water Authoriy. He was also High Sheriff of Dyfed (1982–3) and a leading member of the Congregationalists in Cardiganshire. Having turned down the offer of an honour from the Queen on the grounds that a Welsh Nationalist should have no truck with royalty or empire, he took particular pleasure in being admitted to the druidic order of the Gorsedd of Bards in 1976, which he thought was honour enough for a Welsh patriot devoted to the public life of his country.

Hywel Heulyn Roberts, county councillor: born Liverpool 16 March 1919; married 1944 Margaret Davies (died 2004, one son, two daughters and one daughter deceased); died Tregaron, Ceredigion 30 April 2010.

The Independent (5 June 2010)

WILL ROBERTS

Painter who found grandeur in the industrial landscape of Wales

THE WELSH PAINTER Will Roberts came to prominence in the 1950s, at the same time as his mentor Josef Herman, who died less than a month ago. Their association in the public mind is reinforced by the fact that, in 1945, Roberts sought out the Polish refugee at Ystradgynlais in the Swansea Valley and, for several years, shared a studio with him in that mining village.

Both painted industrial workers, particularly miners – but there the similarity ends. Whereas Herman tended to make massive icons of his colliers, Roberts was more concerned with the gentler, more intimate aspects of working-class life, depicting both men and women not only at work but at leisure and in the semi-rural setting which he found around his adopted town of Neath in Glamorgan and in nearby Gower.

William Roberts was born at Rhiwabon in Denbighshire but moved with his Welsh-speaking family to south Wales while still a child; his father was a railwayman. Except for war service as a technician in the RAF, when he was stationed at Biggin Hill, he lived the rest of his life in Neath, earning his living as a jeweller and optician but with a studio not far from his shop in the town centre.

He abandoned his course at Swansea Art School in 1930 after he discovered the pleasures of the violin, and like Ingres he remained a competent player for the rest of his life. His first public performance was given with Italian prisoners-of-war who had made their own instruments out of Naafi chair-legs and chicken wire. His attempt to enrol at the art school in Bath was thwarted when the building was destroyed by German bombs.

Despite his lack of formal art training, Roberts was a superb draughtsman and had some early success: he sold his first canvas, of Aberdulais Tinworks, to the University College of Wales, Aberystwyth, in 1946. Many of his paintings at that time were of the steel and tinplate works, open-hearth furnaces, rolling mills, canals and marshes which formed the landscape in and around Neath in the days before the rundown of the heavy industries of South Wales.

Of the Glamorgan landscape he once wrote: 'It's not lush and pretty here, but something far grander, heroic – the thumb-print of the 19th century is on every hill and valley.' There may be, too, something remembered from his country childhood in north Wales in his fondness for animals, farmyards, hedges and hills.

The earliest influence on his painting was Picasso, whose work bowled him over when he saw it for the first time in London in 1945. He was fond of quoting the Catalan: 'The man who sees a tree and paints a tree has done nothing, but the man who sees a tree and draws an elephant...' – adding: 'None of my paintings copy nature. Practically everything I do is in some way changed by distortion of shape; then the change of colour might follow; because they have to comply with my feelings about the things. I am trying to get at the greater truth of the thing itself.' In 1954 he held his first one-man exhibition at the Roland, Browse & Delbanco Gallery in London's Cork Street.

A typical painting by Will R. (as he always signed himself) is perhaps divided by a central line of horizon which seems to mark the boundary between Heaven and Earth, between which his figures – the sturdy cockle-gatherers of the Penclawdd Estuary, for example – bend in thought, labour, or worship. The religious element, which entered his work during the 1970s, is not always to the fore, for it is man who takes central place in his scheme of things. He is primarily concerned with the dignity of 'ordinary people', who are revealed as anything but ordinary.

But a series of canvases depicting Christ on the road to Emmaus goes one step farther in declaring the sacramental function of Roberts's art. He once said that, like Dylan Thomas, he worked 'for the love of man and in praise of God', echoing the poet's words with a chuckle, 'and I'd be a damn' fool if I didn't'. A series of charcoal drawings inspired by the Stations of the Cross hang in St David's Anglican Church, Neath, which he attended regularly. His last, retrospective exhibition began touring Wales in 1993 and he was still painting shortly before his death.

Will Roberts married Phyllis Hinds in 1948, and she survives him; they had one daughter, Sian.

William Roberts, painter, was born on 21 December 1907. He died in Neath on 11 March 2000 aged 92.

The Times (18 March 2000)

SELWYN RODERICK

Pioneer television producer in Wales

ONE OF THE first television producers in Wales, Selwyn Roderick had a distinguished career in which he was held in high esteem as much for the programmes he made as for his amiable personality and the unfailingly generous help he gave to younger professionals in the broadcast media.

He joined the BBC in Cardiff early in the 1950s while still in his twenties, working at first in radio, and remained with the Corporation for the rest of his working life. He and his colleagues, who included D.J. Thomas and Dafydd Gruffydd, laid the foundations for what became BBC Cymru/Wales by exercising the talents they had in abundance. Quartered at first in a cluster of huts at Baynton House, which in 1967 metamorphosed into the BBC's splendid broadcasting centre in Llandaf, on Cardiff's north-western rim, these were young men eager to win their spurs in the new medium and Selwyn Roderick was soon regarded as outstanding among them.

In 1954, at the age of 26, he became the Corporation's youngest television producer. The Outside Broadcasting Unit had just arrived in Cardiff and it was his job to use it to make programmes for Wales and the rest of Britain. This he did with commitment and panache. Although he was generally admired by colleagues, including those who worked with the legendary Peter Dimmock, Selwyn Roderick became famous not so much for his grasp of the administrative skills that usually went with being a sober-suited BBC executive, but for the original ideas that sprang from his quicksilver mind.

The historian Dai Smith, with whom he made a lively series entitled *Wales! Wales?* in 1985, described him as 'feisty, intellectually driven, and a passionate (Welsh) patriot. At times he could be irascible, a pain in the neck. He could also be charming and delightful company.' What I recall about Selwyn was his love of good talk: a few years back we met over a liquid lunch to discuss a film he was making with Emyr Daniel about the writer Glyn Jones but, several pints later, we had still not got down to business.

Among his early successes was a series of programmes as diverse as *Come Dancing*, *Songs of Praise* and *Your Life in their Hands*. He also covered umpteen royal events, eisteddfodau and rugby internationals. But he was always looking for opportunities to make better, more serious television, especially documentaries. His big chance came in 1968 when he took his cameras out into the streets of Tiger Bay, as the docklands of Cardiff used to be known before the advent of the National Assembly, to record the break-up of a well-established working-class community that has since all but disappeared.

He was just in time to witness the demolition of the old Bay as buildings were knocked down, roads widened, docks filled in and the people rehoused. The result was his crowning achievement, *Tamed and Shabby Tiger*, an affectionate portrait of a neighbourhood known the world over for its multicultural mix and thriving pub and street-corner culture, then at its last gasp. Selwyn Roderick was the narrator and Shirley Bassey, who is from Tiger Bay, took part.

Born at Cwm-gors on the Glamorgan/Carmarthenshire border in 1928, Selwyn Roderick was a son of the manse, like so many in the early days of broadcasting in Wales. His father was a member of the Independent Labour Party and it was in that colliery village Selwyn learned the Socialism he embraced for the rest of his life. He was very proud of his family's connections with William Williams of Pantycelyn, author of the words of the great hymn, 'Cwm Rhondda', which begin, 'Guide me, O Thou great Jehovah', often to be heard at international rugby matches.

The boy won a scholarship to Caterham School in Surrey, where he acquired, in addition to his rich Welsh, a command of English that was to serve him in good stead. From school he went up to Jesus College, Oxford, then on to the United States with the aid of a Fulbright Scholarship. On his return his sights were firmly fixed on a career in the broadcasting media.

By the 1970s, now an *éminence grise* at the BBC, he was put in charge of a group of producers who were making a range of documentaries and arts programmes. He enjoyed this avuncular role but, once again, he became famous, and admired, for his cavalier attitude to administrative niceties, preferring to strike sparks in discussion with younger men and women than give his attention to mere paper-work. He always staunchly defended his protégés from any meddling from the top floor of Broadcasting House.

His last major programme was *Plant y Paith* ('Children of the prairie'), which he made in 1979 with Owen Edwards, later Controller of BBC Wales and S4C. The film followed in the footsteps of the early Welsh settlers in Patagonia, where they had set up a self-governing, Welsh-speaking community in 1865, and it is still an important record of that quixotic venture, having captured something of the emigrants' radical Nonconformity and the gaucho culture which they adopted in order to survive.

'Information about the world's ways,' he wrote in typically wry fashion while reminiscing about the Patagonian programme in the symposium *Wales in Vision* (1990), 'may come from somewhere else, but Welsh broadcasters have an unchallenged responsibility to keep an eye on our own wherever they may be. Nobody else will do it for us – nobody else would want to.'

One of his sons is Vaughan Roderick, BBC Cymru's Welsh Affairs Editor and renowned blogger.

Selwyn Thomas Roderick, television producer: born Cwm-gors,
Glamorgan 21 August 1928; married 1954 Dilys Owen (two sons,
one daughter); died Penarth, Vale of Glamorgan 12 March 2011.

The Independent (24 May 2011)

VICTOR SPINETTI

Welsh actor who appeared in all three of the Beatles' films

ONCE ASKED BY a young actor how he might make his way in the theatre, Victor Spinetti gave this advice: 'Do everything from pantomime to Shakespeare, and learn the 3 Rs – redundancy, rejection, and resting.' It was something he himself had done during a long and varied career, playing many roles and putting up with the spells of unemployment that are often the actor's lot.

He might have added that a sense of the absurd often comes in handy in the precarious world of acting, for he had this in spades, too. On receiving a Tony Award on Broadway for his part in the stage version of *Oh! What a Lovely War*, he was praised for his eloquent speech in what the audience took to be Italian, only to admit later that it had been in his own made-up version of Welsh, a language he did not speak, but with Italian cadences and appropriate gestures. As a comedian, he had an infectious grin and twinkling eyes even when trying to be serious. When Jane Fonda asked him how it was he could play both comedy and tragedy, he told her earnestly, 'Well, you have to listen,' to which she replied, 'Pardon me?'

Victor Spinetti was born in Cwm, a steel-making village near Ebbw Vale, in 1933. His father was of Italian extraction and his mother Welsh. From one he inherited his hooded eyes and Roman nose and from the other a warm, vivacious personality that delighted in village gossip. The actor was fond of recalling how his grandfather had walked all the way from Italy to south Wales in search of a job in the steelworks. The Spinettis owned a chipshop and the family lived over it, happily enough and glad to be part of the close community, like so many people of Italian origin in the industrial valleys.

Even so, the father was interned as an 'enemy alien' on the Isle of Man during the Second World War. As he was dragged downstairs by the police, his son recalled in his memoirs, 'In that moment I was suddenly flung to the frontier with my passport not quite in order, and that feeling has remained with me for the rest of my life.' He was later beaten up by two neighbours, an attack which left him deaf in one ear.

His parents could afford to send him to the fee-paying Monmouth School, where he played the clown, and later to Cardiff College of Music and Drama, and supported him while he earned a living as a waiter and factory hand. The actor was proud of his Welsh upbringing and made frequent returns to the land of his birth, where he still has relatives. He always acknowledged that his love of acting had first been sparked by watching films in the local Coliseum, by the colourful characters he met in his parents' shop, especially their vivid way of speaking, by his membership of the local drama group and by his student days in Cardiff. His brother Henry Spinetti became a noted drummer.

He shot to prominence in the early 1960s when he was given parts in three films starring the Beatles: *A Hard Day's Night*, *Help!* and *Magical Mystery Tour*. This was a great piece of good fortune for a young actor who was still to land any major roles. Spinetti explained it by recalling how George Harrison had told him: 'You've got to be in all our films. If you're not, me Mam won't come to see them – she fancies you.' If this was not praise enough, Paul McCartney referred to the actor as 'the man who makes clouds disappear'. The glamour of his association with the Beatles was slow to fade: while playing on Broadway in the 1980s he was mobbed in the street by adoring fans wanting to touch the actor who had had such close contact with the Fab Four.

Small parts in about 35 films followed this initial success. They included Zeffirelli's *The Taming of the Shrew*, Dylan

Thomas's *Under Milk Wood*, with Elizabeth Taylor and Richard Burton, *Becket*, *Voyage of the Damned*, *The Return of the Pink Panther* and *The Krays*. If none of these fixed him in the popular view as a star of the large screen, they at least provided him with a living and the experience he always said was a necessary accoutrement of the working actor. During the 1970s he even appeared as a Mexican bandit in a series of television advertisements for McVities' Jaffa Cakes: for him, it was all in a day's work.

Between 1959 and 1965 he trod the boards as a straight actor with Joan Littlewood's Theatre Workshop at Stratford East in such productions as *Fings Ain't Wot They Used T'Be* (1959) and *Oh! What a Lovely War* (1963), in which he played the obnoxious Drill Sergeant. His West End and Broadway appearances included parts in *Expresso Bongo*, *Candide*, *The Hostage*, *Peter Pan*, *Oliver!*, *Cat Among the Pigeons*, *The Odd Couple* and *Chitty Chitty Bang Bang*. One of his most challenging roles was as the principal male character in Jane Arden's radical feminist play *Vagina Rex and the Gas Oven*, which played to packed houses for six weeks at the Arts Lab on Drury Lane towards the end of 1969. He also tried his hand as a director: he adapted *In His Own Write*, a play based on John Lennon's book, which he directed for the National Theatre in 1968.

His acclaimed one-man show, *A Very Private Diary*, first staged at the Edinburgh Festival in 1981 and going on to the Sydney Opera House, featured hilarious accounts of his acquaintance with such stars as Marlene Dietrich, Frank Sinatra, Brendan Behan, Sean Connery, Salvador Dali, Peter Sellers, Richard Attenborough, and Laurence Olivier, and was reprised in 2008. The same delight in anecdote and theatrical gossip informs his memoirs, *Victor Spinetti Up Front* (2006), in which he wrote movingly about the death of his partner, Graham Cumow. In a later chat show he revealed to Michael Ball that Princess Margaret had been instrumental in securing the Censor's permission for some of the more controversial passages in the first run of *Oh! What a Lovely War*. A more sensitive side to his character is shown in his book of poems, *Watchers along the Mall* (1963).

Victorio Georgio Andrea Spinetti (Victor Spinetti), actor: born 2 September 1933, Cwm, Monmouthshire; died Monmouth, 19 June 2012.

The Independent (20 June 2012)

RHOBERT AP STEFFAN

Tireless campaigner for Welsh patriotic causes

THE MAGNIFICENT MENHIR that commemorates Llywelyn ap Gruffudd, killed by English forces at Cilmeri near Builth in the middle March on 11 December 1282, is the focus for several hundred patriots who gather there on the anniversary of his death every year. Drums are beaten, speeches made, books sold and poems read, and some of our bolder politicians address the motley crew who come to remember the last Prince of independent Wales, 'our Prince' as the inscription nicely has it.

Prominent among them was Rhobert ap Steffan, who from his teens was devoted to the memory of Llywelyn and those others who have given their lives in the cause of their country's freedom down the centuries. He never missed the occasion, not once in forty years, and when, last December, he failed to turn up there was a sense of unease in the nearby pub to which the crowd had repaired. Something was seriously amiss if Castro, as Rhobert was known, was not there to join in the act of remembrance. It was he, after all, who had done much to convene the rally over the years. What most present didn't know was that he had just been diagnosed with a particularly virulent form of cancer and had only a month to live.

His zeal for commemorating the heroes of the Welsh Pantheon never faltered. In 2001 he led a campaign to put up a statue of Llywelyn ap Gruffudd ap Fychan in the centre of Llandovery in Carmarthenshire. This man, a local squire, of whom few had heard up to then, was a staunch supporter of Owain Glyndŵr who took the King's men on a wild goose chase across upland mid-Wales in order to buy time for Owain to muster elsewhere.

Captured in 1401, he was hanged, drawn and quartered, and his intestines burnt before his eyes, but refused to divulge Owain's position, and for this reason he has been called 'the Welsh Braveheart'. The splendid stainless steel monument, created by the brothers Toby and Gideon Petersen, is now an admired feature of Llandovery's townscape.

Rhobert was also one of the leaders of the large Welsh contingent who travelled to Mortagne-sur-Gironde, some forty miles south of Bordeaux, for the inauguration of a memorial to Owain Lawgoch, known to the French as Yvain de Galles, a soldier of fortune and claimant Prince of Wales, who was killed during the siege of the castle at Mortagne in 1378. The statue, with a lapidary inscription in Welsh and French, was unveiled by Rosemary Butler, Chair of the National Assembly's Culture Committee, in 2003.

Rhobert was a tireless campaigner in the cause of Wales. He took a very active part in the anti-Investiture campaign of 1969, seeing in the pageantry at Caernarfon castle in July of that year a celebration of English dominion over Wales and a measure of the devastation which had been wrought on the Welsh people's sense of their national identity. His articles in the magazine *Cambria*, of which he was Editor at Large, were informed with a wit and sense of the absurd which made him an attractive commentator on current affairs in Wales and abroad. Conversation with him always ended in laughter.

An associate of Cayo Evans, and other leaders of the Free Wales Army, he was never openly implicated in its clandestine activities, preferring to put his skills to good use in staging processions and rallies. It was on such occasions that the arms of the House of Gwynedd (*'quarterly de Gu et Or en les quartiers leopards passans de contre couleur'*), outlawed after 1282, first made a comeback; the red-and-gold flag is now widely seen in Wales, often flying from public buildings together with the Red Dragon. The same fondness for heraldic devices prompted Rhobert to found the annual St David's Day Parade which, every March, enlivens the streets of Cardiff.

He also supported the Keep Cornwall Whole campaign when, in 2010, it was proposed to move the boundary with Devon some miles to the west, making a comparison with the status of Monmouthshire before it was declared an integral part of Wales. Indeed, he had contacts and friends in all the Celtic lands as well as in Catalonia and the Basque Country.

He shared the general sense of outrage when it was announced that the 2001 Census form would not allow Welsh people to declare themselves to be of Welsh nationality. The way he chose to protest was typically original and effective: he made a coffin in which he collected many thousands of spoiled forms and drove it all over Wales in a hearse, often to applause as it passed through villages and towns. The move contributed to a change of heart by the Office of National Statistics which has given an assurance that there will be a Welsh tick-box in the Census due to take place this year.

Rhobert's energies were sometimes put to purposes charitable rather than patriotic. In 2008, with the naturalist Iolo Williams, he went on a sponsored trek through the Andes in a bid to raise money for Mencap Cymru. Walking twelve miles a day for five weeks, he visited many of the Welsh settlements in Patagonia, taking copies of textbooks and the recently-published *Encyclopaedia of Wales* for presentation to schools and libraries there, and this out of gratitude for having first learnt Welsh in the colony as a young man of 19. A member of the Patagonia Support Group, he was among those who helped Shirley Edwards, a young Welsh-speaker from Patagonia, to spend some time in Wales after she had been refused entry by the Border Agency.

Rhobert ap Steffan was born in Hove, Brighton, in 1948, the son of a Welsh army chaplain named Hinton who was stationed in England and Germany. Brought up in Treorci in the Rhondda, he was educated at Porth Grammar School and Cirencester Agricultural College; after nearly a year in

Patagonia he trained as an Art teacher at Barry College of Education. His first teaching job was at Bishop Hedley Roman Catholic School in Merthyr Tydfil; he took early retirement from a similar post at Ysgol Pantycelyn, Llandovery, where he had been Head of the Art Department, devoting his last years to photography, history and patriotic causes. The decision that defined the course of his life was that, while still in his teens, he changed his name to a patronymic form, using no other thereafter and passing it on to his three children.

Rhobert ap Steffan (formerly Robert Hinton), Welsh patriot: born Hove, Sussex 4 February 1948; married 1977 Marilyn Walters (two sons, one daughter); died Llangadog, Carmarthenshire 11 January 2011.

The Independent (24 January 2011)

ERIC SUNDERLAND

Vice-Chancellor of Bangor University
who brought calm after a period of turbulence

FEW WHO WITNESSED the results of the referendum on Welsh Devolution late on the night of 18 September 1997 will forget the evident relish with which Professor Eric Sunderland, the Chief Counting Officer, announced that the Yes campaign had won by a slim but sufficient majority of 6,721 votes and that the proposal to establish a National Assembly was therefore approved by the people of Wales. The clip has been shown over and over again on television in Wales, and the excitement and historic significance of the occasion, together with the Professor's beaming face, have entered the iconography of recent Welsh politics. It was as if Wales had scored a winning drop-goal in the closing minutes of an international rugby match and the roar was deafening; it gave him special satisfaction that the very last Yes result, which clinched the matter, came from Carmarthenshire, his native county.

Born at Blaenau, near Ammanford, in 1930, he went from Amman Valley grammar school to the University College of Wales, Aberystwyth, where he took a first in Geography and Anthropology, and then a master's degree; he was later awarded his doctorate by University College, London. After military service, he worked for a year as a research scientist with the Coal Board, but took his first academic post in 1958 as a lecturer in the Anthropology department of Durham University, where in due course he was appointed Professor and Head of Department in 1971; he also served as Pro-Vice-Chancellor from 1979 to 1984.

By the time he returned to Wales in 1984 he had a reputation as an anthropologist of distinction, having published such substantial books as *Elements of Human and Social Geography: some anthropological perspectives* (1973), *Genetic Variation in Britain* (with D.F. Roberts, 1973) and *The Exercise of Intelligence: biosocial preconditions for the operation of intelligence* (with Malcolm T. Smith, 1980), to which he later added *Genetic and Population Studies in Wales* (with Peter S. Harper, 1986). He had also held some of the most important posts in his specialist field, including those of Honorary Secretary of the Royal Anthropological Institute, Secretary General of the International Union of Anthropological and Ethnological Societies and Chairman of the Biosocial Society.

His appointment as Principal at Bangor in 1984 followed a turbulent phase in the history of the University College of North Wales, as it then was, and much was expected of the new man in healing the schisms caused by his predecessor, the autocratic Sir Charles Evans, whose tenure had come to what Dr David Roberts, Bangor's Registrar, in his history of the institution published in 2009, called 'a bitter and querulous end'. Evans, best-known for his role as deputy leader of the team that conquered Everest in 1953, had shown 'a cold indifference' to the wider use of Welsh in the college's affairs and, moreover, had been highly unpopular among both staff and students during these 'dark and divisive days, the darkest in the University's history', on account of his vindictive attitude towards those who disagreed with him.

Eric Sunderland, like his predecesssor a Welsh-speaker, was much better disposed towards the growing demand for teaching in Welsh, his first language, which he spoke fluently and elegantly, and in this and many other ways he proved to be the very antithesis of Evans. Although a patriotic Welshman, it had taken some persuasion to entice him from Durham, where his family was happily settled, but in the end he accepted the post with pleasure and took office just weeks before the college's official centenary celebrations. The appointment proved a popular one and, with his genial personality and abundant communication skills, he soon won over a wide swathe of the academic staff.

At ease in social gatherings, and ably supported by his wife, Patricia, he took his role as ambassador for the college seriously and few could fail to respond to his broad grin and friendly nature. He even made a point, early in his principalship, of going to speak to students at Neuadd John Morris-Jones, the hostel for Welsh-speakers where many of those who had been protesting against the former principal were housed, thus spiking the guns of the Young Turks who had been disrupting the campus. His lecture 'Esblygiad Dyn' ('Man's evolution'), delivered at the National Eisteddfod in 1985, demonstrated his ability to treat complex scientific topics in his first language.

Slowly the acrimony began to subside and a new mood of optimism started to be felt. Even so, and despite some gratifying achievements, Sunderland had to preside over a raft of administrative problems, not least those having to do with funding cuts by the University Grants Committee, and some hard choices about whether to maintain teaching in certain disciplines. This he did with sympathy and common sense and always with regard for the human cost involved. Despite his warm engagement with people, he had a tough inner core which stood him in good stead in the piranha pools of Academe. That the college survived the troubled years of the 1970s and 1980s and the financial stresses of the 1990s was in large measure due to him and his senior officers.

Sunderland also played an active part in public life, and served on myriad bodies across the UK, where his skills were always appreciated. In Wales alone he was Chairman of the Local Government Boundary Commission (1994–2001), a member of the Welsh Language Education Development Committee (1987–94), the British Council (1990–2001), the Court of Governors of the National Museum (1991–94), and the Broadcasting Council (1996–2000).

He was keenly interested in the arts: he was Chairman of

the Welsh Chamber Orchestra, Vice-President of the Welsh Music Guild, and patron of Artworks Wales. I first met him when he was chairman of the Gregynog Press Board in the 1980s, where we often talked about our love of books and fine editions in particular. After his retirement he liked nothing better than attending concerts at the University and was involved in fostering its art collection.

Many honours came his way, including the Mahatma Gandhi Freedom Award from the College of William and Mary in Virginia (1989). He served as High Sheriff of Gwynedd (1998–99) and Lord Lieutenant of the county from 1999 to 2006, and was awarded the honorary degree of LLD by the University of Wales in 1997 and the Queen's Golden Jubilee Medal in 2002.

Eric Sunderland, anthropologist and Vice-Chancellor of Bangor University: born Blaenau, Carmarthenshire 18 March 1930; Professor of Anthropology, University of Durham (1971–79); Pro-Vice-Chancellor, University of Durham (1979–84); Principal, later Vice-Chancellor, University College of North Wales, later Bangor University (1984–95); Emeritus Professor, University of Wales; married 1957 Patricia Watson (two daughters); OBE 1999; CBE 2005; died Beaumaris, Ynys Môn 24 March 2010.

The Independent (17 May 2010)

Aeronwy Thomas

Daughter of Dylan Thomas and promoter of his work

DYLAN THOMAS'S DAUGHTER was only ten when the writer died in a New York hospital. Yet she had vivid memories of her early childhood, four years of which were spent in Laugharne, on the Towy estuary in Carmarthenshire, and of the man who enjoyed a reputation as one of the twentieth century's greatest poets in English, and certainly the most rumbustious. In later life she acknowledged that he was a drunkard, a spendthrift and a womaniser but remembered him as a loving father who was always full of fun and ready to talk and read to her. His death, she said, was a terrible blow which left her, even as a grown woman, craving the affection he had given her. 'I never really got over it,' she said in a BBC Wales interview in 2003. 'I always feel there's something missing in my life.'

She had been born in London in 1943 and christened Aeron after the river in Cardiganshire on the banks of which she had been conceived, but chose to be known by the dimunitive of her name, Aeronwy. Her birth inspired Thomas to write the poem 'Vision and Prayer'. Six years later she was taken to Laugharne, where the Thomases lived at the Boathouse, Dylan's 'seashaken house on a breakneck of rock', which remained for her a magical place. She wrote about it with almost total recall, notably in *Christmas in the Boathouse* (2003), one of several attempts to capture the special quality of the place that attracts thousands of tourists every year. 'Some of my best memories are when we walked back silently to the Boathouse and I just felt so comfortable with him and he obviously felt comfortable with me, because there wasn't any need to speak,' she said.

For all the bohemian ambience of their home, with her father in the village pubs and her mother having little taste for housework, she was never neglected but grew up with an independent outlook and a sturdy ability to look after herself. Paul Ferris, biographer of Dylan Thomas, has said, 'She was a tough little customer and knew her own mind. I liked her. She was friendly and quite assertive. She would look you in the eye if she thought you were wrong about something.' A self-assured woman, from her father she inherited a sense of mischief and something of his charm, and from her mother a sharp tongue which she used on occasion when approached by the importunate. She received the rudiments of a good education at the Arts Educational School in Tring, Hertfordshire, where she also acquired a cutglass English accent.

Not that her parents' way of life impinged much on her own poems, published in *Later than Laugharne* (1976), for they celebrate the natural scene and her growing awareness of a wider world rather than domestic quiddities. She spent her teenage years in Italy with her mother and became a competent translator from the Italian, notably in *I Colori della Parole* – 'The colour of saying', after one of her father's poems.

Although she made strenuous efforts to be taken seriously as a writer in her own right, she was not averse to reminding her readers that she was her father's daughter – indeed, his admirers the world over expected it of her – and with such books as *Christmas and other Memories* (1978) she began mining a seam of which neither she nor they ever tired. Whereas her two brothers showed little interest in his work, there was nothing that could be said about her father's fecklessness that deterred her. She thus revealed aspects of Thomas which were relevant to a fuller understanding of the man and poet. In appearance, too, she had the curls and cherubic features which made Dylan Thomas such a recognizable icon for the poetry-reading public. Her last book, *My Father's Places*, was chosen by BBC Radio 4 as Book of the Week.

From the 1970s on, Aeronwy was often in the public eye. I first met her at the opening of the Arts Council's exhibition, 'Welsh Dylan', which was mounted in Cardiff's Sherman Theatre to mark the twentieth anniversary of his death in November 1973. As soon as it was known that she was interested in the literary life of Wales she was much in demand from literary societies seeking her patronage. She became a patron of the Dylan Thomas Society, a keen supporter of the Dylan Thomas Centre in Swansea, one of the best of its kind in Britain, and of the Dylan Thomas Trust which awards a prize to writers under the age of thirty. A tireless lecturer on the American circuit, she launched the Dylan Thomas Trail in New York which takes acolytes on a tour of the poet's watering-places. She even backed *The Edge of Love*, a film starring Matthew Rhys and Sienna Miller. For her contribution to Dylan Thomas studies she was awarded an Honorary Fellowship by Swansea University in 2003.

She also gave freely of her time to less grand bodies such as local literary groups, speaking and reading and sometimes adding lustre simply by turning up. I last saw her at the London Welsh Club, where, though frail and clearly unwell, she showed a lively interest in the poetry reading and seemed to be enjoying the fun. Her ashes were scattered near the Boathouse in Laugharne.

Aeron (Aeronwy) Thomas, writer: born Chelsea, London 3 March 1943; married Trefor Ellis (one son, one daughter); died New Malden, Surrey 27 July 2009.

The Independent (7 August 2009)

ANEURIN M. THOMAS

First Director of the Welsh Arts Council

ANEURIN M. THOMAS was appointed first Director of the Welsh Arts Council in 1966 when it was merely the Welsh Committee of the Arts Council of Great Britain. He had responsibility, on taking up his post in the year following, for overseeing the change of status and internal restructuring which the new arrangements required.

One of his first initiatives, which the Council's new royal charter allowed, was the appointment of a Literature Director and a Committee whose brief was the formulation of a policy for the financial support of writers, books, magazines and publishers in Wales. A highly literate man, he was especially keen that the Literature Committee's work should succeed, and in both the languages of Wales, because he had argued consistently for the devolution of arts funding and here was an opportunity to prove that it made sense. From modest beginnings – the grant in 1968/69, its first full year, was £18,000 – the Literature Department's work grew rapidly and its policies, tentative though they were, were soon adopted by other arts bodies in the United Kingdom.

Although Thomas's own training and background were in the visual arts, he was perfectly content to let his subject Directors pursue their own notions of what their art-forms needed, and to back them to the hilt, and for this he earned the respect of his colleagues and the members with whom they had to work. As a consequence, the real power, or at least the responsibility for gathering new ideas and seeing them through the grant-making process, lay with the

Council's specialist officers and their committees, in whose business he rarely intervened.

Towards the end of his career, however, he felt as if he had little to do in its day-to-day affairs and this weighed on him heavily. He did a great deal of reading from books which he purchased, at staff discount, from the Council's Oriel Bookshop. He also managed, on one famous occasion, to raise the hackles of underfunded actors with a comment, during a television interview, to the effect that at a conference of seals the delegates will always call for more fish.

In 1972 he served as a member of the Committee of Inquiry into Bilingual Traffic Signs, publishing a one-man minority report in which he argued for dropping anglicized place-names such as Bridgend, Fishguard, Holyhead and Cardigan, in favour of their Welsh forms. The committee eventually agreed to recommend the bilingual signs that are now seen in all parts of Wales.

Aneurin Thomas had come back to Wales on his appointment to the Arts Council post after spending seven years as Vice-Principal of Hornsey College of Art and thirteen as Lecturer and Vice-Principal at Somerset College of Art. His time at Hornsey preceded the student troubles there.

He was born to working-class parents at Cilybebyll, a Welsh-speaking village near the tinplate town of Pontardawe in Glamorgan. His own Welsh was rudimentary and, after long years in England, he was never confident enough to use it except for mundane purposes. He received his secondary education at Ystalyfera Intermediate School and from there went on to the Swansea School of Art and Crafts. The war broke out while he was still at Swansea and, as soon as he qualified in 1941, he enlisted in the army. For the next five years he served in the British and Indian Armies, ending his military career with the rank of Major. He never spoke to colleagues about his war-service but, despite his egalitarian instincts, his time in the army sometimes showed in his imperious manner and insistence on protocol.

His love of strategy, not to say plotting, was often put to good effect in his dealings with the Arts Council of Great Britain, of which the Welsh Arts Council was technically only a consultative committee, albeit with a very wide degree of autonomy and its own budget. In this delicate and sometimes daunting relationship – the Welsh members were once described by Lord Goodman as robber barons who grabbed what spoils they could from London before making their way home over the hills on their mules – he had the staunch backing of three successive Chairmen, namely Professor Gwyn Jones, Colonel Sir William Crawshay and the Marchioness of Anglesey.

During the years of their stewardship in Wales the Council's grant-in-aid grew from £320,000 in 1967 to £6,451,000 in 1984, the year of Aneurin Thomas's retirement. Among the many successes in which he and his colleagues played a leading role were the work of the various bodies which were called into existence or developed from small beginnings to become part of the artistic landscape of present-day Wales. These included the Welsh National Opera Company, the BBC Welsh Symphony Orchestra, the Welsh Books Council, the Welsh Academy, and the three Regional Arts Associations, as well as myriad projects in Drama, Film, Crafts and the Visual Arts – though the dream of a National Theatre remained beyond the Council's reach.

With hindsight, the years from 1967 to 1984 now seem like a golden age of arts funding in Wales, for they saw rapid and substantial growth in all areas, which slowed down thereafter. Aneurin Thomas would not have claimed credit for this huge improvement in the nation's artistic affairs, for he was by nature self-effacing and somewhat laconically detached from the artistic community, but it cannot be denied that he played a key role in it.

In retirement he lived quietly in the seaside town of Penarth, near Cardiff, where he continued to take keen pleasure in the arts and kept up his hobby of painting in water-colours, an activity at which, despite the loss of sight in one eye, he had excelled since his student days.

Aneurin Morgan Thomas, arts administrator, born Cilybebyll, near Pontardawe, Glamorgan 3 April 1921; Lecturer and Vice-Principal, Somerset College of Art (1947–60), Vice-Principal, Hornsey College of Art (1960–66), Director, Welsh Arts Council (1966–84); married 1947 Mary Dineen (one son, one daughter); died St Hilary, Vale of Glamorgan 16 January 2009.

The Independent (28 April 2009)

CRAIG THOMAS

Author of Cold War spy stories and inventor of the techno-thriller

CRAIG THOMAS WROTE eighteen novels, six of which were best-sellers. But the book that brought him global fame was *Firefox*, after it was adapted for a Hollywood film directed by and starring Clint Eastwood. The blockbuster sold so well its author was able to give up teaching in 1978 and live as a full-time writer.

Both book and film have as their main character a U.S. fighter-pilot named Mitchell Gant who steals a Soviet MiG-31 with spectacular consequences. Meticulously researched and featuring cutting-edge technology, like all Thomas's books, the novel spins a gripping yarn that draws the reader into a world of chilling Cold War espionage. It was the first techno-thriller and the first action story to be set mainly in the Soviet Union.

The hero-spy appeared in several more of Thomas's novels and established their author as a leading exponent of the genre, on a par with, though perhaps not quite as famous as his fellow countryman Ken Follett. In *A Different War* Gant appears as an air accident investigator in the corrupt world of global aircraft manufacturing during the 1990s. The novel is set at the end of the Cold War and reflects on the demise of the old political and moral certainties.

Craig Thomas was born and brought up in Cardiff and educated at the city's High School and University College, where he read English. His father was the rugby journalist J.B.G. Thomas from whom he inherited a delight in vivid language. After graduating in 1967 he wrote an MA dissertation on Thomas Hardy and then taught English at various schools in the West Midlands, including the Shire

Oak School in Walsall Wood and King Edward VI School in Lichfield. He ended his career as Head of Department.

Having made an unsuccessful start as a scriptwriter for radio, he soon turned to writing novels, beginning with *The Rat Trap* (1976). His wife Jill acted as his amanuensis and editor of all his books. She has said, 'He had a great passion for his writing and for music. Even when he was in hospital undergoing chemotherapy, he was still scribbling away until it just got too much for him.' The couple moved from Lichfield to Somerset in 2010. He died after a short battle with acute myeloid leukaemia.

The *violon d'Ingres* in which Thomas found deep satisfaction was his writing about philosophical subjects. His volume of essays, *There to Here: Ideas of Political Society*, appeared in 1991 and he finished a two-volume commentary on the writings of the German philosopher Friedrich Nietzsche shortly before his death. He regarded philosophy as 'the greatest adventure of all'.

But his life's work was done as a master storyteller. His other books in the spy genre include his fourth novel, *Snow Falcon* (1980), which was favourably reviewed by none less than C.P. Snow, together with *Sea Leopard*, *Jade Tiger* and *Firefox Down*, all of which made him an international best-seller; the last-named was dedicated to Clint Eastwood. His books have sold more than two million copies. He also wrote, as David Grant, *Moscow 5000* (1979) and *Emerald Decision* (1980).

Asked why he was drawn to the thriller, Thomas said, 'Because of its evident sense of tension and danger, the deliberate structure of the plots, and perhaps the emphatic moral framework, just as many writers of detective fiction are drawn to the sense of justice their books demonstrate towards good and evil. There is an attraction in the thriller or adventure story, for both the writer and the reader, in knowing which side one is supposed to be on. And thrillers are optimistic. Their problems are soluble and they are resolved by individuals. As Oscar Wilde said, "The good end happily, the bad unhappily." That is the meaning of fiction.' Few writers have provided such a succinct and lucid guide to their work.

Most of his novels in his favourite mode are set within MI6 and have Sir Kenneth Aubrey and Patrick Hyde as their main protagonists. Although the invention of the techno-thriller is sometimes attributed to Tom Clancy, aficionados of the genre believe Craig Thomas to have been its true originator. 'Plotted to absolute perfection' was the observation made by Peter Finch, chief executive of Literature Wales, on hearing of the writer's death.

In *Snow Falcon*, Thomas speculated on a possible Soviet invasion of Western Europe via Finland. He found his own voice in writing out of this preoccupation with geopolitical problems and conflicts. He believed that the kind of books he wrote had not been consigned to history by the fall of the Berlin Wall. 'Just watching the evening news or picking up a newspaper ought to make it obvious that the world may now be a more, rather than a less dangerous place,' he said.

A formal man, courteous and amiable, Craig Thomas took a lenient view of humankind but did not flinch from recording some of the atrocities of which we are capable.

David Craig Owen Thomas, novelist: born Cardiff 24 November 1942; married Jill Whittington; died Bath, Somerset 4 April 2011.

The Independent (13 May 2011)

TASKER WATKINS

Victoria Cross holder who became a distinguished judge
and Welsh Rugby Union President

GENERAL THOMAS PICTON, Wellington's second-in-command
at Waterloo, was of the view that the ideal infantryman
was the Silurian type of Welshman, still to be found in his
indomitable thousands in the valleys of south Wales to this
day – dark, stocky, thick-necked and about five feet two
inches in his socks – or, in other words, the sort that usually
plays behind the scrum for Wales. Tasker Watkins was
the perfect embodiment of the short, tough, bright-eyed,
mercurial, gallant Silures who were the aborigines of these
islands before the coming of the fair-haired Celts, and what
he lacked in inches he made up for in courage under fire.

Watkins won the Victoria Cross in action against
the retreating Germans near the Normandy village of
La Fresnaye on 16 August 1944. It was an incident about
which he was famously reticent in public, choosing not
to talk about it for reasons of natural modesty, delicacy
and tact. But the official citation makes it clear with what
extraordinary bravery he behaved on that occasion.

In command of a company of the Welch Regiment,
Lt Watkins was ordered to attack enemy positions near the
railway at Balfour which lay across open cornfields where
booby-traps had been set. As dusk fell, his company came
under fire and many lives were lost in the first few minutes
of the engagement. The only officer left, Watkins placed
himself at the head of his men and, under short-range
bombardment, charged two German posts, killing and

wounding the occupants with his Sten gun. As he pushed on towards an anti-tank gun emplacement, his weapon jammed, so he hurled it in a German's face and, before his opponent had time to recover, shot him with his revolver.

The company, now with only 30 men left, was counterattacked by about 50 Germans, against whom Watkins led a bayonet charge which wiped most of them out. Orders for the battalion to withdraw were not received and the Welshmen now found themselves surrounded, cut off from their comrades, short of ammunition and in failing light. The lieutenant decided to rejoin his battalion by passing around the enemy's flank through which he had advanced an hour before. As they made their way back across the same cornfields they were challenged by a German position. Ordering his men to scatter, Watkins charged the post with a Bren gun, silenced it and then led the remnants of his company back to battalion headquarters. He had managed to save the lives of half his men.

Tasker Watkins, the son of a miner at the Ocean Colliery, Treharris, was born in Nelson, Glamorgan, in 1918. His father and grandfather had both fought in Kitchener's Army and two of his uncles had been killed while fighting with the Welsh Guards. Tasker won a scholarship to Pontypridd County School and I remember in what awe this diminutive man with the huge reputation was held by boys and teachers alike when he spoke as guest of honour at our Speech Day there in the early 1950s.

After the war, which he finished in the rank of Major, Tasker Watkins took up the legal studies which had always been his ambition and soon became a distinguished member of his profession. Called to the Bar by the Middle Temple in 1948, he took silk in 1965, and served as Deputy Chairman of Radnor Quarter Sessions from 1962 to 1971, of Carmarthenshire Quarter Sessions from 1966 to 1971, and then as Recorder of Merthyr Tydfil and Swansea. From 1971 he was a Judge of the High Court of Justice and from

1974 to 1980 Presiding Judge of the Wales and Chester Circuit. He was a Lord Justice of Appeal, 1983–93, and Deputy Chief Justice of England and Wales from 1988 until his retirement in 1993.

Among the other bodies on which he served were the inquiry into the Aberfan disaster of 1966, the Mental Health Review Tribunal for Wales, the Judicial Studies Board, the University of Wales College of Medicine and the Territorial Army Association. Many honours came his way: he was knighted in 1971, appointed GBE in 1990, an Honorary Fellow of the Royal College of Surgeons in 1992 and a Knight of St John in 2000; he received an honorary doctorate from the University of Wales in 1979 and from the University of Glamorgan in 1996.

But perhaps the appointment that gave him most pleasure was his presidency of the Welsh Rugby Union from 1993 to 2004, after which he was made Honorary Life Vice-Patron. In 2006 he was made a Freeman of the City and County of Cardiff, to general acclaim, thus joining a select band that includes David Lloyd George, Winston Churchill, Pope Paul John II and Nelson Mandela. His VC is displayed in the Welch Regiment Museum housed in the city's castle. On that occasion, too, he showed himself to be a man of dignified manner and unfailing courtesy, with an outstanding intellect and an impeccable command of spoken English.

Tasker Watkins, soldier and judge: born Nelson, Glamorgan 18 November 1918; VC 1944; called to the Bar, Middle Temple 1948, Bencher 1970; Deputy Chairman, Radnor Quarter Sessions 1962–71; QC 1965; Deputy Chairman, Carmarthenshire Quarter Sessions 1966–71; Recorder, Merthyr Tydfil 1968–70; Recorder, Swansea 1970–71; Leader, Wales and Chester Circuit 1970–71, Presiding Judge 1975–80; Kt 1971; Judge of the High Court of Justice 1971–80; PC 1980; a Lord Justice of Appeal 1980–93; Senior Presiding Judge for England and Wales

1983–91; Deputy Chief Justice of England and Wales 1988–93; GBE 1990; President, Welsh Rugby Union 1993–2004; married 1941 Eirwen Evans (one daughter and one son deceased); died Cardiff 9 September 2007.

The Independent (10 September 2007)

HUW WEEKES

Television journalist with HTV

Huw Weekes, who has died aged 43, fronted the nightly news programmes *Wales Tonight* and *Wales At Six* on HTV and became one of the company's senior reporters. His interviewing technique won HTV's news programmes a reputation for being well-informed and authoritative.

Born in Newport, Weekes was brought up in Aberdare, the son of a senior National Coal Board official. Fascinated by the power of television, Weekes set his heart on entering the industry. He began his journalistic career aged 18 on the *Weston Mercury* weekly in Weston-super-Mare and then joined the *Evening Post* in Bristol. A highly respected hard news man, he was professional to his fingertips.

His broadcasting career started as a reporter on BBC Radio Newcastle in 1980. Two years later he joined Yorkshire Television as a sub-editor and then made his mark as a presenter for the nightly news magazine *Calendar*. After a stint at Tyne Tees Television, he joined HTV in 1988.

Weekes became the cornerstone of HTV's news operation. He presided over a team of reporters in whom he encouraged the highest standards of diligent, accurate and balanced reporting.

Bespectacled and genial in his screen manner, he brought a dignified delivery to the most trivial of stories. His Welsh accent made no concession to the estuarine cadences now penetrating south Wales – there is still a widespread belief among Welsh viewers that news delivered in a Welsh accent is more credible.

He had a puckish sense of humour and a penchant for

telling appalling jokes. His leisure interest was following Cardiff City football club.

The affection in which he was held by colleagues at HTV was apparent when a clearly upset Juliet Piper and Jonathan Hill announced the news of his death: unusually, the BBC *Wales Today* programme also carried a warm tribute. The circumstances of Weekes' death remain unclear, but are not regarded as suspicious by the police. His body was found on the beach at Boverton, near Llantwit Major.

He leaves a wife, Sue, a son and two daughters.

Huw Weekes, television presenter, born 22 January 1957; died 18 January 2001.

The Guardian (12 February 2001)

BRYNLE WILLIAMS

Fuel protest leader and popular member
of the National Assembly of Wales

THE FARMER BRYNLE Williams shot to public prominence in 2000 when he was among those who led protests at the gates of the Stanlow oil refinery at Ellesmere Port in Cheshire. The week-long blockades in which road hauliers and others demonstrated against escalating petrol prices that were ruining their businesses brought the country to a standstill and challenged the economic policies of the Labour government of the day. He was proud that the demonstrations, though raucous, had not turned violent and he advocated such direct action as a means of making a political point. 'The aim of our protests,' he said, 'was to bring to Tony Blair's attention that all was not well in the countryside.'

He admitted privately that before 2000 he had never seen himself as a politician or even as someone who would ever stride upon a public stage, but as a Member of the National Assembly he was often in the news on account of his forthright opinions. He had been thrust into the limelight, he thought, because he cared passionately about issues that impacted upon his livelihood as a farmer and cattle breeder and because, unlike some politicians, he was prepared to speak up and take action on behalf of the farming industry.

The protest at Stanlow was not the first in which Brynle Williams had been involved. He had also taken part in demonstrations against the importation of beef from Ireland in 1997 when forty tons of meat were thrown into the sea at Holyhead. But it was the fury of the televised scenes in Ellesmere Port and the masterly way in which he acted as spokesman for his fellow protesters which made his name as a farmers' leader. It seemed inevitable that he would be persuaded to stand for public office.

Born at Cilcain near Mold in Flintshire in 1949, he had begun working on the land at the age of 15 and, after studying at the Welsh College of Horticulture in Northop, spent the rest of his life at Cefn Melyn, the farm where he and his wife Mair raised sheep and cattle. He made his name as a beef producer and as a breeder and judge of Welsh ponies and cobs. The delight of his life was in the showing of these beautiful creatures, both at home and abroad, and he was often to be seen winning rosettes in the ring at the Royal Welsh Show or, natty in a bowler hat, judging the entries of others.

First elected to the National Assembly in 2003, he won a regional seat for the Conservatives again in 2007 and was hoping to return to political life when the Fourth Assembly, rejuvenated for having been given law-making powers by the people of Wales, is convened after the elections on 5 May. He chaired the North Wales Regional Committee during the First Assembly of 1999–2003 and also sat on the Sustainability, Local Government, Rural Development and Standards of Conduct Committees.

His transparent honesty made him many friends in political circles. His ruddy complexion, large frame and earthy manner were in contrast with the sleeker, sharper-suited politicos now to be seen in Cardiff Bay. Although he had made his name with his outspoken responses to journalists' questions during the fuel protests, he was, as it turned out, no rabble-rouser and there was nothing of the rantipole about him. His Welsh was rich in idiom redolent of the Clwydian hills and he listed the language as one of the causes in which he had a special interest as an Assembly Member. It was his amiable nature that always came to the fore when he got to his feet.

His speeches in the chamber were not much given to rhetoric or point-scoring but had a certain bluntness in their homely turn of phrase that many found refreshing, even charming. Some of his fellow AMs have said they will miss his larger-than-life presence in the Senedd, as the Assembly is generally known, especially his singing and whistling in the corridors and his infectious sense of humour during debates.

Brynle Williams was, by common assent, an honest man speaking up for the rural communities of Wales of which he was such a splendid representative and in whose way of life he believed passionately. As Shadow Minister for Rural Affairs from 2007 to 2011, he had an excellent working relationship with Elin Jones, the more politically experienced Plaid Cymru Minister, each holding the other in high regard. We have it on the good authority of Betsan Powys, the BBC Wales political editor, that he was the only AM who would dare wink at female journalists in the press gallery.

Among the many posts he held in the agricultural community was the chair of the Flintshire branch of the Farmers' Union of Wales, to which he devoted a great deal of his time and energies. He also served as a member of the Council of the Royal Welsh Show and the Welsh Pony and Cob Society.

The affection in which he was held by Welsh Conservatives and political opponents alike was borne out by the many tributes paid by such prominent figures as Lord Dafydd Elis-Thomas, Presiding Officer of the National Assembly in its most recent incarnation, Carwyn Jones the Labour First Minister, Nick Bourne the leader of the Welsh Conservatives, and Ieuan Wyn Jones the Plaid Cymru Deputy First Minister who called him 'a thoroughly honourable and decent man'.

Brynle Williams, farmer, fuel protester and Conservative Member of the National Assembly of Wales; born Cilcain, Flintshire 9 January 1949; married Mair (one son, one daughter); died Wrexham 1 April 2011.

The Independent (7 April 2011)

ORIG WILLIAMS

Wrestler and fights promoter known as El Bandito

WHEN THE DEATH of the wrestler Orig Williams was announced on Radio Cymru's mid-day news programme *Taro'r Post* on 12 November the phone-lines were kept busy for nearly an hour by listeners wanting to share their memories of a much-loved character. Known as El Bandito, he had entertained wrestling fans for forty years with his burly physique, Zapata-style moustache, and flamboyant showmanship in the ring. He would hurl himself at his opponents with such devastating effect they fell like ninepins and, up close, delivered punishing blows with what seemed to be real relish.

He was tough, mighty tough, and not averse to pitting his physical prowess against opponents with all the tricks in his repertoire. It was said he liked hurting them, his foot-stomps compared with being hit by a concrete block. Billed as one of 'the best villains in the business', he had a mean streak that often served him in good stead against men with more experience but less stamina and inventiveness.

He was also a footballer who had played for Dyffryn Nantlle, Oldham Athletic and Shrewsbury Town, where he held the record for the number of red cards in a season. On one famous occasion the Prestatyn goalkeeper walked off the field in protest against Orig Williams's rough tactics. Whenever one of his side's players took a tumble he would say of the perpetrator, 'Leave him to me!', and within minutes there would be cries of 'Foul!'. He had to retire from the game after an injury received during one such bruising encounter.

For all his reputation as a wild man in the ring and 'dirty' player on the soccer field, Orig Williams was a gentle man whose greatest pleasure was in reading poetry and putting the world to rights in a quiet pub, especially in Ireland. He had great admiration for the Irish and named his daughter, a talented singer and actor, Tara Bethan; she was a contender for the part of Nancy in the programme *I'd do Anything*. Among the poets he often quoted was Cynan, who wrote some of the finest lyrics in the Welsh language, which was always close to his heart. His private persona was calm, reflective, and fundamentally serious, especially about the claims of Wales to be a nation with its own unique culture and right to govern itself.

Wherever he went, and he wrestled in about 30 countries, he wore the Welsh colours and sported the Red Dragon flag; when he came to publish his autobiography in 1985 he gave it the title *Cario'r Ddraig* ('Carrying the Dragon'). He was given the sobriquet El Bandito while wrestling in America, where he was first taken to be a Mexican on account of his trademark moustache. The highlight of his career was when he wrestled the legendary Bholu Brothers in Pakistan, men who were treated like gods but who accepted him as their equal. He spent several years in their country and was at his happiest there.

Orig Williams was firmly rooted in the Welsh-speaking society into which he had been born in 1931. He always returned from his trips abroad to the small village of Ysbyty Ifan, near Betws-y-coed, where he had been born, but after his marriage in 1983 he settled in Llanfair Talhaearn, to be nearer his promotions business in Rhyl. At Llanrwst Grammar School he excelled at sport and kept fit by running six miles a day. He learned to box when, at the age of ten, the journalist Terry Lloyd, who was serving in the RAF, brought home the first pair of gloves to be seen in Ysbyty Ifan and let the village boys try them on.

Orig's first opponents were Liverpool evacuees, who were even tougher than he was. 'They couldn't speak Welsh,' he recalled, 'and we couldn't speak English, so fighting came naturally to us.' His first appearances in the ring were at Ffair y Borth, the fair held in Porthaethwy/Menai Bridge, where he soon learned how to take care of himself and win monetary prizes. He continued to box after being called up for military service with the RAF in 1949.

It was the rough-and-tumble of the Fair which he brought to the series *Reslo*; when screened on S4C in the 1980s, the show boosted the channel's ratings and made El Bandito a household name, a folk-hero even, in Wales. He went on to promote cage matches, pole matches and even women wrestlers such as Tina Starr, Rusty Blair, Carla Sanchez and Bella Ogunlana. Among the male wrestlers who worked for him were Adrian Street, Mighty John Quinn, Tommy St Clair, Mark Rosco and Johnny Saint.

Some viewers were appalled by the apparent violence that took place in the ring, and the debate raged as to whether the wrestlers were really using physical force to poleaxe and pin down their opponents or whether it was all just a show which would have been balletic if it hadn't been so physical. He repaid his debt to Welsh audiences by organizing charity wrestling matches for the youth organization Urdd Gobaith Cymru and the Welsh Schools movement. El Bandito was the Big Daddy and Giant Haystacks of Wales.

Outspoken in his non-P.C. political views, which ranged broadly to take in foreign affairs and the world of sport from hurley to the Olympic Games, he wrote a much-read column, *Siarad Plaen* ('Plain Speaking') in the *Daily Post*, in which he displayed journalistic skills of a high order. He was anxious to take Wales and the Welsh to the wider world and, although keenly committed to the principle of self-government, urged his compatriots to broaden their horizons in order to see their country in a clearer light. He often expressed frustration that they didn't share his sunny confidence in the ability of the Welsh people. His own heroes were the patriots of the Welsh pantheon such as Owain Glyndŵr and Gwynfor Evans.

A big-hearted man, hospitable and generous to all who asked for his help, he was also an astute businessman who understood what the crowd wanted and had no hesitation in providing it: entertainment, with a villain to boo and a hero to cheer, slogging it out on a canvas square. Yet he was, too, a family man, literate and cultured, and with a social conscience, a rare combination for which he will long be remembered.

Orig Williams, wrestler known as El Bandito: born Ysbyty Ifan, Denbighshire 20 March 1931; married 1983 Wendy Young (one daughter); died St Asaph, Clwyd 12 November 2009.

The Independent (22 December 2009)

PHIL WILLIAMS

Plaid Cymru strategist and member of the Welsh Assembly

PHIL WILLIAMS COMBINED a distinguished career as a space physicist with a whole-hearted commitment to the cause of Plaid Cymru, which he served for more than 40 years as strategist and latterly as a member of the Welsh Assembly.

He put his formidable intellectual gifts into thinking not only about what the party should adopt as its economic policies but also, as the momentum for self-government gathered pace, into what kind of democratically elected body was needed by the people of Wales. Dr Phil, as he was widely known, often joked that his eyes might be on outer space but his feet were firmly planted on Welsh ground, and he threw himself into the hurly-burly of political life with great verve and relish.

His academic career began at Lewis School, Pengam, in Glamorgan, from where he went up to Clare College, Cambridge, winning the Greene Cup and the Mugorki Prize for Physics in 1964, the year he took his doctorate in Physics. A brilliant student, he stayed on at Cambridge for another seven years, first as a research worker at the Cavendish Laboratory and then as a Fellow of his old college.

He had already discovered an interest in left-wing politics and had joined the Labour Party in 1955, at the age of 16, an occasion made all the more memorable by Aneurin Bevan's signing his copy of Marx's *Das Kapital*. From a working-class background, he had a fund of anecdotes about the mutual incomprehension that dogged relations between Cambridge left-wingers from more privileged backgrounds and those who, like himself, were rooted in socialism as lived by the people of the south Wales valleys.

He had been born in Tredegar in Monmouthshire, and brought up in nearby Bargoed, a town with an enormous slag-tip almost in its main street, and had seen the consequences of economic decline and social deprivation at first hand. While still in Cambridge he was the joint author of *Socialism for Tomorrow*, a manifesto published by *Socialist Commentary* which stressed the importance of decentralizing power from London to the regions and nations of Britain.

It was the Labour Party's failure to get to grips with the blight that was settling on Wales during the 1950s and the brutish behaviour of certain leading lights of that party which eventually drove Phil Williams out of Labour's ranks and into Plaid Cymru's in 1961. In this he came under the influence of nationalist leaders such as Gwynfor Evans and Emrys Roberts and of the poet Harri Webb, in whose convivial company he was often to be found. For a while he belonged to the New Nation group within Plaid Cymru, which was calling for more realistic economic policies for the industrial parts of Wales.

An English-speaker in those days, he attracted like-minded young people in the valleys of the south-east for whom he was something of a local hero. His own odyssey from Labour to Plaid Cymru – he described himself as a Welsh internationalist – is described in his book *Voice from the Valleys* (1981), a refreshingly rigorous account of radical politics in Wales and a disarmingly honest statement of his own views.

By the late 1960s he was back in Wales, teaching in the Physics Department at the University College, Aberystwyth, where he set about learning Welsh, a language he spoke with some fluency and in which his two children were reared; he was appointed Professor of Solar Terrestrial Physics in 1991. He played an active role in the affairs of the college and the university, serving on the Court and as Chairman of the University Forum.

He was also involved in many scientific projects on a

wider stage, notably the European Incoherent Scatter Facility (Eiscat), of which he became Scientific Director and later Chairman, and in the work of the Royal Astronomical Society. His main contribution as a physicist was in pioneering the study of solar wind using interplanetary scintillations. He published more than a hundred papers on radio astronomy, space and atmospheric physics and was due to return in August to Arctic Scandinavia, where he was taking part in a major astronomical project.

His career as a scientist went hand in hand with his political commitments. He stood in Plaid Cymru's name at six elections for the Westminster parliament, all in the Caerphilly constituency. At one of these his supporters devised the election slogan 'Who put the Phil in Caerphilly – hush, you know who'.

But it was not to be. It was at the by-election of July 1968 that he came closest, with only some 1,800 votes fewer than the Labour candidate. His share of the votes cast, some 40 per cent, represented a swing of 29 per cent, at the time the second largest ever recorded in UK elections. It was this close shave for Labour, together with another in Rhondda in the previous year, and Gwynfor Evans's victory in Carmarthen in July 1966, that concentrated the Government's mind on the case for a more effective measure of administrative devolution than Wales had hitherto been given. Phil Williams also stood in Mid and West Wales in the European Elections of 1984 and 1989.

As Vice-President of Plaid Cymru he chaired the Strategy Committee whose main achievement was the decision to recognise the European Community, despite its shortcomings, as the only realistic context for the UK's economic policies. As National Chair he concentrated his energies on promoting the party in the English-speaking areas of south Wales such as Aberdare, Merthyr and Caerphilly, which were his natural base and where the nationalist vote increased significantly. As spokesman on the environment he developed an energy plan for Wales and played a key role in encouraging discussions between Plaid Cymru and the Green Party, which led to the election of Plaid's Cynog Dafis as MP for Ceredigion.

His major contribution to the development of Plaid Cymru's economic policies was made in *An Economic Plan for Wales* (1970), which he co-wrote with Dafydd Wigley, the substance of which was duly adopted by the party, and *The Welsh Budget* (1998), in which he demonstrated that Wales, far from being subsidized by England, was more than paying its way in the economy of the United Kingdom. These publications, widely circulated and discussed, were typical of Williams's thinking: well-informed, strictly analytical and rich in the ideas sparked by the main tenets of his thesis – that Wales could become a prosperous, progressive society if freed from the shackles of London control.

He had the satisfaction of being elected as a list candidate for the South Wales East region at the first election held for the Welsh Assembly in 1999 and was voted AM of the Year for his work on the Objective One European funding programme. Among the matters on which he put his keen intellect to work was the Barnett formula by which Wales is funded by the British Exchequer, inadequately and unfairly in his view. His decision to retire from the Assembly before its second term was greeted with dismay by all sections of the party, since he was one of the few figures of national stature to sit in Cardiff Bay.

He remained, however, an influential figure in Plaid Cymru's affairs and continued to be held in high esteem across the political spectrum in Wales. His sudden death from a heart attack is a severe blow to the political life of Wales at a moment when the fortunes of Plaid Cymru, the official Opposition, are at a low ebb after its loss of five seats and the impending resignation of its leader, Ieuan Wyn Jones.

Philip James Stradling Williams, physicist and politician: born Tredegar, Monmouthshire 11 January 1939; Lecturer, then Senior Lecturer in Physics, University College of Wales, Aberystwyth (later University of Wales, Aberystwyth) 1967–86, Reader 1986–91, Professor of Physics 1991–2003; Vice-President, Plaid Cymru 1968–70, 1976–8, 1982–4, National Chair 1970–6; AM (Plaid Cymru) for South Wales East 1999–2003; married 1962 Ann Green (one son, one daughter); died Cardiff 10 June 2003.

The Independent (13 June 2003)

STEWART WILLIAMS

Publisher of books about the history of Cardiff

'I'M CARDIFF BORN and I'm Cardiff bred, and when I dies I'll be Cardiff dead.' Although Stewart Williams died a few miles outside the city's boundaries, Frank Hennessy's song always brings him to mind. For the publisher and local historian who devoted his energies, and in the early days a lot of his own money, to recording Cardiff's growth from sleepy fishing village to the largest coal-exporting port in the world and then, in our own time, to administrative capital of Wales, was a proud Cardiffian.

In all he published more than a hundred books that are admired by general readers and academic historians alike, in particular the 36-volume series *Cardiff Yesterday*, which includes an important archive of some 7,500 black-and-white photographs. The first volume, published in 1980 to coincide with the 75th anniversary of Cardiff's elevation to city status, was the template for the rest in that it illustrated various aspects of the city's life, in war and peace, the photos arranged chronologically and with captions providing valuable information about the places, buildings and people who appeared in its pages.

From the start, Stewart Williams's enthusiasm for his birthplace was to the fore: 'Cardiff is a city of contrasts, a sprawling amorphous mass of vowel-flatteners chanting CARDIFF on cold, wintry Saturday afternoons at Ninian Park; it is Roath Park in all its colourful glory at rose blooming time; or its less perfumed backstreet pubs where old timers sup the familiar local brew with dedicated single-mindedness; or it is the marble splendour and magnificence of the still beautiful Civic Centre.' One heard the famous vowel-flattening in everything he wrote, so that 'Cardiff', for example, in the local dialect, is invariably pronounced 'Kairdiff'.

Stewart Williams was born in Roath, Cardiff, but brought up in Ely, one of the less affluent suburbs mostly made up of housing estates on the city's western side, but taught himself the rudiments of historiography the better to understand the wider urban context and present his research in ways accessible to readers with little or no academic backgrounds. His passion for sharing his knowledge with ordinary readers was the lodestar of his career but he was also a director of the Glamorgan County History Trust and a Vice-President of the Glamorgan History Society, at whose meetings he rubbed shoulders with the great and the good.

He had begun by producing bootleg football programmes and souvenirs for Cardiff City, the Bluebirds, a team that commanded his lifelong support. Having moved from the Engineering Department of the City Council to a job as publicity officer with the Western Welsh bus company, he found himself learning skills such as layout, point-size and caption-writing that are the foundation of the printer's and journalist's craft.

The runaway success of the *Cardiff Yesterday* series enabled him to take up full-time publishing in 1977 and by 1980 he had published fifty books from his home in Barry. His children, Robert and Diane, together with his wife Betty, helped with everything from proof-reading to deliveries, so that the business was very much a kitchen table affair at the outset. By the time the thirty-sixth volume appeared Stewart Williams was one of the largest publishers of local history anywhere in Britain but still operated from home.

I saw him last at a book fair in Cardiff at which I recall discussing with him how, while human memory is notoriously fallible, photographs record the changing scene with a degree of accuracy. He told me there was no shortage of material because his books had opened the flood-gates of reminiscence and people kept on offering him images that he could weave into a rich gallery of places and scenes reflecting the life of the city over a century and a half. Profit was never one of his aims, he said: his was a mission to educate his fellow Cardiffians, and anyone else with an interest in the history of the Welsh capital.

Although he had had no higher education beyond the age of 16, Stewart Williams enjoyed the confidence and esteem of academic and professional writers such as Ewart Parkinson, Director of Environment and Planning for South Glamorgan, the architect John B. Hilling, D. Morgan Rees of the National Museum of Wales, and Geraint Talfan Davies, Assistant Editor of the *Western Mail*, all of whom contributed to his symposia, *The Cardiff Book*. A similar roster of distinguished names contributed to his series *Glamorgan Historian*.

Such was the popularity of his Cardiff books that Stewart Williams was asked to produce similar volumes on the Rhondda, Ebbw Vale, Cowbridge, Abergavenny, Bridgend, Caerffili, Barry and Aberystwyth, and another on Welsh rural life. Among reprints were his editions of Rice Merrick's *Booke of Glamorganshires Antiquities* and the classic book by Wirt Sikes, American Consul in Cardiff, *Rambles and Studies in Old South Wales*. He also published Herbert Williams's *Stage Coaches in Wales* and *Vintage Buses and Trams in South Wales*, which again appealed to specialist enthusiasts and readers nostalgic for a bygone age.

Stewart Williams, publisher: born Cardiff 12 December 1925; married Betty Stocker (deceased; one son, one daughter); died Llandough, Vale of Glamorgan 13 January 2011.

The Independent (17 February 2011)

HOWARD WINSTONE

Featherweight champion of the world

IN BOXING'S HALL of fame, and especially in south Wales, where he was idolized, Howard Winstone has a secure place as one of the most skilful pugilists of his day.

He won the world featherweight title in 1968 after defeating Mitsunori Seki, the world's number two, taking the crown left vacant by Vicente Saldivar. But he had become a legend long before, as the gallant challenger who had fought Saldivar on three occasions, narrowly losing on points.

His first victory came in 1958 when he won a gold medal as a bantam fighter at the Empire Games in Cardiff, beating Ollie Taylor of Australia. He went on to win the British title at the Royal Albert Hall by defeating Terry Spinks and the European title against Alberto Sarti in Cardiff.

He kept the world title for only six months before losing it to the Cuban fighter Jose Legra in Porthcawl, after which he retired from the ring.

Winstone was born and bred in Merthyr Tydfil, the former iron town at the head of the Taff valley, which has produced a number of champion boxers, including Eddie Thomas, his manager, who died three years ago, and the bantam-weight Johnny Owen, 'The Matchstick Man', who died from his injuries in 1980 after fighting the Mexican Lupe Pintor.

During a short but brilliant career, Winstone fought 67 matches, losing only six. His appearances in the ring included seven British title fights, nine European title fights and five world championship fights.

A terrifying puncher, he stopped most of his opponents inside the distance, displaying footwork that few aficionados of the game had seen since the days of Peerless Jim Driscoll and Freddie Welsh. He developed a devastating left jab after three fingers of his right hand were amputated in a factory accident when he was 15.

At Eddie Thomas's gym in Penydarren, crowds would gather just to watch Winstone train and young hopefuls came from afar in the hope of going a few rounds with the world champion.

Out of the ring, he was a gentle, charming and generous man who devoted himself to quiet good works in his native town. With Don James, a former Welsh flyweight champion, he worked for the Welsh Ex-Boxers' Association, raising money for good causes such as the Aberfan Disaster of 1966.

His hospitality was legendary and his home, Lonsdale House, in Twynyrodyn, high above the old town, became a Mecca for boxers and enthusiasts of the game. A regular visitor was his old opponent Vicente Saldivar, who remained a friend despite not being able to speak directly to Winstone, since neither knew a word of each other's language.

The purses Winstone won were very small compared to what boxers earn today. The Legra fight brought him only £11,000, and a large slice of that went to his manager and promoter.

After his retirement, he set himself up as manager of a pub, the Gadlys Arms in Aberdare, but candidly admitted that he was not cut out to be a businessman and the enterprise failed. One of the occupational hazards of the job was that so many of his customers insisted on buying the champion drinks. For a while he was a boxing manager but then opened a haberdashery shop in Merthyr and ran a café near the town's bus-station, which was known as the Lonsdale bar.

He was appointed MBE for services to boxing in 1968 and published a ghosted autobiography, *The Welsh Wizard*, in 1976. But the honour of which he was most proud was the Freedom of Merthyr, the town of which he seemed, in his pluck and democratic nature, a typical son.

Winstone's last public engagement was at the unveiling of

a bronze statue erected in memory of his former manager, Eddie Thomas. It seems only a matter of time before he is commemorated in the same way. His funeral at St Tydfil's Parish Church on Saturday is expected to draw friends and admirers from the world of boxing in their thousands.

Howard Winstone, boxer: born Merthyr Tydfil, Glamorgan 15 April 1939; world featherweight champion 1968; MBE 1968; married first Benita Howells (two sons, two daughters; marriage dissolved), second 1971 Bronwen Williams (one son, one stepson); died Merthyr Tydfil 30 September 2000.

The Independent (3 October 2000)